THE UNITED STATES
AND THE
CARIBBEAN AREA

RECENT
WORLD PEACE FOUNDATION PUBLICATIONS

ഇൽ

THE UNITED STATES

AND THE

CARIBBEAN AREA

By

DANA G. MUNRO

PROFESSOR OF LATIN AMERICAN HISTORY AND AFFAIRS
PRINCETON UNIVERSITY

WORLD PEACE FOUNDATION
BOSTON
1934

CONTENTS

CONTENTS

PAGE

CONTENTS

THE UNITED STATES
AND THE
CARIBBEAN AREA

THE UNITED STATES AND THE CARIBBEAN AREA

CHAPTER I

CUBA AND THE PLATT AMENDMENT

THE SPANISH–AMERICAN WAR

It would be hard to find any single statement of public policy [wrote Mr. Elihu Root in 1901] which has been so often officially declared by so great an array of distinguished Americans authorized to speak for the Government of the United States, as the proposition stated, in varying but always uncompromising and unmistakable terms, that the United States would not under any circumstances permit any foreign power other than Spain to acquire possession of the island of Cuba.

Jefferson and Monroe and John Quincy Adams and Jackson and Van Buren and Grant and Clay and Webster and Buchanan and Everett have all agreed in regarding this as essential to the interests and the protection of the United States.[1]

With the exception of the smaller island of Puerto Rico, Cuba was the only Spanish colony in America which did not become independent during the first quarter of the nineteenth century. The mother country's hold upon these last remaining possessions seemed precarious, because of the weakness of the home government itself, and several other powers besides the United States would have been very glad to relieve her of them. This very fact, however, had played a part in enabling Spain to retain the islands, for neither England nor France nor the United States was willing to see them pass from her hands into those of any other power. In the United States, suggestions for the purchase, or even the conquest, of Cuba were made from

[1] Extract from Mr. Root's letter of February 9, 1901, to General Wood, printed in Annual Report of the Secretary of War for 1901, p. 43.

1

time to time, notably in the Ostend Manifesto of 1854, but interest in the acquisition of the island had decreased, although American investments there had increased, after the Civil War.

In Cuba itself there were occasional revolts, culminating in the destructive Ten Years' War (1868–1878). This struggle was ended by the defeat of the rebels and the granting of minor concessions by Spain, but the reluctance with which these concessions were put into effect, combined with the political discontent caused by the exclusion of native-born Cubans from participation in the government of the colony and by the corruptness and inefficiency of the officials sent from Spain, kept the revolutionary spirit alive.

Cuba was nevertheless a prosperous colony during the latter part of the nineteenth century. Sugar production in 1894–5 exceeded 1,000,000 tons,[2] and the tobacco and mining industries were flourishing. A considerable amount of American and other foreign capital had been invested in the island. The sugar industry, however, which was largely dependent upon the American market, suffered a serious setback when the tariff concessions granted by the United States in the reciprocity treaty signed in 1891 were withdrawn after the enactment of the Wilson Tariff in 1894. The resulting decline in the prices of the island's chief product was one of the causes of the revolt which began in the following year.

When a new revolution began in 1895, Spain was unable to restore order although large forces were sent to the island. As the months passed the struggle became increasingly bitter and both sides adopted measures which bore heavily on the noncombatant population. The insurgents systematically destroyed property and murdered those who attempted to trade with the towns still under Spanish control, while the Government's forces, under the "reconcentration" orders, compelled the

[2] Rowan and Ramsey, *The Island of Cuba*, p. 43.

country people to move with their livestock into garrisoned towns, where great numbers died of starvation
and disease. American commerce and interests suffered heavily, and American public opinion was profoundly affected by reports of the appalling conditions
among the noncombatant population.

The Government of the United States had repeatedly
urged Spain to take more adequate measures to terminate
the revolt. Under the Cleveland administration it had
offered its good offices to bring about an agreement with
the insurgents, but the Spanish Government had insisted
that the island could be pacified only by the submission of
the rebels.[3] Subsequently a more liberal policy was
adopted. Spain offered to grant a substantial measure of
autonomous government, and General Weyler, who had
been much criticized for his ruthless policy, was replaced
by an officer of more liberal views. The insurgents, however, refused to be satisfied with anything short of complete independence, and the numerous pro-Spanish party,
which opposed the granting of any concessions, organized
demonstrations at Habana not only against the revolutionists but against the United States. It was the disorders
thus created which led the American Government to send
the battleship *Maine* to Habana in January 1898.[4]

President McKinley had opposed insistent demands for
the recognition of the independence of the insurgents or
for the forcible annexation of the island to the United
States, but after the explosion of the *Maine*, with the loss
of two officers and 258 enlisted men, the public demand
for intervention became almost irresistible. When an

[3] *Foreign Relations of the United States, 1897*, p. 540, 544.
[4] The account here given of events leading up to the Spanish-American
War is based mainly on the correspondence published in *Foreign Relations*
for 1898, and upon the Spanish Government's correspondence published under
the title Spain, Ministerio de Estado, *Spanish Diplomatic Correspondence and
Documents 1896–1900*. Presented to the Cortes by the Minister of State.
(Translation) Washington, Government Printing Office, 1905. This is subsequently cited as *Spanish Documents*.

American board of investigation reported that the explosion had been caused by a submarine mine or some other external cause, the American Minister at Madrid made a formal demand for reparation, on the ground that the Spanish Government had failed to provide the protection which a warship of a friendly power had a right to expect in a Spanish port. On the following day, March 29, 1898, a virtual ultimatum was presented. The United States demanded an immediate armistice, to permit negotiations through the mediation of the United States, and the revocation of the reconcentration order. The Spanish Government replied on March 31. Maintaining that its own investigation indicated that the *Maine* had been destroyed by an internal explosion, it proposed to arbitrate the question of responsibility. It refused an immediate armistice, saying that it would look to the new insular parliament, which would meet on May 4, to take steps for the pacification of the island.

On April 6, the "great powers" of Europe addressed a joint note to the Government of the United States urging further negotiations with Spain in an effort to prevent war. Meanwhile, the Captain General at Habana discontinued the reconcentration system, and on April 9, in response to pleas from the Pope and the "great powers," the Spanish Government ordered a general armistice. President McKinley, however, had apparently reached the conclusion that Spain's efforts to pacify Cuba through the establishment of autonomous government would be ineffective, because they were opposed both by the revolutionists and by the pro-Spanish party, and that the war could be terminated only by the independence of Cuba.[5] On April 11, 1898, in a special message to Congress, he requested authority to intervene by force to terminate the war in Cuba and to establish a stable government there.

[5] In this connection see the instructions sent to the Minister at Madrid on March 26 and 28, 1898, *Foreign Relations, 1898*, p. 704, 713.

The response was a joint resolution, approved by the President on April 20, which declared: [6]

First. That the people of the Island of Cuba are, and of right ought to be, free and independent.

Second. That it is the duty of the United States to demand and the Government of the United States does hereby demand, that the Government of Spain at once relinquish its authority and government in the Island of Cuba and withdraw its land and naval forces from Cuba and Cuban waters.

Third. That the President of the United States be, and he hereby is, directed and empowered to use the entire land and naval forces of the United States, and to call into the actual service of the United States the militia of the several states, to such extent as may be necessary to carry these resolutions into effect.

Fourth. That the United States hereby disclaims any disposition or intention to exercise sovereignty, jurisdiction or control over said Island except for the pacification thereof, and asserts its determination, when that is accomplished, to leave the government and control of the Island to its people.

After about three months of war, the Spanish Government asked the United States to suggest terms of peace. The preliminary protocol signed on August 12 provided that "Spain will relinquish all claim of sovereignty over and title to Cuba." [7]

During the preliminary peace negotiations, the Spanish Government stated that it would accept any disposition of Cuba "which may please the United States—absolute independence, independence under the protectorate, or annexation to the American Republic, preferring definite annexation, because it would better guarantee the lives and estates of Spaniards established or holding property there." [8] Efforts were made during the subsequent negotiations at Paris to persuade the United States to accept a renunciation of sovereignty in its favor. The Spanish

[6] United States Statutes at Large, 30, p. 738.
[7] Foreign Relations, 1898, p. 828.
[8] Spanish Documents, p. 209.

Government desired especially some assurance of the payment of the Cuban debt, but the American commissioners refused to assume any responsibility for this debt, either on behalf of the United States or on behalf of the future government of Cuba. With regard to proposals for annexation to the United States, they were instructed by Secretary Hay that "we must carry out the spirit and letter of the resolution of Congress." The first article of the Treaty of Paris, signed on December 10, 1898, provided:

Spain relinquishes all claim of sovereignty over and title to Cuba.

And as the island is, upon its evacuation by Spain, to be occupied by the United States, the United States will, so long as such occupation shall last, assume and discharge the obligations that may under international law result from the fact of its occupation, for the protection of life and property.

The Spanish commissioners did, however, obtain one important concession. They had insisted that Spanish citizens and interests in Cuba must be given guaranties of some sort against unjust action by future Cuban Governments, and the United States finally agreed to the incorporation in the treaty of Article XVI, which read:[9]

It is understood that any obligations assumed in this treaty by the United States with respect to Cuba are limited to the time of its occupancy thereof; but it will upon the termination of such occupancy advise any Government established in the island to assume the same obligations.

THE MILITARY GOVERNMENT

Upon the evacuation of Habana by Spanish troops on January 1, 1899, a United States Military Government was established under General John R. Brooke, who was suc-

[9] The correspondence relating to the peace negotiations is printed in the Spanish Documents and also in *Foreign Relations* for 1898. The text of the Treaty of Paris is printed in *Foreign Relations, 1898*, p. 831.

ceeded in December 1899 by General Leonard Wood. The first tasks undertaken by the American authorities were the relief of the starving civilian population, and the disarmament both of the Cuban rebels and of the large native forces which had fought for Spain. Subsequently, a rural guard of native Cubans was created, municipal governments were set up, the financial administration and the administration of justice were reorganized, and a modern school system was established.

The American authorities also undertook the improvement of sanitary conditions, which were and have continued to be a matter of international importance. Yellow fever had made Habana notoriously unsafe for foreigners, and was a constant menace to the health of near-by ports in the United States. Its control and almost complete eradication was made possible by the work of a commission appointed by General Wood and headed by Dr. Walter Reed, which proved the truth of a theory already elaborated by Dr. Finlay, a Cuban physician, that the disease was carried by the *stegomyia* mosquito. The discovery was made possible by the heroism of several American physicians and enlisted men who permitted themselves to be exposed to the disease, of whom one, Dr. Jesse Lazear, died as the result of the experiment. The conquest of yellow fever was of vast importance not only for the future of Cuba, but for all tropical countries; and the building of the Panama Canal a few years later would have been difficult if not impossible without it.

The chief object of the Military Government, however, was to establish the Republic of Cuba as an independent nation. The attitude of the United States was expressed by Mr. Root in his report as Secretary of War for the year 1899:

The control which we are exercising in trust for the people of Cuba should not be, and of course will not be, continued any longer than is necessary to enable that people to establish a suitable government to which the control shall be transferred, which shall really represent the people of Cuba and be able to maintain order and discharge international obligations. . . . Our present duty is limited to giving every assistance in our power to the establishment of such a government and to maintaining order and promoting the welfare of the people of Cuba during the period necessarily required for that process.

The feeling that the United States was exercising merely a trusteeship for the people of Cuba found further expression in the Foraker amendment to the Military Appropriation Act for the Fiscal Year 1900 which provided: [10]

That no property, franchises, or concessions of any kind whatever shall be granted by the United States or by any military or other authority whatever in the Island of Cuba during the occupation thereof by the United States.

As a first step toward the establishment of a Cuban Government, a census was taken in 1899, to secure information needed in drafting an electoral law. The electoral law was promulgated on April 18, 1900, and municipal officials were chosen on June 16 of the same year. [11]

Shortly afterward the Military Governor issued a proclamation calling for the election on September 3, 1900, of a convention

to frame and adopt a constitution for the people of Cuba, and, as a part thereof, to provide for and agree with the Government of the United States upon the relations to exist between that Government and the Government of Cuba, and to provide for the election by the people of officers under such constitution and the transfer of government to the officers so elected.

The convention, when it met on November 5, was informed by the Military Governor that it should first

[10] United States Statutes at Large, 30, p. 1074.
[11] For the events of this period, see *The Establishment of Free Government in Cuba,* compiled in the United States Bureau of Insular Affairs, Washington, 1904. The more important documents are also published in the *Annual Reports of the Secretary of War.*

frame a constitution "adequate to secure a stable, orderly, and free government," and that it should subsequently "formulate what in your opinion ought to be the relations between Cuba and the United States." After this had been done, the Military Governor said

the United States will doubtless take such action on its part as shall lead to a final and authoritative agreement between the people of the two countries to the promotion of their common interests.

THE PLATT AMENDMENT

When the Convention had nearly completed the first part of its task, the views of the United States Government regarding the future relations between the two countries were communicated to the Military Governor in a lengthy instruction from the Secretary of War. While pointing out that the final decision might depend upon the action of the American Congress, Mr. Root indicated that the general principles which must govern the future relationship between the two countries must necessarily be determined by the obligations already specifically assumed by the United States in the Joint Resolution of April 20, 1898, and in the Treaty of Paris, which had been construed as imposing upon the United States the obligation to

cause or permit the establishment of a government to which we could in good faith commit the protection of the lives and property and personal rights of those inhabitants from whom we had compelled their former sovereign to withdraw her protection.

Steps having been taken to establish an adequate government, the "remaining duty" of the United States was clear. The authorized spokesman of the United States Government had repeatedly "stated in varying but always uncompromising and unmistakable terms, that the United States would not under any circumstances permit any foreign power other than Spain to acquire possession of the island of Cuba."

It would be a most lame and impotent conclusion if, after all the expenditure of blood and treasure by the people of the United States for the freedom of Cuba and by the people of Cuba for the same object, we should, through the constitution of the new government, by inadvertence or otherwise, be placed in a worse condition in regard to our own vital interests than we were while Spain was in possession, and the people of Cuba should be deprived of that protection and aid from the United States which is necessary to the maintenance of their independence.

Mr. Root stated, therefore, that

the people of Cuba should desire to have incorporated in her fundamental law

a series of provisions, which were set forth in the instruction, and which were substantially similar to Articles I, II, III, IV and VII of the Platt Amendment as subsequently adopted.

When General Wood presented the views of the Secretary of War to the convention's Committee on Relations to Exist between Cuba and the United States, he found some objection to the provision giving the United States the right to intervene to maintain a stable government in Cuba, and a more serious objection to the proposed grant of naval stations, chiefly on sentimental grounds.[12] The opposition to the American proposals subsequently became more formidable, and on February 26 the committee which considered Mr. Root's communication presented an unfavorable report to the convention, expressing the belief that the proposed limitations upon the Republic's freedom of action in foreign relations, the recognition of the right to intervention, and the grant of naval stations would constitute an impairment of sovereignty.[13]

[12] Wood's letter to Root, February 19, 1901, quoted in Root, *The Military and Colonial Policy of the United States*, p. 186-7.
[13] *Foreign Relations, 1902*, p. 360.

The problem of relations with Cuba had meanwhile received consideration in the United States Congress, which gave its approval on March 2, 1901, to a proviso attached to the Military Appropriation Bill, which has since become famous as the "Platt Amendment." This enactment, which has formed the basis of the relations between Cuba and the United States down to the present time, read as follows:

Provided further, That in fulfillment of the declaration contained in the joint resolution approved April twentieth, eighteen hundred and ninety-eight, entitled, "For the recognition of the independence of the people of Cuba, demanding that the Government of Spain relinquish its authority and government in the island of Cuba and to withdraw its land and naval forces from Cuba and Cuban waters, and directing the President of the United States to use the land and naval forces of the United States to carry these resolutions into effect," the President is hereby authorized to "leave the government and control of the island of Cuba to its people" so soon as a government shall have been established in said island under a constitution which, either as a part thereof or in an ordinance appended thereto, shall define the future relations of the United States with Cuba, substantially as follows:

I. That the Government of Cuba shall never enter into any treaty or other compact with any foreign power or powers which will impair or tend to impair the independence of Cuba, nor in any manner authorize or permit any foreign power or powers to obtain by colonization or for military or naval purposes or otherwise, lodgement in or control over any portion of said island.

II. That said Government shall not assume or contract any public debt, to pay the interest upon which, and to make reasonable sinking-fund provision for the ultimate discharge of which, the ordinary revenues of the island, after defraying the current expenses of Government shall be inadequate.

III. That the Government of Cuba consents that the United States may exercise the right to intervene for the preservation of Cuban independence, the maintenance of a government adequate for the protection of life, property, and individual liberty, and for discharging the obligations with respect to Cuba imposed

by the treaty of Paris on the United States, now to be assumed
and undertaken by the Government of Cuba.

IV. That all acts of the United States in Cuba during its
military occupancy thereof are ratified and validated, and all
lawful rights acquired thereunder shall be maintained and
protected.

V. That the Government of Cuba will execute, and as far
as necessary, extend, the plans already devised or other plans
to be mutually agreed upon, for the sanitation of the cities of
the island, to the end that a recurrence of epidemic and in-
fectious diseases may be prevented thereby assuring protection
to the people and commerce of Cuba, as well as the commerce
of the Southern ports of the United States and the people residing
therein.

VI. That the Isle of Pines shall be omitted from the proposed constitutional boundaries of Cuba, the title thereto being
left to future adjustment by treaty.

VII. That to enable the United States to maintain the independence of Cuba, and to protect the people thereof, as well as
for its own defense, the Government of Cuba will sell or lease
to the United States lands necessary for coaling or naval stations
at certain specified points, to be agreed upon with the President
of the United States.

VIII. That by way of further assurance the Government of
Cuba will embody the foregoing provisions in a permanent treaty
with the United States.

Besides the new requirement that the articles to be
incorporated in the Cuban constitution should also be
embodied in a permanent treaty with the United States,
the Platt Amendment covered two other matters which
had not been dealt with in Mr. Root's instruction to
General Wood. Article V, regarding sanitation, had been
inserted at the suggestion of General Wood, who had
pointed out in a letter to Mr. Root the danger that sanitary
conditions in Cuba would revert to their former state,
with consequent danger to the southern ports of the
United States.[14] Article VI, referring to the Isle of Pines,
was inserted by the Senate Committee on Cuban Relations,
presumably because there was some doubt whether this

[14] Root, *op. cit.*, p. 187.

island was an integral part of Cuba or was to be considered as one of the islands which had been ceded to the United States by the Treaty of Paris.

When the Constitutional Convention was formally advised of the provisions of the Platt Amendment, and informed that the President of the United States awaited its action thereon, its members were still reluctant to accede to the demands of the United States. The feeling was expressed that the acceptance of such demands would deprive the new government of all real independence, and would open the way for constant interference in its internal affairs. In an effort to allay this feeling, the following telegram was sent to the Military Governor on April 3: [15]

Wood, Habana.

You are authorized to state officially that in view of the President the intervention described in the third clause of the Platt amendment is not synonymous with intermeddling or interference with the affairs of the Cuban Government, but the formal action of the Government of the United States, based upon just and substantial grounds, for the preservation of Cuban independence and the maintenance of a government adequate for the protection of life, property, and individual liberty, and adequate for discharging the obligations with respect to Cuba imposed by the treaty of Paris on the United States.

ELIHU ROOT, *Secretary of War.*

Subsequently, a committee of the convention conferred with the President and the Secretary of War in Washington. In reporting upon their mission, the committee stated that Mr. Root had indicated to them that one of the main purposes of Article III of the Amendment was to place the United States in a stronger legal position, in the eyes of other foreign powers, if action for the preservation of Cuban independence should become necessary. The Secretary of War was quoted as saying that

[15] *The Establishment of Free Government in Cuba,* p. 12.

intervention will occur only to prevent foreign attacks against the independence of the Cuban Republic or when a veritable state of anarchy exists within the Republic,

and that the sending of troops to Cuba under any other circumstances would be incompatible with the independence which the Platt Amendment itself was designed to secure. Mr. Root also pointed out that the obligations assumed by the United States under the Treaty of Paris would not be extinguished merely by advising the new government to take them over, but that the United States must see that these obligations were carried out, because of the responsibility which it had assumed in creating a new republic. With respect to Articles I and II of the Amendment, Mr. Root was reported to have said that they should be considered as "purely internal constitutional limitations," like those imposed by Congress in the American Constitution, and that they referred only to Cuba and should be applied by the Cubans themselves. Speaking of Article VII, he said that the proposed naval stations were desired solely to aid in the defense of both countries, and not to serve as a base for interference in Cuban affairs, and that the question of their establishment would be settled in any event by agreement between the two Governments.[16]

On June 12, 1901, after it had been made clear that the United States would not withdraw from Cuba until the requirements laid down by the American Congress had been fulfilled,[17] the convention accepted the provisions of the Platt Amendment as an annex to the constitution which it had already signed. The Permanent Treaty, embodying the same provisions word for word, was signed

[16] No record of these conversations appears to have been published by the United States Government. The report of the Committee was published by the Cuban Government in a volume entitled Senado, *Memoria de los trabajos realizados* . . . 1902–4, Habana, 1918, and extracts are given in James Brown Scott, *Cuba, La América Latina, y Los Estados Unidos*. The quotations in the text are translations from the Spanish.

[17] Martinez Ortiz, *Los Primeros Años de Independencia*, Vol. I, p. 311.

on May 22, 1903, and was proclaimed by the President of the United States, after ratification by both Governments, on July 2, 1904.

THE ESTABLISHMENT OF THE CUBAN REPUBLIC

At a general election held on December 31, 1901, Tomás Estrada Palma, who had been the principal representative of the Cuban revolutionists in the United States during the war of independence, was chosen as the first President of the Republic. When he was inaugurated on May 20, 1902, the Military Governor formally transferred to him "the government and control of the island" and declared "the occupation of Cuba by the United States and the military government of the island to be ended." In accepting the transfer, the new President formally assumed "each and every one of the obligations concerning Cuba" imposed upon the United States by the Treaty of Paris, and agreed also to carry out certain specified plans for the sanitation of the cities of the island, in accord with the fifth article of the Platt Amendment.[18]

On the day following the inauguration the Cuban House of Representatives passed a resolution [19]

that a solemn vote of thanks be passed, a sincere expression of heartfelt gratitude to the Government and people of the United States of North America for their earnest sympathy, their efficient aid, and for the sacrifices made by them in behalf of the independence and freedom of Cuba.

Although the Platt Amendment had laid down the general principles which were to govern the relations between the United States and Cuba, several questions vitally affecting these relations were necessarily left to be dealt with after an independent Cuban Government had

---

[18] The documents relating to the transfer are printed in the Appendix of the Annual Report of the Secretary of War for 1902.

[19] *Foreign Relations, 1902*, p. 325,

been established.   The most important of these were the establishment of commercial relations which would assure the new republic's economic stability, and the execution of those provisions of the Platt Amendment which contemplated the establishment of American naval stations in the island, the determination of the status of the Isle of Pines, and the completion of the sanitation work which had been begun under the Military Government.

THE RECIPROCITY TREATY

Immediately after the establishment of the Military Government, the American authorities at Washington and at Habana began to emphasize the necessity for giving Cuba assured markets in the United States.   The delegates from the Constitutional Convention who visited Washington in April 1901 had discussed the question of commercial preferences in connection with the provisions of the Platt Amendment and had received assurances of the sympathy with which the Cubans' desires were regarded in official circles in the American capital.   President Roosevelt subsequently advocated reciprocity with Cuba in his annual messages of 1901 and 1902, saying on the latter occasion:

Cuba lies at our doors, and whatever affects her for good or for ill affects us also.   So much have our people felt this that in the Platt Amendment we definitely took the ground that Cuba must hereafter have closer political relations with us than with any other power. Thus in a sense Cuba has become a part of our international political system.   This makes it necessary that in return she should be given some of the benefits of becoming part of our economic system.

Mr. Root wrote in his Annual Report for 1901:

The same considerations which led to the war with Spain now require that a commercial arrangement be made under which Cuba can live.

The Commercial Convention signed December 11, 1902, which is still in force, provided in general for a twenty per cent reduction in customs duties upon all importations from Cuba into the United States, and for reductions ranging from twenty to forty per cent upon importations from the United States to Cuba. It was stipulated that the preference thus granted to Cuba by the United States should continue during the life of the convention as against all like imports from other countries, and that the duty on sugar imported into the United States should never be less than that imposed by the Tariff of 1897. The convention was to remain in force for five years, and from year to year thereafter until denounced by one of the contracting parties. The advantages assured to Cuban sugar by the reciprocity provision made possible the rapid growth of the industry, with an expansion of production from 1,124,327 short tons in 1902–3 to 2,909,460 in 1913–14.[20] Recent developments in the sugar industry, however, have made the reciprocity clause of less value to the Republic.[21]

NAVAL STATIONS

Under the Platt Amendment, Cuba had agreed to sell or lease to the United States the lands necessary for the establishment of coaling or naval stations at points subsequently to be agreed upon. The United States appears at first to have proposed the cession of lands for this purpose at Guantánamo, Bahía Honda, Cienfuegos and Nipe [22] but to have subsequently consented to reduce the scope of its demands in deference to the wishes of the Cuban Government. An agreement for the cession of specified areas at Guantánamo and Bahía Honda was consequently signed by President Estrada Palma on February 16,

[20] Wright, *The Cuban Situation and Our Treaty Relations*, p. 50.
[21] See *infra*, p. 58–62.
[22] Martinez Ortiz, *Los Primeros Años*, Vol. II, p. 40.

1903, and by President Roosevelt on February 23. The United States recognized Cuba's ultimate sovereignty over these areas, but was granted complete jurisdiction and control over them during the period of its occupancy. In a more detailed agreement, in the form of a lease, signed at Habana on July 2, 1903, boundaries of the areas ceded were set forth in detail and the United States agreed to pay rent for them at the rate of $2,000 annually.[23] Neither of these agreements was regarded as a treaty which required ratification by the United States Senate.

Under a subsequent agreement, signed December 27, 1912, the United States gave up its rights at Bahía Honda in return for an enlargement of the area at Guantánamo. The amount of the rent was increased to $5,000, but the other provisions of the original lease remained in force.

THE ISLE OF PINES

Under Article VI of the Platt Amendment, the status of the Isle of Pines, a small island some fifty miles from the south coast of Cuba, had been left for future adjustment. Although this territory had been an administrative subdivision of the Province of Habana under Spanish rule, there was at first some doubt as to its status under the Treaty of Paris, and numerous inquirers had been informed in writing during 1899 and the early part of 1900 that it had been ceded by Spain to the United States and was therefore American territory.[24] A better understanding of the facts in the case led to a subsequent change in point of view, and there appears to have been no real intention on the part of the Government of the United States after 1900 to claim the island for the United States. At the time of President Estrada Palma's inauguration it had been agreed that the Isle of Pines would remain *de facto* under

[23] *Foreign Relations, 1903*, p. 350–351.
[24] For these letters and other documents relating to the earlier phase of the Isle of Pines question see 59th Cong., 1st Sess., Senate Doc. No. 205.

Cuban jurisdiction pending the determination of its status by treaty.[25]

A treaty definitely recognizing Cuba's sovereignty over the island was signed on July 16, 1903, but failed to obtain the approval of the United States Senate within the time stipulated in its provisions. A new treaty, including no specific time limit for ratification was signed on March 2, 1904, but its ratification was delayed for many years. Under the Military Government, American real estate promoters had brought to the island a considerable number of American colonists, who had believed that they were settling under the American flag. These settlers not unnaturally objected to being left under Cuban jurisdiction, and their influence repeatedly blocked the efforts of successive administrations at Washington to have the treaty ratified. The statement in Article II that the relinquishment of the United States' claim to the island "is in consideration of the grants of coaling and naval stations in the Island of Cuba heretofore made to the United States of America by the Republic of Cuba" made the long delay especially embarrassing. On March 13, 1925, the Senate finally gave its consent to ratification, with reservations which were accepted by the Cuban Government.[26]

SANITATION

Another question left by the Platt Amendment to be dealt with by the first Cuban administration was the obligation to "execute, and as far as necessary extend the plans already devised, or other plans to be mutually agreed upon, for the sanitation of the cities of the Island." In the letters exchanged by General Wood and President

[25] This agreement was embodied in the letters exchanged at the time of the transfer of government.

[26] For a brief history of the whole Isle of Pines question see James Brown Scott's article in the *American Journal of International Law*, Vol. XVII, p. 100–104.

Estrada Palma at the time of the transfer of the government, the Military Governor had stated that the "plans already devised," as the United States understood them, included projects for the paving and sewering of Habana and for the establishment of water works and sewers at Santiago, the quarantine regulations established by the Military Government in the Cuban ports, and the sanitary rules and regulations in force in Habana and other cities.

The most important of the contemplated measures of sanitation was the paving and sewering of Habana. Although an American firm had entered into a contract with the city government to carry out this work, actual construction was delayed because the municipality found itself unable to borrow the necessary funds. After waiting for some time, the contractors applied to the Department of State at Washington for assistance, and on March 10, 1905, Secretary Hay instructed the American Minister to lay the matter before the Cuban Government and to impress upon the latter its obligation to see that the work was carried out.[27]

The ports and commerce of the United States [Mr. Hay wrote] have heretofore suffered immense losses through the prevalence of yellow fever in Cuba and the importation of the same into the United States from such sources of infection. The result has been that certain portions of the South, at different times, have been completely cut off by quarantine and other regulations from all social and commercial intercourse with the other sections, with a resulting great loss and damage to the people of the United States. In consequence, the United States Government, in granting liberty to Cuba, provided, by the covenants contained in the Platt Amendment, that the evil arising from the unsanitary conditions of the ports of the Island should be remedied as soon as possible by proper sanitary works.

Although the American Minister made representations on several occasions and the Cuban President sent messages

[27] *Foreign Relations, 1905*, p. 267.

urging the Cuban Congress to take action, nothing was accomplished. Sanitary conditions in the island as a whole became gradually worse. The problem was not dealt with effectively until after the American intervention in 1906. Under the Provisional Government, a new contract for the paving and sewering of Habana was executed with the same firm, and work was begun in 1908. A National Board of Sanitation was also created to replace the ineffective local municipal boards, and yellow fever was again wiped out.[28] Although sanitary conditions in the island have not always been satisfactory since the reëstablishment of Cuban control in 1909, they have apparently not again created serious difficulties.

THE INTERVENTION OF 1906

President Estrada Palma endeavored during the first three years of his term of office to conduct his administration without affiliating himself with any one political party. Toward the end of this period, however, disappointed at his inability to obtain action from the Congress even on important and urgent questions, he definitely affiliated himself with the so-called Moderate party and for the first time appointed a definitely partisan cabinet. Soon afterward he permitted this party to nominate him for reëlection. His opponent in the contest was José Miguel Gómez, the candidate of the Liberal party.

The difficulty of holding a fair election in Cuba had already been demonstrated when a part of the membership of Congress was renewed in 1904. The existing law placed the direction of elections largely in the hands of the *alcaldes,* or mayors, in each municipality, and each party was said to have resorted to extensive fraud in those

[28] Republic of Cuba, *Report of Provisional Administration, 1907–8,* p. 132, 142.

districts where it had control. The local officials elected under the Military Government were still in office in many of the towns, for the Cuban Congress had failed to enact a law providing for new elections. Under the old Spanish law, however, the Executive Power had appointed and removed municipal officials when it considered such action necessary. With the approach of the presidential election, the new Secretary of Government proceeded to remove a large number of Liberal *alcaldes,* ostensibly on grounds of misconduct. This aroused bitter resentment among the Liberals, and they responded with threats and acts of violence which in turn brought forth repressive measures by the Government. On the day of the primary election to select the boards which were to direct the registration and voting for the national officials, the Liberals withdrew from the contest, refusing also to participate in the principal election held on December 31, 1905. Secretary Taft later reported that the registration conducted by the Moderate electoral boards had reached a total of 432,000, whereas he believed that the total number of voters in the Republic could not by any possibility have exceeded 300,000. Not one Liberal candidate was successful in any province in the general election.[29]

Although a small revolt occurred in February, it was easily suppressed, and Estrada Palma was inaugurated for a second term on May 20, 1906. In the following August, another revolt started suddenly and spread so rapidly that the Government soon exercised little control except in the more important cities. The Government had no strong forces at its disposal, for President Estrada Palma, relying probably upon the eventual support of the

[29] See Secretary Taft's report of his mission to Cuba, printed as an appendix to the Annual Report of the Secretary of War, submitted December 12, 1906. The above description of the events leading up to the American intervention is based largely on this report, on Martinez Ortiz' book already cited, and on Charles E. Chapman's *History of the Cuban Republic* (New York, 1927), which is the best history of modern Cuba in English.

United States under the Platt Amendment, had made no adequate military preparations. On September 8, the President informed the American Consul General that he was unable either to quell the rebellion or to afford proper protection to life and property, and stated that he was about to convene Congress in order that that body might request the forcible intervention of the United States. The President also asked that American warships be sent at once to Habana and to Cienfuegos.[30]

The Acting Secretary of State replied on September 10 that the warships would be sent. The Consul General was informed, however, that the American Government was not prepared to consider intervention until the Cuban Government should have made every effort either to suppress the revolution or to come to an agreement with the rebels.

The President directs me to state [Mr. Bacon said] that perhaps you do not yourself appreciate the reluctance with which this country would intervene. . . . It is of course a very serious thing to undertake forcible intervention, and before going into it we should have to be absolutely certain of the equities of the case and the needs of the situation.

Two days later, the President officially requested the intervention of the United States, stating that he had decided to resign and to deliver the government to the representative whom the Government of the United States might designate. Without accepting this invitation, President Roosevelt announced on September 14 that he was sending Mr. Taft, the Secretary of War, and Mr. Bacon, the Assistant Secretary of State, to render such aid as might be possible. At the same time, the President wrote and immediately published a letter to be transmitted by the Cuban Minister at Washington to President Estrada Palma, informing him of this action and saying:

[30] The diplomatic correspondence here referred to is printed in *Foreign Relations* for 1906, and also as an appendix to Secretary Taft's report.

I solemnly adjure all Cuban patriots to band together, to sink all differences and personal ambitions, and to remember that the only way that they can preserve the independence of their Republic is to prevent the necessity of outside interference, by rescuing it from the anarchy of civil war.

The American commissioners reached Habana on September 19. Hostilities had in the meantime been suspended, but the city of Habana was surrounded by a revolutionary force of from eight to ten thousand men, who appeared likely to encounter little effective opposition if they should decide to march into the city.[31] One of the commissioners' first acts was to bring about an agreement for a more formal truce, based on rules laid down by themselves.

The commissioners announced immediately after their arrival that they wished to consult with the leaders of both parties and with Cuban and foreign business men who were not in politics. They gathered a great body of information from sources of all kinds, working as rapidly as possible because of the constant danger of a recurrence of hostilities and also because the need for reëstablishing order was repeatedly impressed on them by appeals for help from American citizens in the interior. At the suggestion of President Estrada Palma, they discussed the situation especially with accredited representatives of the two political parties in an effort to find a basis for a compromise.

After a careful investigation, the commissioners reached the conclusion that it would not be fair or advisable for the Government of the United States to attempt to uphold the régime resulting from the 1906 elections. The outcome had been too clearly vitiated by violence and fraud. They would much have preferred to support the constituted government, and they were fully aware of the

---

[31] The description here given of the work of the commissioners is based mainly on Mr. Taft's report.

bad precedent which would be set by negotiating with rebels under arms, but, as Mr. Taft pointed out, they had to take the situation as they found it.

> We cannot maintain the Palma Government, [he said] except by forcible intervention against the whole weight of public opinion in the island.

This would have involved "fighting the whole Cuban people." Even though American troops could easily have defeated the revolutionists in battle, guerrilla warfare might have continued indefinitely at a heavy cost in lives and money. Two hundred thousand Spanish troops had been inadequate to deal with a similar situation a few years before. The commissioners were not, on the other hand, willing to consider turning the Government over to the revolutionists, who were "only an undisciplined horde of men" whose leaders were not even the more prominent members of the opposition party. A compromise appeared to be the only possible solution. Mr. Taft's discussion of the considerations which guided the commissioners in the course of action which they adopted is especially interesting in view of the apparently different attitude which the Government of the United States assumed on subsequent occasions.[32]

The compromise which the commissioners proposed was substantially similar to one which had already been proposed before their arrival by the Veterans of the War of Independence, who had maintained an influential organization, and who had endeavored without success to bring about a settlement when the war first started. Believing that the President himself would probably have been reëlected without the use of force or fraud, and that the continuance of the constituted government was necessary for the good name of Cuba, they proposed that Estrada

[32] Mr. Taft discussed the subject in p. 457–8 of his report and also in his letters of September 21 and September 26 to President Roosevelt, printed in the report, p. 469 and 475.

Palma should remain in office. On the other hand, the newly elected congressmen, governors and provincial councillors were to resign, and their successors were to be chosen after the revision of the electoral and municipal laws and the formulation of laws placing the judiciary and the civil service on a better basis should have been effected by a commission of which the chairman should be an American. The rebels were to lay down their arms immediately after these resignations had been obtained. Changes in the President's cabinet were suggested, but not as an essential part of the compromise plan.

The Liberal leaders seemed inclined to accept the commissioners' proposal, but the Moderates refused to consider it. On September 24, the President said that it would not be consistent with his dignity and honor to acquiesce in the resignation of the congressmen who were members of his own party and who had been elected on the same ticket with himself. He maintained this position, and reiterated his intention to resign from the presidency, in spite of a strong appeal in writing from the commissioners and a personal message from President Roosevelt urging him to remain in office either under Mr. Taft's plan or under any other practicable arrangement which he could suggest. In reply to Mr. Roosevelt, he said:

the bases proposed by Mr. Taft and Mr. Bacon in order that the rebels should lay down their arms would, if accepted, simply be giving these the victory, encouraging them, once they had put aside their arms, to continue in the same spirit of rebellion and laying the foundation for revolt in the future.

It seems clear that Estrada Palma and his advisers in the Moderate party desired to force intervention by the United States. There were many other influential Cubans, however, who wished to avoid intervention, and strenuous efforts were made at the last moment to bring about a compromise by establishing a provisional government supported by both parties. While the commissioners had some doubt as to the propriety of an arrangement which would have no constitutional basis, President Roosevelt insisted that every expedient, whether constitutional or not, be tried before intervention should become inevitable. The Cuban leaders were unable, however, to agree upon a provisional president, and the Minister of Government told Mr. Taft on September 28 that the Moderates desired intervention and that there was no other possible solution.

On the same day, the President and the Vice-President submitted their resignations to the Cuban Congress. The members of the Cabinet had already resigned, in order to leave no successor to the presidency, for the Cuban law provided that one of the ministers should assume the executive power in default of the President and Vice-President.[33] The Congress, in an effort to avoid the appearance of responsibility for what would inevitably follow, requested Estrada Palma to reconsider his decision, but when he refused to do so the Moderates broke the quorum and thus made it impossible even to consider the possible establishment of a provisional administration. Cuba was left literally without a government, and on the evening of September 28, Estrada Palma asked the American commissioners to assume the custody of the funds in the Treasury and to "put an end to the present unfortunate conditions of the country."

On the next day, Secretary Taft issued a proclamation establishing an American Provisional Government, under his own direction, to be

maintained only long enough to restore order and peace and public confidence, and then to hold such elections as may be necessary to determine those persons upon whom the permanent Government of the Republic should be devolved.

The new régime was to be a Cuban Government, conforming so far as possible to the Cuban Constitution and

---

[33] Martinez Ortiz, *Los Primeros Años,* Vol. II, p. 354.

laws, and with the executive departments administered as they had been under the Republic.[34]

THE PROVISIONAL GOVERNMENT, 1906–1909

The new Provisional Government faced an extremely critical situation. There was no certainty that the large forces still under arms on both sides would accept peacefully the new régime or submit to being disarmed. The Government of the United States had no desire to become involved in a costly campaign of pacification, and President Roosevelt was therefore especially pleased when Mr. Taft reached an agreement with the insurgent leaders on September 29, by which the latter were to surrender their arms and disperse their forces upon the understanding that the terms of the compromise arrangement proposed by the commissioners before Estrada Palma's resignation should be carried out so far as they were now applicable.[35] The disarmament of the former rebels, and also of the militia which the Cuban Government had hastily organized during the revolution, was a delicate task, but it was carried out without very serious difficulty.[36] The Cuban Rural Guard, reorganized by American officers, assumed the duty of maintaining order, and there was no occasion to call upon the American forces which were sent to Cuba immediately after the establishment of the Provisional Government for any active military duty.[37]

Mr. Taft was succeeded as Provisional Governor on October 13, 1906, by Mr. Charles E. Magoon. Before his departure he issued a decree providing that the Cuban Congress should remain in recess during the continuance of the American administration and that the legislative

[34] Annual Report of the Secretary of War, Dec. 12, 1906, p. 463.
[35] Roosevelt to Taft, Sept. 30, 1906, quoted in Taft's report, p. 487. For the terms of the agreement see the same report, p. 464.
[36] Ibid., p. 487.
[37] Charles E. Magoon, Republic of Cuba, Report of Provisional Administration, 1907–8, p. 109.

power should be exercised by the Provisional Governor. The duties of the Cabinet devolved upon the chief clerks in the respective departments, each of whom was placed under the general supervision of an American officer. An Advisory Commission of nine Cubans and three Americans, under the chairmanship of Colonel E. H. Crowder, was appointed to draft the legislation which was to be enacted before new elections were to be held.[38]

Mr. Magoon's conduct of affairs has been severely criticized by certain Cuban writers. It has been asserted that he permitted a reckless and corrupt expenditure of public funds, and that he was unduly generous in the distribution of offices to Cuban politicians and in the granting of pardons.[39] While it is clear that the advisability or propriety of some of the policies adopted by the Provisional Government was open to question, it may be said that American historians who have investigated the matter have reached the conclusion that the more serious charges, at least, are not borne out by facts. Even a writer who is somewhat prone to place the policy of the United States Government in an unfavorable light on other occasions states that "no evidence has been adduced to convict either Magoon or any other American official of the intervention of corruption in the exercise of his office," [40] and the chief American authority on the history of Cuba points out, not only that there is clear evidence that the Provisional Governor did not himself profit from his service in Cuba, but also that the policy which he followed was in reality directed from Washington.[41]

[38] The work of the Provisional Government is described in Mr. Magoon's reports for the period from October 13, 1906, to December 1, 1907, and for the period from December 1, 1907, to December 1, 1908, published in English at Habana in 1908 and 1909 respectively.

[39] A discussion of the charges against Mr. Magoon will be found in Jenks, *Our Cuban Colony*, pp. 95–103, and in Chapman, *History of the Cuban Republic*, Chapter X. For a Cuban account see Martinez Ortiz, *op. cit.*, Vol. II, p. 487.

[40] Jenks, *op. cit.*, p. 98.

[41] Chapman, *op. cit.*, p. 232.

Charges that the Provisional Government was guilty of reckless expenditure of Cuban funds do not seem to be substantiated. President Estrada Palma had left approximately $13,600,000 in the Cuban Treasury, but this sum seems to have been more than offset by outstanding obligations and special appropriations. In the year following his resignation, the financial position of the government was adversely affected by the world depression of 1907 as well as by loss and expense resulting from a hurricane. The Provisional Government had to meet not only the ordinary expenses of government, but also the cost of the 1906 revolution, which was estimated as reaching $8,634,116.64 up to October 31, 1907.[42] It also embarked on a very ambitious program of public works. The condition of the Cuban Treasury appears nevertheless to have been fairly satisfactory when the Provisional Government came to an end in 1909.[43]

It is more difficult to ascertain the truth regarding the charges that the Provisional Governor was unduly generous in awarding contracts, particularly at the end of his administration, and that he failed to exercise a proper supervision over expenditures. It seems very possible that the Provisional Governor and the relatively small number of Americans serving under him failed in many cases to exercise sufficient supervision over some of their Cuban subordinates.

The Provisional Government's freedom of action was limited to a considerable extent by the fact that it took over an organized administration, permeated by politics, and that it was compelled to give weight to purely political considerations in making appointments. There had appeared to be a real necessity when the Provisional régime

[42] Magoon, Report for 1906–7, p. 84.
[43] Chapman, p. 246, says: "An expert accounting of the books of the Estrada Palma and the Magoon administrations might even show that the latter *saved* something, for the actual deficit with which it began may well have been greater than the one it left."

was established to placate the Cuban leaders, and especially the Liberal leaders, in order to obtain their coöperation in the pacification of the island. Many of Mr. Taft's dispatches in September 1906 reflect his anxiety that the American intervention might meet with serious armed resistance. Consequently, when the Liberals protested that nearly all of the government posts were held by Moderates, and that the latter had thus an unfair advantage through their ability to influence the conduct of the Provisional Government, Mr. Taft had promised that Liberals would be appointed to vacancies which might occur until an approximate equality was established.[44] Such appointments were made by Mr. Magoon upon the recommendation of a Liberal Committee, and it was charged that positions with generous salaries were even created in some cases for the benefit of prominent politicians.

The charge that pardons were granted with reckless generosity was important chiefly because of its bearing upon the efforts later made by the Government of the United States to prevent the passage by the Cuban Congress of amnesty bills which would have released large numbers of criminals. Mr. Magoon explained his conduct on the ground that the severity of penalties under the old Spanish law and the lack of discretion given to the judges in cases where there were mitigating circumstances had made it customary to rely upon the pardoning power as a sort of court of final appeal for the correction of obvious injustices; and he sought to show by figures that the Provisional Government had not been more generous to criminals than had the Military Government or the administration of Estrada Palma.[45]

Whatever the conclusion regarding these criticisms of the Provisional Government, it seems clear that the work of the Advisory Commission under the Chairmanship of

[44] Taft, Report, p. 466.   [45] Magoon, Report for 1907–8, p. 87–94.

Colonel Crowder conferred a lasting benefit upon the Republic. Beside the laws contemplated in the peace agreement, governing elections, municipal and provincial government, the judiciary, and the civil service, the commission drafted much other legislation of permanent value, including a much needed organic law for the armed forces of the Republic.

The peace agreement had contemplated the holding of elections immediately after the preparation of the necessary legislation by the Advisory Commission, but the program was changed somewhat by Mr. Taft after he had conferred with the leaders of the various Cuban parties during a visit to Habana in April 1907. It was found necessary to have a census for electoral purposes, and this was taken in the latter part of 1907. Provincial and municipal elections were held on August 1, 1908, and the national elections on November 14, under the immediate control of purely Cuban electoral boards but under the effective supervision of a central board headed by Colonel Crowder. The Liberal party had divided after the revolution of 1906 into two factions, headed respectively by José Miguel Gómez and Alfredo Zayas. This made it possible for the new Conservative party, which had been organized in 1907 by several of the leaders of the now defunct Moderate party, to obtain victories in three of the six provinces at the first election. The Liberals thereafter united upon the Presidential candidacy of José Miguel Gómez, who defeated General Menocal, his Conservative opponent, by a vote of 201,199 to 130,256 in the election of November 14.[46] The new President was formally installed, and the American intervention terminated, on January 28, 1909.

INTERPRETATION OF THE PLATT AMENDMENT, 1909–1913

Although the Government of the United States has not again actually intervened in Cuba, there were several oc-

[46] Ibid., p. 73.

casions in the years immediately following 1909 when urgent representations were made to the Cuban Government to prevent the development of conditions which might have brought about another intervention. This "preventive policy," as it came to be called, was followed particularly during the administration of President Taft, and in a somewhat different form under that of President Wilson.

THE VETERANS' MOVEMENT

A serious situation was created in the latter part of 1911, when the Veterans of the War of Independence began a violent agitation for the removal from public office of all Cubans who had fought on the Spanish side in that conflict. Their attitude became increasingly threatening, in spite of concessions made by the administration, and the American Minister finally recommended that the Government of the United States take a "decided stand." On January 16 he was authorized to hand to the President and to make public the following unsigned note:

The situation in Cuba as now reported causes grave concern to the Government of the United States.

That the laws intended to safeguard free republican government shall be enforced and not defied is obviously essential to the maintenance of the law, order and stability indispensable to the status of the Republic of Cuba, in the continued well-being of which the United States has always evinced and cannot escape a vital interest.

The President of the United States therefore looks to the President and Government of Cuba to prevent a threatened situation which would compel the Government of the United States, much against its desires, to consider what measures it must take in pursuance of the obligation of its relations to Cuba.

This pronouncement was greeted in Cuba by expressions of resentment at American "interference" but it forced both sides to recognize the necessity for a peaceful settlement, and on January 20 the veterans promised to suspend their political agitation. One article of the agreement which they signed with President Gómez stated significantly that: [47]

The Government of the Republic shall publish this agreement so that all may know that those who sacrificed themselves to Independence are the most stable support of the Republic, and that law and order and the stability of our institutions are henceforth guaranteed and peace assured; wherefore there will be no justification for any intervention in our internal affairs by the United States, to whose honor and loyalty as well as to its own patriotism the Cuban people trusts its peaceful development.

THE NEGRO REVOLT

The existence of the Cuban Government was more seriously threatened later in the same year, when Negro political leaders started a revolt for the ostensible purpose of obtaining more recognition for members of their race in the distribution of government positions. The movement soon assumed a dangerous character, and the Cuban Government admitted that it was unable to guarantee full protection to foreign interests in the regions most affected.

In May, therefore, "in the hope of somewhat steadying the situation and thereby assisting the Government of Cuba to put down" the uprising, the Department of State announced that war vessels and marines were being sent to the naval station at Guantánamo to afford protection to Americans in that vicinity in case of necessity. Subsequently, the Cuban Government was informed that the United States, "pursuant to its uniform custom in such cases" would land forces for protection, if the Cuban Government failed to prevent injury to American lives and property. It was pointed out that "this is not intervention." When President Gómez protested to President Taft in a personal cable that

[47] The correspondence regarding the Veterans' Movement was published in *Foreign Relations, 1912*, p. 236 ff. A brief account is also given in Chapman, p. 306–8.

A determination of this serious character alarms and injures the feelings of a people loving and jealous of their independence, above all when such measures were not even decided upon by previous agreement between both governments,

Mr. Taft replied that the purpose of the United States was

merely to be able to act promptly in case it should unfortunately become necessary to protect American life and property by rendering moral support or assistance to the Cuban Government.

He reiterated that "these ordinary measures of precaution were entirely disassociated from any question of intervention." The distinction between a formal intervention under the permanent treaty on the one hand and the temporary landing of forces for purposes of protection on the other was subsequently set forth in more detail by Secretary Knox and was apparently recognized by President Gómez. When four companies of marines were landed at Guantánamo, President Gómez expressed gratification and sent word to the American Minister that their arrival would free Cuban forces for operations against the rebels. The revolt was soon afterward suppressed.[48]

THE AMNESTY BILLS

Secretary Knox also interposed on several occasions to dissuade the Cuban Government itself from proceeding in a manner which might affect the political and financial stability which the Permanent Treaty was intended to safeguard. It will be sufficient to describe briefly three typical cases when action of this nature was taken.

Toward the end of the Gómez administration, the Cuban Congress passed a bill granting a general amnesty not only to participants in the recent Negro Revolt but also to a large number of persons guilty of common crimes, including especially many government officials

[48] The correspondence regarding the Negro Revolt will be found in *Foreign Relations, 1912*, p. 242 ff.

who had been accused of corruption or embezzlement. While the bill was still pending, the American Minister was instructed on January 6, 1913, to protest orally that its enactment would create the impression that crimes were not dealt with in Cuba "in the manner found necessary in all countries to the adequate protection of life, property, and individual liberty." Subsequently, when President Gómez seemed inclined to promulgate the law, the Minister was instructed by cable to

inform the Cuban Government that the amnesty bill seems to be not only an injustice to the American citizens affected but also to effect such a withdrawal of due protection to property and individual liberty of Cuba as to excite this Government's concern. In view of its rights and obligations under the Treaty of Relations of 1903, the Government of the United States expresses its firm conviction that upon final study of this harmful measure the President of Cuba will not permit it to become a law.

President Gómez subsequently returned the bill to Congress for amendment and differences between the two houses delayed further action until after the inauguration of President Menocal. The latter vetoed an amnesty bill which was submitted for his signature later in the year. He also prevented the passage of another bill in 1914, after the Department of State, which adopted a somewhat different tone under Mr. Bryan, had instructed the American Minister to point out informally the bad impression which such a law would cause, saying that this "suggestion arises from the friendly interest taken by the United States in matters affecting Cuba's standing before the world." [49]

THE CUBAN PORTS COMPANY

A case of a different nature arose in 1911, when a contract was entered into with the Cuban Ports Company

[49] For correspondence regarding the Amnesty Bill, see *Foreign Relations, 1913*, p. 354 ff. and *Foreign Relations, 1914*, p. 187–9.

under which tonnage and port dues were to be greatly increased and the proceeds were to be turned over to the company for a period of thirty years in payment for work to be done in improving several harbors. The business appeared likely to be very profitable to the promoters, several of whom were American citizens, and to the Cuban politicians who were associated with them. When London bankers who had been asked to underwrite bonds to provide funds for the work made inquiries as to the views of the Department of State, the latter objected to the plan as "wasteful and against the best interests of Cuba." The contract was therefore substantially modified before the bonds were issued. At a later date, when the Cuban Government cancelled the concession, the Department made energetic representations to bring about a fair settlement with the bondholders, more apparently to protect Cuban credit and to prevent complications with the British Government than for the benefit of any American interests.[50]

THE ZAPATA SWAMP CONCESSION

In July 1912 the American Minister reported that the Cuban Government had granted a concession for the reclamation of the vast Zapata Swamp on the south coast of the island. He expressed doubt of its legality, and said that the reclamation project was merely a specious pretext for giving away "incalculable millions in timber and charcoal woods." The Department of State instructed him to say to the Cuban Government that the concession seemed "so clearly ill advised a project, so improvident and reckless a waste of natural resources," that the Government of the United States was compelled to express "emphatic disapproval" and a conviction that the Cuban Government

[50] The diplomatic correspondence about the Ports Company case appears in *Foreign Relations, 1917*, p. 431 ff. Chapman, *op. cit.*, p. 332–339 gives a more complete account of some aspects of the question, and it is also discussed in Jenks, *op. cit.*, p. 119 ff.

would not put it into operation. President Gómez in reply defended the concession and asserted in rather offensive language that the Platt Amendment did not authorize interference in such a case by the United States. This called forth a strong statement from Secretary Knox. If the apprehension as to the effect of the concession was well founded, he said, ultimately a situation would result requiring intervention by the United States. "In any event," he continued, referring apparently to the corrupt practices which had notoriously characterized the Gómez régime,

this Government believes that the Cuban Government is pursuing a fiscal policy which will ultimately lead to a situation requiring intervention, and therefore, inasmuch as from the standpoint of both governments intervention is not desired, it must be evident to the Cuban Government that the United States is not only justified but is acting in accordance with its rights and obligations in warning the Cuban Government against the course it is pursuing.

President Gómez still disagreed with the United States Government's interpretation of the Platt Amendment, but nevertheless repealed the decree granting the concession. It subsequently appeared, however, that the information upon which the Department of State had based its protest had not been entirely correct, and the objection to the concession was withdrawn when the Americans who were interested agreed to accept modifications protecting the interests of the Cuban Government and of private owners in the swamp.[51]

THE REVOLUTION OF 1917

General Mario García Menocal had become President of Cuba on May 20, 1913. The victory of the Con-

[51] A large amount of correspondence regarding the Zapata Swamp project is published in *Foreign Relations, 1912*, p. 309 ff., and *Foreign Relations, 1913*, p. 365 ff.

servative party in the preceding election had been made possible, in part at least, by a break between President Gómez and the Liberal candidate, Señor Zayas, which had prevented the latter from receiving the customary support from the administration.[52] When General Menocal was a candidate for reëlection in 1916, however, the Liberals were again united. The electoral campaign was marked by violence, and there was some disorder and much fraud on election day. Both sides appear to have been to blame, for several provinces were under the control of Liberal governors and municipal authorities. It is significant that approximately 800,000 votes were cast, and that they were fairly evenly divided between the two parties, whereas a census three years later showed only 477,786 eligible voters in the Republic.[53]

It was at first believed that the Liberals had won. Subsequently, however, the Government began to intercept returns coming in from the provinces to the Central Electoral Board, and the Liberals asserted that the returns were being falsified. The Central Electoral Board and the Supreme Court sustained their appeals and awarded to them the electors from Habana and Camaguey. New elections were ordered in a few precincts in Santa Clara and Oriente provinces, but it seemed impossible that their result could overcome the Liberal majority in Santa Clara, which, with Habana and Camaguey, would give Zayas a majority in the electoral college.[54] The Liberals, however, regarded the elaborate military precautions adopted by the Government as evidence of its intention to win the election at any cost. After the Administration rejected their proposal that the voting be supervised by a commission of six designated persons,

[52] The following account of political events in 1916 is based mainly on Chapman's book. The account of the revolution is based on *Foreign Relations, 1917.*

[53] Chapman, *op. cit.*, p. 353-4.

[54] *Foreign Relations, 1917*, p. 350.

four of whom were Conservatives,[55] they resorted to armed revolt, without even awaiting the new elections.

The revolt had practically started when the Department of State, on February 10, 1913, instructed the American Minister to communicate to President Menocal a lengthy statement, intended for publication in Cuba, saying in effect that it hoped that the dispute about the election would be settled by legal means. This was followed on February 13 by another public statement making it clear that the Government of the United States would give its support only to a government established by legal and constitutional means. A third statement, sent to the American Minister on February 18, was more definite. The "Cuban people" were informed that: [56]

1. The Government of the United States supports and sustains the Constitutional Government of the Republic of Cuba.

2. The armed revolt against the Constitutional Government of Cuba is considered by the Government of the United States as a lawless and unconstitutional act and will not be countenanced.

3. The leaders of the revolt will be held responsible for injury to foreign nationals and for destruction of foreign property.

4. The Government of the United States will give careful consideration to its future attitude towards those persons connected with and concerned in the present disturbance of peace in the Republic of Cuba.

Meanwhile the revolutionists, under the leadership of Ex-President Gómez, had obtained control of a large part of the eastern end of the island. There was grave doubt for a time as to the loyalty of the Cuban army and much fear of an uprising in Habana,[57] but the substantial victories won by the Government in the field, culminating with the capture of Gómez with his entire staff on March 8, soon gave it control of the situation except in the

[55] Chapman, op. cit., p. 360.
[56] For the text of these statements, see Foreign Relations, 1917, p. 351 356, 363.
[57] Ibid., p. 359.

province of Oriente. The Liberals, who had apparently hoped for a repetition of the events of 1906, were profoundly discouraged by the attitude assumed by the United States, and there is no question but that the public statements issued by the American Legation did much to contribute to their defeat.

The Department of State, however, obviously did not wish simply to support the Cuban Government without regard to what might have been the outcome of the election if the Liberals had not resorted to arms before the electoral process was completed. On March 1, it had urged General Menocal to offer to hold new elections in Santa Clara and Oriente and to grant an amnesty if the rebels would lay down their arms. Nothing came of this suggestion, because General Menocal objected on grounds of policy to proposing an armistice, and pointed out that the suggestion for new elections was based on a misconception of the situation. The new election had already been held in Santa Clara province, giving the Conservatives some 2,000 votes in precincts where the number of voters had previously been estimated at about 1,500, and military conditions made it impossible to hold elections in Oriente. The Cuban President also failed to act on a suggestion made on March 10, that he should "ask for an investigation and adjustment of the election question by General Crowder and other representative Americans." The new elections subsequently held in a few precincts in Oriente did not affect the majority already obtained by the Conservatives in that province, and the election of General Menocal was duly proclaimed by the Cuban Congress on May 7.

Throughout the revolt, the Department of State had been besieged by requests for protection from American sugar producers and other interests, and American marines had been landed at several points when it seemed probable that the Cuban Government's forces could not prevent the destruction of foreign property. Even after the revolt was practically crushed, several marauding bands continued to cause anxiety to property owners. In May 1917 the United States indicated that it contemplated sending a considerable force to assist in preventing any interference with the production of sugar, which had acquired a new importance since both the United States and Cuba had entered the World War. President Menocal, although at first expressing the opinion that such action was unnecessary, subsequently gave his cordial approval, and a force of marines was therefore stationed in Cuba during the war and for some time after its close.

The American Minister reported on June 18, 1917, that the revolt could be considered as entirely suppressed. The defeated rebels were treated with conspicuous leniency. Although several leaders had been condemned to death, the penalties were reduced in every case by executive clemency, and even Ex-President Gómez, the leader of the revolt, was released from prison in March 1918.[58]

THE WORLD WAR AND ITS RESULTS

Cuba's declaration of a state of war with Germany on April 7, 1917, led the United States to extend an even more emphatic support to the constituted government, and helped to discourage those Liberals who were still under arms. In a public statement issued May 15, 1917, the Cuban people had been told that "the time has now arrived when all internal political questions must be set aside in the face of the grave international danger." [59]

. . . In the present war [Mr. Lansing said], in order to insure victory, Cuba, as well as the United States, has two great obligations, one military and the other economic. Therefore, as the Allied Powers and the United States must depend to

[58] *Foreign Relations, 1918*, p. 283.
[59] *Foreign Relations, 1917*, p. 407.

a large extent upon the sugar production of Cuba, all disturbances which interfere with this production must be considered
as hostile acts, and the United States Government is forced to
issue this warning that unless all those under arms against the
Government of Cuba return immediately to their allegiance it
may become necessary for the United States to regard them as
its enemies and to deal with them accordingly.

It was recognized from the first, as Mr. Lansing indicated, that Cuba's principal contribution to the Allied
cause would be the production of sugar to supply the
deficiency caused by the devastation of the beet producing
areas of Europe. It seemed probable during the first sum-
mer of the war that an acute sugar shortage might develop
if the available supply were not increased and placed under
some form of control. On September 30, 1917, therefore, the United States Food Administration announced
that an International Sugar Committee, with American
and British members, had been created to arrange for the
distribution of the available supply of sugar in the entire
world.[60] This committee subsequently purchased the
Cuban crops of 1917–8, and 1918–9 at fixed prices.
Financial assistance was extended to the sugar industry
through American banks, and production was increased
from less than three million tons before the war to nearly
four and one half million tons in 1918–9. In 1918, Cuba
received a loan of $15,000,000 from the United States
Treasury, a part of which was used for the rehabilitation
of railroad lines needed for the transportation of the sugar
crop.[61]

At the end of the war, the control of sugar prices in the
United States ceased, and the Sugar Equalization Board
made no arrangement to buy the Cuban crop of 1919–20.
As world production was still below normal, prices increased, and within a short time speculation in sugar had

[60] *Foreign Relations, 1918*, p. 340.
[61] For the correspondence regarding this loan, see *Foreign Relations, 1918*,
p. 284–339.

reached almost incredible proportions. At one time in May, 1920, sugar was sold f.o.b. Cuban ports at 22.5 cents per pound.[62] Cuba enjoyed for a time an unexampled prosperity, and both the Government and private citizens indulged in an orgy of reckless spending, "the Dance of the Millions." Within a few months, however, there was a disastrous collapse. The price of sugar declined as rapidly as it had risen until it reached four cents per pound in December 1920, and the sugar producers who had purchased or improved properties on the basis of inflated values and the banks which had financed them were very seriously affected. A general moratorium was put into effect by the Government on October 10.

It was under these conditions that the presidential election of 1920 took place. The administration candidate was Alfredo Zayas, whose followers had abandoned the Liberals and formed a new organization, the "Popular" party, which now joined with the Conservatives. The Liberals nominated Ex-President José Miguel Gómez. In an effort to prevent a repetition of the disorders which had occurred four years before, both parties had united in inviting General Crowder, the head of the Advisory Commission under the Provisional Administration, to visit Cuba in 1919 to revise the electoral law. The Liberals, however, had little confidence in the Administration's willingness to assure fair play and in August 1920 they threatened to withdraw. They were dissuaded from doing so by a statement issued by the American Legation, in which it was indicated that the United States would have observers at hand to discourage intimidation or fraud.[63] When the election took place, however, the American supervision, confined as it was to the presence

[62] Philip G. Wright, *The Cuban Situation and Our Treaty Relations* (Washington, the Brookings Institution, 1931), p. 56.

[63] This statement was given to the Cuban press by the American Chargé d'Affaires on August 30, 1920.

of observers without effective control, was insufficient to insure satisfactory conditions. Seventy-three out of one hundred and twelve municipalities were placed under the control of military supervisors, and much intimidation and fraud appears to have occurred on November 1, when the voting took place. The Liberals were excited and bitter, and the situation became more tense when the electoral boards and the courts for various reasons failed to act promptly upon the appeals which were at once laid before them.[64]

GENERAL CROWDER'S MISSION

The Republic was therefore in a state of economic collapse which almost made certain an early default upon the foreign debt, and was also threatened with civil war. It was under these circumstances that President Wilson sent General Crowder to Habana as his personal representative in January 1921.

Through General Crowder's efforts, the machinery for settling the electoral dispute was at once put in motion. The Supreme Court annulled the elections in about one-fifth of the voting districts, and it was arranged that new partial elections should be held on March 15. The President and the two candidates were brought together in a "Pact of Honor" which sought to assure fairness and freedom when the elections took place. The Liberals, however, refused at the last moment to go to the polls, alleging that the guaranties offered were not sufficient, and the result was naturally a victory for Señor Zayas, the Government candidate. General Gómez went to Washington to ask the United States to compel the holding of new elections under an American provisional government, but his mission was unsuccessful.

General Crowder endeavored also to assist the Cuban

[64] Chapman, p. 399–409, gives a good account of the 1920 election.

Government in dealing with the economic situation. The first step toward the establishment of more normal conditions was obviously the raising of the moratorium. Under three acts of Congress known as the Torriente Laws, banks and merchants who were solvent were permitted to resume payments gradually over a period of months, and a commission was created to liquidate banks which were not solvent.[65] This legislation, partly because it was ineffectively administered, failed to prevent the complete collapse of nearly all of the banks in the island. The Banco Nacional, an important institution with many branches, closed its doors on April 9, 1921, a few days after its chief stockholder had committed suicide, and other failures followed rapidly during the next two months. Two foreign institutions, the National City Bank and the Royal Bank of Canada, were the only important banks to survive. Excessive expansion, mismanagement, and in many cases actual dishonesty, had apparently brought all of the others to a situation where nothing could have saved them.

More success attended the effort to improve the very critical situation of the Cuban Government's own finances. The revenues during the fiscal year 1920–21, had been the largest in the Republic's history, reaching $108,000,000, but expenditures had been $182,000,000.[66] The Government had lost many millions of dollars which had been deposited in the closed banks, and its revenues were decreasing to little more than fifty per cent of the total for the preceding year. There was a floating debt of an indeterminate amount resulting largely from contracts granted by the Menocal Administration, and the Government had defaulted on the bonded debt, both foreign and internal, early in 1921.[67] President Zayas had recognized

[65] Translations of the Torriente Laws were furnished to the press by the Department of State on February 5 and February 17, 1921.

[66] Chapman, p. 424.

[67] Ibid., p. 425.

in his inaugural address the urgent need for an immediate reduction in the Government's expenditures as a first step toward the reëstablishment of the national credit, but it was not until several months later, and until after prolonged and earnest representations by General Crowder, that any effective reduction took place. It is said that the reduction of the budget for the fiscal year 1921–22 to $59,000,000 and for 1922–23 to $55,000,000 was one of the conditions under which the Cuban Government obtained an Emergency Loan of $5,000,000 from American bankers in January 1922.[68]

This Emergency Loan, which made possible the resumption of payments on the bonded debt, was intended to be merely the first step in a general program of financial rehabilitation. A larger loan was contemplated for the refunding of the floating debt, but the United States Government took the position that it could not approve such a loan until the Cuban Government had placed its financial administration on a sounder basis and had eliminated the administrative evils and the corruption which were largely responsible for the difficulties in which it found itself.[69] General Crowder, who had made a careful study of the problem during the first year of his mission, began early in 1922 to set forth his views in a series of fifteen memoranda which he laid before President Zayas. While very little information regarding the contents of these memoranda has been divulged,[70] the main features of the program which General Crowder sponsored were fairly clear. They included the reduction of the

[68] Jenks, op. cit., p. 253.

[69] It is very difficult to discuss authoritatively the events of the past fifteen years in Cuba, because little of the official correspondence has been published and such accounts as exist are based on inadequate source material, in so far as they deal with the policy of the United States Government. Chapman, op. cit., Chapter XVIII, perhaps gives the most reliable account of General Crowder's mission, based chiefly upon information obtained in Cuba.

[70] Chapman, p. 426–437, gives such information as was available in Cuba regarding their contents. What purported to be the text of memorandum No. 13 was published in August 1922 by a Cuban newspaper.

budget, the rescinding of extravagant or improper contracts, and in general the elimination of corruption from the national administration.

General Crowder insisted especially upon a reform in the National Lottery, which was perhaps the most important source of graft. The lottery brought great profits to favored politicians because the tickets, which were disposed of at a fixed price to agents called "collectors," could usually be sold to the public at a considerable advance over the legal price. Politicians who were given one or often several collectorships were thus able to turn over the tickets assigned to them, without labor or risk on their part, to professional wholesalers, with a profit which is estimated at more than three thousand dollars a year for each collectorship. It is said that the Cuban people paid approximately $30,000,000 annually for lottery tickets in normal times, of which less than $15,000,000 was returned in prizes and $4,000,000 went into the national treasury. The remainder, after paying the cost of administration, was available for political purposes, and the distribution of collectorships, controlled as it was by the President of the Republic, proved to be a most effective means of obtaining political support.[71]

Presumably as a result of General Crowder's representations, President Zayas accepted the resignations of several of his ministers in June 1922 and appointed what has since been referred to in Cuba as "the Honest Cabinet." The new ministers energetically effected such reforms as were possible by administrative action, including some improvement in the Lottery, and the Department of State announced two months later that advices from Cuba indicated substantial progress toward a definite and satisfactory solution. It was stated that the Cuban leaders

[71] A detailed description of the Cuban lottery and its relation to Cuban politics is given in Chapter XXIII of Chapman's *History of the Cuban Republic.*

after full discussion had evolved a definite program embracing the following fundamental measures: [72]

1. The modification of certain provisions of the civil service law and the temporary suspension of others to permit the reorganization of the executive departments and particularly of the services collecting revenues and controlling expenditures.

2. A law establishing a better and stricter system of accounting.

3. A law to create a commission to investigate and determine the amount of the floating debt.

4. A law to improve judicial procedure and to facilitate the removal of certain members of the judiciary.

5. A law providing for a foreign loan to settle the floating debt to make possible the initiation of public works, and creating new taxes for the service of the loan.

On September 14, however, a less optimistic statement was issued: [73]

Reports from Cuba are to the effect that considerable opposition has developed in the Cuban Congress to the reform program of the Cuban Government. Amendments have been made which, if finally enacted, would render nugatory the reform measures which it is hoped will be adopted, and which are essential to Cuban prosperity.

The Department was very gratified that President Zayas had undertaken to carry out the reform measures proposed, but is now very much concerned at the obstructionist action of the Cuban Congress. All well wishers of Cuba, including most of the leading Cuban citizens and the Cuban press, have realized for some time that the plan as presented to the Cuban Congress is vitally necessary for stamping out corruption. No progress can be made towards the financial rehabilitation of the Island until this program is carried out.

While the situation presented by this opposition in Congress is most serious and is causing the Department a great deal of concern, the Department is, nevertheless, still confident that the matter will be satisfactorily adjusted. General Crowder has the complete confidence and support of the American Government in his difficult mission and the Department hopes and believes

[72] Department of State Press Release, August 22, 1922.
[73] Department of State Press Release, Sept. 14, 1922.

that it will still be possible for Cuba to carry out the reforms in the manner suggested by him, and in this way avoid the serious situation which would otherwise inevitably arise.

Subsequently the Congress passed the proposed legislation in a satisfactory form. On October 18 the Cuban Government formally advised the Department of State that it desired to float a loan of $50,000,000 in pursuance of its program for the solution of its economic difficulties, and inquired, in view of Article II of the Permanent Treaty, whether the United States had any objection. A favorable reply was received on November 4,[74] and arrangements for the loan were completed early in 1923.

Although there had been much opposition in Cuba to a large foreign loan, President Zayas had apparently felt that the Government's financial difficulties could not be solved without it and had therefore been willing to accept the program of reform upon which General Crowder had insisted. With the loan in hand, his attitude rapidly changed. Although he is said to have promised both the United States Government and the issuing bankers, at the time when the loan was floated, that the Honest Cabinet would remain in office indefinitely,[75] he removed four of its members on April 3. There was a rapid reversion to the conditions which the reform program had sought to eliminate, accompanied by emphatic public assertions that the Cuban Government would no longer submit to foreign interference in its internal affairs. While the diplomatic correspondence of this period has not been published, it is clear that the United States did not actively attempt to influence the policy of the Cuban Government, once the crisis which had led to General Crowder's appointment as Personal Representative of the President had passed. General Crowder's own status had changed

[74] Department of State Press Release, Nov. 4, 1922.
[75] Chapman, p. 440, 443.

with his appointment as American Ambassador in January 1923.

Certain large financial transactions which took place after the resignation of the Honest Cabinet aroused strong opposition to President Zayas' administration and led the Veterans' and Patriots' Association to start a movement for the ostensible purpose of terminating the alleged wholesale corruption in the Government. This led to a small revolt in April 1924, which was easily put down after the Government of the United States had placed an embargo on the shipment of arms to the revolutionists and had itself sold war equipment to the Cuban Government.[76] President Zayas was not, however, able to bring about his own reëlection later in the same year, because he was defeated by General Menocal for the nomination of the Conservative party, which had been his chief support in 1920. Consequently, he gave his support to General Gerardo Machado, the Liberal candidate, who was elected.

PRESIDENT MACHADO'S ADMINISTRATION

Although overproduction of sugar and the resulting weakness of prices began to make the situation of Cuba's chief industry extremely precarious some years before the advent of the world depression, President Machado's first term was on the whole a period of general prosperity. Business activity was stimulated by the inflow of large sums borrowed in the United States for road construction and other purposes, and there was a notable development of the tourist trade. There was less interest in partisan politics than at times when economic conditions were more difficult.

A constitutional convention which met in April 1928 changed the presidential term from four to six years and provided that while future presidents should not be

[76] *Ibid.*, p. 469–480.

eligible for reëlection this prohibition should not apply to the President then in office. In the meantime, by a policy of *rapprochement* in which the distribution of lottery collectorships seems to have played an important part, the President had been able to obtain the support of all of the three regular party organizations. He was aided in this by the fact that the provisions requiring a periodical reorganization of the political parties had been eliminated from the Crowder Electoral Law, thus perpetuating the control of each by a small group of men. Prohibitions against the nomination of the same candidate by different political parties had also been removed, and the organization of independent parties had been made more difficult. General Machado was, therefore, the only candidate on the ballot at the presidential election in November 1928.

There was nevertheless some opposition to the President's reëlection, although the impossibility of placing another candidate on the official ballot had prevented its expression at the polls. As time went on, disaffection became more and more evident, and there were allegations that the Administration was discouraging open manifestations of discontent by harshly repressive measures. The desperate economic situation, brought on by the collapse of sugar prices and the general effects of the world depression, created unrest as it did in many other Latin American countries. With the approach of the congressional elections of 1930, disturbances and political arrests became increasingly frequent, and the students at the University of Habana, who had been among the most outspoken opponents of the President's reëlection, staged a series of riots which resulted in loss of life and in the closing of the University by the President's order. Efforts to bring about an agreement between the President and his opponents proved unsuccessful, and an armed revolt occurred in August 1931, but was easily suppressed. Aside from the enforcement of the neutrality laws, to prevent the departure of armed expeditions from American ports, the Government of the United States took no action in connection with this revolt.

Feeling, apparently, that a revolution of the ordinary type would be hopeless so long as the Cuban army remained loyal, President Machado's opponents inaugurated a new form of campaign, which assumed serious proportions in the spring of 1932. Secret revolutionary organizations, among which one called the A.B.C. was the most prominent, attempted to make the situation of the Administration intolerable by murdering public officials, obstructing the operation of the government by propaganda and sabotage, and creating minor disorders throughout the country. The Administration retaliated by making great numbers of political arrests, and several political agitators, including a number of students, were killed by the police. A veritable reign of terror resulted.[77]

REVOLUTION OF 1933

In June 1933 it was announced that both the Government and the A.B.C. had accepted the mediation of the American Ambassador, Mr. Sumner Welles, in an effort to terminate this situation. Several other revolutionary groups subsequently agreed to participate in the negotiations, although others, including the University students and the followers of Ex-President Menocal, were reported to be holding aloof. Professor McBain, of Columbia University, was employed by the Cuban Government to draft a new electoral law in preparation for a free election at the end of the President's term. For a time there appeared to be a good prospect for an agreement between the President and his adversaries.

Early in August, however, all forms of transportation were paralyzed by a general strike, organized as a protest

[77] The above account is based mainly on press reports. It is impossible to give a satisfactory or authoritative account of recent political events in Cuba, and no effort has therefore been made to discuss these events in detail.

against General Machado's continuance in power. As the movement spread, commercial activity in Habana ceased altogether. On August 7 a false report that the President had resigned brought rejoicing crowds into the streets and many were killed in resulting clashes with the police and the troops. The American Ambassador appears to have suggested that the President withdraw from office as the only means of assuring peace. The President refused at first to do so, but on August 11 the Army, which had been his main support, abandoned him and demanded his resignation. General Machado fled from Habana by airplane on August 12, leaving the presidency to Dr. Carlos Manuel de Céspedes, who had been appointed by agreement as Minister of Foreign Affairs. For a day or two there was much disorder in Habana, and several police officers of the former régime were killed by mobs in the streets.

Under these conditions three small American war vessels were sent to Habana and Manzanillo on August 13, but one of these was withdrawn on the following day and the others shortly afterward. In a statement issued when the vessels were sent, President Roosevelt said:

Latest advices are to the effect that domestic disturbances, including acts of violence, are occurring in some parts of Cuba among certain elements of the population.

In these circumstances, I feel constrained as a matter of special precaution and solely for the purpose of safeguarding and protecting the lives and persons of American citizens in Cuba, to order certain vessels to points on the Cuban Coast.

The change of government now taking place in Cuba is in entire accord with the recognized Constitution and laws of that country, and no possible question of intervention or of the slightest interference with the internal affairs of Cuba has arisen or is intended by this precautionary step to protect, if necessary, the lives of American citizens, pending the restoration of normal conditions of law and order by the Cuban authorities.

I am giving strict instructions accordingly to the commanders of each vessel.

The American people deeply sympathize with the people of Cuba in their economic distress and are praying that quiet and strict order may soon prevail in every part of Cuba. The American Government will lend all aid feasible, through constituted Cuban authorities, for the relief of the distressed people of the island.

Although the Provisional President endeavored to have all of the principal revolutionary groups represented in his cabinet, he was unable to obtain the coöperation of the followers of Ex-President Menocal, the Communists or the students. His administration was unsatisfactory to the more radical revolutionary leaders, who felt that he did not proceed fast enough in effecting political and economic reforms, and who also asserted that his connection with the elements which had hitherto dominated political affairs and his friendly relations with the United States would be an obstacle to the realization of the ultra-nationalistic program which the principal revolutionary organizations had advocated.

On September 5, the Provisional President was overthrown by a revolt of the enlisted men of the Army and Navy, working in concert with the students' organization, the Directorio Estudiantil. Dr. Ramón Grau San Martín, former dean of the medical school of Habana University, was chosen as President by the revolutionary council on September 10. The new administration, which had no claim to be regarded as the constitutional successor of the De Céspedes régime, was not recognized by the United States, although it was intimated in Washington that purely constitutional considerations would not be a bar to eventual recognition if the new government should show itself able to maintain order and to discharge its international obligations. Its ability to meet these requirements seemed questionable. The Army, which had mutinied against its officers, had been reorganized under a group of sergeants, but its discipline and efficiency had been seriously affected. The treasury was empty and governmental machinery seemed to have broken down in the interior provinces. Nearly all of the political factions withheld their coöperation. Efforts which were made during September and October to obtain their support were unsuccessful. Five hundred officers of the Army, who had been displaced from their commands by the mutiny, established themselves, heavily armed, in the National Hotel, where they defied the authority of the new government until they were compelled to surrender on October 2 after a battle in which many lives were lost. The Communists also actively opposed the new régime, and created disturbances in Habana and the interior.

Under these conditions, a number of American warships had again been sent to Cuban ports. American citizens were obviously in grave danger, for political agitators were violently denouncing the supposed disposition of the United States to interfere in Cuba's internal affairs, and such propaganda for a time at least was evidently fomented by the faction which controlled the new administration. In the interior a number of American sugar mills and other enterprises were seized by the workers, and in some cases the foreign staffs were imprisoned or threatened in an effort to compel the management to agree to higher wages or new working conditions. It was reported on September 20 that the representatives of the Department of State were advising Americans in the troubled areas to take refuge on the war vessels. American marines had not, however, been landed in Cuba up to November 2.

The possible effect of these events in Cuba upon relations with the other Latin American countries evidently caused concern in Washington. On September 6 President Roosevelt invited the diplomatic representatives of Argentina, Brazil, Chile and Mexico to the White House to tell them that he wished their governments to have the fullest information about the situation and to explain to them the attitude of the United States. His statement was summarized as follows for the press:

1. That he wanted them to have complete and constant information about the Cuban situation to the fullest extent that the United States has such information.

2. That the United States has absolutely no desire to intervene in Cuba and is seeking every means to avoid intervention.

3. He expressed to them the very definite hope on the part of the United States—what might be called the key to this country's policy—that the Cuban people will obtain as rapidly as possible a government of their own choosing and, equally important, a government that will be able to maintain order.

Of course, the President added, if a government is constituted as quickly as possible that will maintain order, it will have the happy effect of obviating the thought or the necessity for intervention by the United States.

Inspired apparently by the President's action, the Mexican Government on September 8 invited the Argentine, Brazilian and Chilean Governments to bring pressure upon the new régime in Cuba to maintain order and protect foreign lives and property. Brazil and Chile, at least, appear to have approved this suggestion, although the result of any representations which they may have made was not immediately apparent. The Argentine Government, in a statement made public on September 8, expressed its gratification at President Roosevelt's expressed purpose to avoid intervention in Cuba and indicated its own opposition to intervention in the internal affairs of a Latin American country under any conditions.

Unlike previous political conflicts in Cuba, the revolution of 1933 seems to be something more than a mere contest for power and office. Such organizations as the A.B.C. and the Directorio Estudiantil professedly seek to eliminate completely both the party leaders who have hitherto been prominent in political affairs and the evils which have hitherto characterized Cuba's political life.

Many of them advocate also the adoption of radical measures to free the Republic from what they believe to be the political and economic domination of the United States. A movement of this nature will obviously create new and difficult problems in Cuban-American relations, especially if the permanent government which emerges from the present situation is controlled by the elements which have hitherto taken the leading part in the revolution. It is not improbable, for example, that an effort will be made to abrogate the Platt Amendment. There is also a possibility that legislation seriously affecting American interests in Cuba will be adopted in an effort to change the economic and social conditions created, in part at least, by the dominance of American capital in the island's commerce and industry.

CUBAN–AMERICAN ECONOMIC RELATIONS

From an economic and commercial standpoint, Cuba is far more important than any other Caribbean country. The volume of its commerce with the United States exceeds that of any other Latin American republic, and American investments in the island, variously estimated at from one to one and a half billions of dollars,[78] are

[78] Dr. Max Winkler, in his *Investments of United States Capital in Latin America* (World Peace Foundation, Boston, 1928), estimated the total American investment in Cuba as $1,505,000,000, divided as follows:

Sugar industry	$800,000,000
Real estate	150,000,000
Railroads	120,000,000
Government bonds	110,000,000
Public utilities	110,000,000
Industrials	50,000,000
Tobacco	50,000,000
Commercial	40,000,000
Mines	35,000,000
Banks	25,000,000
Miscellaneous	15,000,000
Total	$1,505,000,000

Other estimates are somewhat lower, and the actual value of American investments at the present time is probably far less than the total given.

greater than in any other country except Canada and Germany. A large amount of American capital had gone into Cuba before the Spanish-American War, mainly for the development and modernization of the sugar industry, and there was a further steady increase in the early years of the Republic. It was during and immediately after the World War, however, that the greatest expansion of American investments occurred, for many sugar properties were purchased by American interests during the war and American banks were compelled to take over many others during the collapse of 1920–21. The proportion of the crop manufactured by American-owned mills is estimated to have increased from 35% shortly before the war to 62½% in 1926–27, with an additional 8% produced by mills in which American capital had a part interest.[79] Much American capital was also invested in the island's other industries and in real estate.

Although the Republic possesses great mineral deposits, especially in the province of Oriente, and there is an important tobacco industry in the western provinces, the overwhelming relative importance of sugar production makes Cuba practically a one-crop country. So much of the arable soil is devoted to cane as to make it necessary to import great quantities of food supplies.

Under these conditions, the control of an increasing proportion of the sugar mills by foreign capital has created social problems of an increasingly serious nature. Much of the cane itself is still produced by Cuban owners, called *colonos,* but these have been more and more reduced to a position of dependence upon the great sugar *centrales,* which control manufacturing and transportation facilities and afford the only outlet for the crop. A large proportion of the *colonos* find themselves compelled not only to

[79] Jenks, in *Our Cuban Colony,* presents a detailed study of the growth of American investments, especially in Chapter XV. The figures here given are taken from him.

sell their product to the local *central*, but to purchase their supplies at the company store, and there have been complaints of extortion and abuses such as inevitably arise under such a system. With the extreme depression through which the sugar industry has been passing in recent years, dissatisfaction among the native planters has naturally become stronger; and one of the objectives of some of the present revolutionary groups in Cuba is the restoration of the control of the sugar industry to Cuban hands. While the inflow of American capital into Cuba, and the largely involuntary taking over of sugar properties by American banking interests since 1920 have been a purely economic movement which neither government could well have attempted to control, it is evident that any effort through legislation or other political action to reverse the process would almost inevitably create diplomatic problems of a most troublesome nature. Even a continuance of the present situation will have an unfortunate effect upon the relations between the two countries, particularly if some means cannot be found to bring about at least a partial return of prosperity to the sugar industry.

Cuba's economic welfare depends upon her ability to sell sugar to the United States. The recognition of this fact led the American Government to grant preferential treatment to her principal crop when the Republic was first established. So long as the entire production of Cuban sugar could be sold in the American market, as it was until just before the World War, there could be no question as to the benefit which the Reciprocity Clause conferred. When increased production made it necessary to sell a part of the crop elsewhere, however, competition among Cuban growers tended to reduce the price in Cuba to the price on the world market rather than in the protected market in the United States, with the result that a substantial part of the advantage formerly derived from the Reciprocity Clause disappeared.[80] The effects of the change were not, of course, felt so long as war conditions created a serious shortage in the world as a whole, but with the resumption of beet production in Europe, the Cuban planters found themselves in an increasingly difficult situation. In recent years, especially, prices have fallen far below the cost of production and the Government's efforts to improve the situation, first by curtailing the Cuban crop, and later by entering into crop-restriction agreements with other producing countries, have met with little success. The marketing of Cuban sugar has been made especially difficult by the increasing prevalence of high protective tariffs for the benefit of local producers in other countries.

This has been especially true with respect to the tariff imposed upon sugar by the United States. Whereas Cuba might have benefited from a high tariff so long as duty-paid sugar from other countries was going into the American market, she is handicapped by such a tariff when she is competing solely with sugar which is duty-free. Production in the United States and its possessions increased from 2,198,000 tons in 1922–3 to 3,800,000 tons in 1929–30 [81] partly as a direct result of the tariff, and the apparent beginning of a great sugar industry in the Philippines has given Cuban planters great concern. There is an increasingly strong feeling that the Reciprocity Clause in its present form no longer affords Cuba the economic security intended by its signers. Several plans have been discussed in recent years for giving Cuba a fixed quota in the American market, or for otherwise enabling her to obtain the full benefit of the preferential duty, but no practical result has thus far been achieved.

[80] This situation is fully discussed in Wright, *The Cuban Situation and Our Treaty Relations*. In an interesting table on p. 59, Dr. Wright shows the proportion of the total Cuban output exported to the United States in each year from 1900 to 1929.

[81] Wright, *op. cit.*, p. 85.

Recent press reports, however, have indicated that the American Government realized the importance of extending economic assistance to Cuba as a means of promoting more stable political conditions there, and the Department of State announced on June 9, 1933, that the American Ambassador had been instructed to proceed with negotiations for the revision of the Reciprocity Treaty in connection with the Administration's general policy of obtaining reciprocal trade agreements with other countries. It was added that the revised treaty would be submitted to the United States Senate at the next session of Congress.[82] Subsequent developments in Cuba, however, have prevented the conclusion of a new agreement.

[82] State Department, *Press Releases*, June 9, 1933, p. 434.

CHAPTER II

PANAMA AND THE CANAL

Earlier Canal Projects

Early in the nineteenth century, the Government of the United States became interested in the possibility of building a transisthmian canal. It was equally concerned with the problem of assuring to American citizens the free use of any canal which might be built. A treaty concluded with New Granada in 1846, stipulated "that the right of way or transit across the Isthmus of Panama upon any modes of communication that now exist, or that may be hereafter constructed, shall be open and free to the Government and citizens of the United States," in return for which the United States guaranteed the neutrality of the isthmus and the freedom of transit there, as well as the rights of sovereignty and property of New Granada therein.[1]

In 1850, after a controversy arising from the activities of Great Britain on the Mosquito Coast, the United States entered into the Clayton-Bulwer Treaty, which provided that neither the American nor the British Government would seek any exclusive control over a canal through Nicaragua. Other agreements regarding the proposed

[1] The text of all treaties entered into by the United States Government up to 1923 will of course be found in Malloy's *Treaties, Conventions, International Acts, Protocols and Agreements, between the United States of America and Other Powers,* 3 vols., Washington, 1910–1923.

The treaties relating to the Panama Canal will also be found in a publication entitled *Treaties and Acts of Congress Relating to the Panama Canal,* published in Washington at the Government Printing Office, 1917.

waterway were made from time to time with Nicaragua and with Costa Rica. A commission created by Act of Congress in 1872 gathered information regarding the various routes proposed and reported in 1876 that a canal through Nicaragua offered greater advantages with fewer difficulties than any other project thus far studied. Further investigations in Nicaragua were made by commissions appointed in 1895 and 1897.

Several unsuccessful attempts to construct a canal had been made by private companies, both American and European. Repeated efforts were made in Congress to obtain official assistance for the Maritime Canal Company of Nicaragua, an American concern which had obtained a concession from Nicaragua in 1887, but which ceased work because of financial difficulties in 1893. Meanwhile, a French company had been endeavoring to construct a canal in Panama, under a concession granted by Colombia in 1878. The company had failed after some years because of financial mismanagement, but a new company had taken up the work, and the Colombian Government had thrice granted extensions of the time within which the canal was to be completed. The first company had done a very large amount of excavation, but its successor, unable to obtain capital, was obviously unable to make further progress. It had become evident by the end of the century that the canal would be built only if the power and resources of the United States Government itself were devoted to the task. During the Spanish-American War, the spectacular voyage of the *Oregon* around South America strikingly demonstrated the necessity for a canal from the standpoint of national defense, and stimulated American interest in the project. An Act of Congress, approved March 3, 1899, authorized a full investigation of all practicable canal routes, including particularly those in Nicaragua and Panama, with a view to the construction of a canal by the United States.

THE HAY-PAUNCEFOTE AND HAY-HERRÁN TREATIES

The Clayton-Bulwer Treaty, which would have been an obstacle to American control of the canal, was abrogated by the Hay-Pauncefote Treaty, signed November 18, 1901, in which it was agreed that the canal might "be constructed under the auspices of the Government of the United States" and that "subject to the provisions of the present treaty, the said Government shall have and enjoy all the rights incident to such construction, as well as the exclusive right of providing for the regulation and management of the canal." Article III laid down rules for the neutralization of the canal, providing especially that "the canal shall be free and open to the vessels of commerce and of war of all nations observing these Rules, on terms of entire equality," and that no right of war should be exercised nor any act of hostility committed within it.

On November 16, 1901, the commission appointed in 1899 recommended that the canal be built in Nicaragua, because it considered excessive the price demanded by the French company for the transfer of its rights and property at Panama.[2] Upon learning of this report, however, the French company offered to reduce its price from $109,141,-500 to $40,000,000, the amount estimated by the commission as reasonable, and a supplementary report, submitted January 18, 1902, recommended the Panama route.[3] An Act of Congress approved June 28, 1902, provided for the construction of the canal and created an Isthmian Canal Commission to conduct the work. The President was authorized to acquire the rights and property of the French company at a cost of not over forty million dollars, and to acquire from Colombia, upon such terms as he might deem reasonable, the perpetual control of a strip of land and the right to construct a canal therein. If it

[2] Senate Doc. No. 54, 57th Congress, 1st Session.
[3] Senate Doc. No. 123, 57th Congress, 1st Session.

should prove impossible to obtain a satisfactory title from the French company, or to reach an agreement with Colombia, the canal was to be constructed in Nicaragua.[4]

An agreement with Colombia was reached in the Hay-Herrán Treaty, signed at Washington on January 22, 1903. Colombia authorized the French company to sell all its rights and property, including the Panama Railroad, to the United States. For a term of one hundred years, renewable indefinitely at the sole and absolute option of the United States for similar periods, the American Government was granted the exclusive right to "excavate, construct, maintain, operate, control, and protect" the canal, as well as the use of a zone extending three kilometers on each side of the canal, but excluding the cities of Panama and Colon. The sovereignty of Colombia over this zone, however, was explicitly recognized. Her courts were to exercise jurisdiction there over controversies between her citizens or between Colombians and citizens of foreign powers other than the United States, while American courts were to have jurisdiction over controversies between Americans or between Americans and other foreigners, and courts established jointly by the two governments were to have jurisdiction in other civil cases and in all criminal cases. Colombian forces were to protect the canal under ordinary circumstances, although the United States was to assist if requested and might in an emergency act of its own accord. Colombia was to receive ten million dollars upon the ratification of the treaty, and an additional sum of $250,000 annually, beginning nine years from the date of ratification.[5]

The treaty was ratified by the United States Senate on March 17, 1903, and was submitted to a special session of the Colombian Congress which convened on June 20.

[4] *Treaties and Acts of Congress Relating to the Panama Canal*, p. 27.
[5] For the text, see *Diplomatic History of the Panama Canal*, Senate Doc. No. 474, 63rd Congress, 2nd Session, p. 277.

Before the Congress met, however, it was learned that the Colombian Government had notified the French Canal Company and the Panama Railroad Company that it would expect additional payments from them, in return for its permission to transfer their rights to the United States.[6] Secretary Hay, who had declined to accept a similar proposal during the treaty negotiations, protested that the attempt to impose an additional burden on the companies would destroy the whole basis of the agreement. While the Congress was in session, the Government of the United States again stated that no amendments increasing its own payments or imposing additional burdens upon the French company could be considered, and urged the necessity for a prompt ratification of the treaty as signed. The Colombian Government, however, apparently made no serious effort to obtain ratification, although its supporters were in the majority in both houses of Congress, and on August 12 the treaty was disapproved.

THE REVOLT IN PANAMA

The people of Panama, who were already feeling severely the commercial depression which had followed the suspension of work by the French company, felt that the construction of the canal by another route would deprive them of the transit trade which was the very basis of their economic existence. They had insistently demanded the ratification of the Hay-Herrán Treaty, and the danger of a separatist movement on the isthmus if the treaty were defeated had been realized at Bogotá and had in fact been discussed in the Congress while the treaty was under consideration. It was in anticipation of a probable revolt that the Colombian Government ordered a force of four hundred men to Colon in the early days of November.[7]

---

[6] The correspondence with Colombia regarding the Hay-Herrán Treaty is printed in *Diplomatic History of the Panama Canal.*

[7] *Diplomatic History*, p. 481; *Foreign Relations, 1903*, p. 190.

The arrival of this force precipitated the movement which disaffected leaders in Panama had already planned. With the aid of the commander of the principal Colombian force at Panama City, revolutionists seized control of the city on the evening of November 3, and the independence of Panama was proclaimed on the following day. The United States Government had sent the U.S.S. *Nashville* to Colon just before the outbreak. It had taken similar action in fulfillment of its obligations under the treaty of 1846 on many previous occasions when disorder or impending revolution threatened the freedom of transit or the safety of the Panama Railroad, which was still an American corporation. On November 2 instructions had been sent to the commander of the *Nashville* to maintain free transit, to occupy the railroad line if interruption of the service was threatened by armed forces, and to prevent the landing of armed forces either of the government or of insurrectionists if such forces arrived with hostile intentions. The Colombian forces had landed before these instructions were received, but the commander of the *Nashville* prevented their proceeding to Panama and thus made impossible the suppression of the revolt. Three days later the independence of the Republic of Panama was recognized by the United States, and on November 18 the Hay–Bunau Varilla Treaty, providing for the construction of a canal through Panama by the United States, was signed at Washington. Since this agreement guaranteed Panama's independence, the Colombian Government was given to understand that no effort to recover her former territory by force of arms would be permitted.

The propriety of President Roosevelt's action in connection with the independence of Panama has been severely criticized. It is impossible to attempt any adequate discussion of the question here. Colombia protested vigorously that her Congress was entirely within its rights in rejecting the Hay-Herrán Treaty, and expressed the belief that a satisfactory agreement might still have been reached if it had not been for the uncompromising attitude of the United States. Her representative at Washington insinuated that the revolutionary movement at Panama had been instigated and encouraged by interests in the United States and by American officials, and insisted that the "premature recognition" of Panama's independence and the military measures which had been taken were violations of the treaty of 1846, under which the United States had guaranteed "the rights of sovereignty and property" of Colombia in the isthmus. Secretary of State Hay, on the other hand, emphatically defended the legality and fairness of the course pursued. He denied that any responsible official of the United States Government had been in communication with the revolutionists in Panama. Characterizing the action of the Colombian Government in connection with the Hay-Herrán Treaty as equivalent under the circumstances "to a refusal of all negotiation with this Government," Mr. Hay said that "the people of Panama rose against an act of the Government at Bogotá that threatened their most vital interests with destruction and the interests of the whole world with grave injury." This created a situation which deeply concerned the United States, especially in view of its obligation under the treaty of 1846, the main purpose of which had been the construction of an interoceanic canal.[8]

THE SETTLEMENT WITH COLOMBIA

Although Secretary Hay had refused to admit that the action of the United States had not been entirely justifiable, he had nevertheless recognized that Colombia had "suffered an appreciable loss" and indicated a willingness to exercise good offices to bring about negotiations between

[8] *Foreign Relations, 1903*, p. 284, 294.

Colombia and Panama for the "possible apportionment of their mutual pecuniary liabilities." [9] This suggestion led, after prolonged negotiations, to the signature on January 9, 1909, of the so-called Root-Cortés-Arosemena treaties, between Colombia and Panama, the United States and Panama, and the United States and Colombia. Colombia was to recognize Panama's independence, and Panama was to transfer to Colombia the first ten installments of the $250,000 canal annuity, in return for the mutual release of all pecuniary claims. The boundary between the two republics was fixed except with regard to a small area on the Pacific, the ownership of which was to be submitted to arbitration. Colombia was to be granted certain privileges in the use of the canal, and the United States also agreed to begin the payment of the annuity five years earlier than required by the treaty of 1903, thus providing half of the money to be paid to Colombia by Panama. Popular opposition in Colombia caused the abandonment of these treaties, after their ratification had been approved both by the Panaman Congress and by the United States Senate.[10]

When Mr. Bryan became Secretary of State, he obtained proposals from the Colombian Government on the basis of which the treaty of April 6, 1914, was finally signed. As originally drawn, the first article contained an expression of regret on the part of the United States, but this was later eliminated because of opposition in the Senate. Approval of the treaty was again delayed when the Colombian Government promulgated certain decrees adversely affecting American interests,[11] but ratification was finally obtained in 1921. Under the treaty, Colombia and her citizens were assured the same treatment as the

[9] *Ibid.*, p. 306.

[10] For the texts of these treaties and the correspondence regarding them, see *Diplomatic History of the Panama Canal.*

[11] See Senator Lodge's speech in the Senate, April 12, 1921. *Cong. Rec.*, Vol. 61, Pt. 1, p. 157.

United States Government and American citizens with respect to the use of the Canal and the entrance of persons and goods into the Canal Zone, and Colombia also received from the United States a payment of $25,000,-000 in five annual installments. The Colombian Government recognized the independence of Panama and accepted a definitive boundary line between the two countries.

THE CANAL TREATY

The Convention for the Construction of a Ship Canal, which was signed at Washington on November 18, 1903, provided that "the United States guarantees and will maintain the independence of the Republic of Panama." Panama granted to the United States in perpetuity "the use, occupation and control" of a Zone ten miles wide "for the construction, maintenance, operation, sanitation, and protection" of the canal, and the use, occupation and control of any other lands outside of the Zone which might be needed for these purposes. Panama further granted to the United States all the "rights, power and authority" within the Zone and its auxiliary lands and waters "which the United States would possess and exercise if it were the sovereign of the territory within which said lands and waters are located, to the entire exclusion of the exercise by the Republic of Panama of any such sovereign rights, power and authority." In return for these grants, Panama was to receive ten million dollars in cash, payable immediately, and an annual payment of $250,000 during the life of the convention, beginning nine years after the exchange of ratifications. Owners of private lands taken by the United States for Canal purposes were to be compensated for the value of the land, as of the date of the convention, after appraisal by a joint commission. The Canal was to be neutral in perpetuity and was to be open to the ships of all nations, as provided in the Hay-Pauncefote Treaty, but the United States was to have the right to protect and fortify it and Panama agreed to sell or lease land for naval stations for this purpose. Some of the other provisions of the treaty, which is too long and detailed for full and accurate summarization, will be discussed below in connection with specific aspects of the relations of the United States and Panama.[12]

The Canal Treaty took effect upon the exchange of ratifications on February 26, 1904. On April 28 the United States Congress authorized the President to take possession of the Canal Zone and to establish there a provisional government "protecting the inhabitants thereof in the free enjoyment of their liberty, property and religion." [13] The boundaries of the Zone were established by an agreement signed on June 16, 1904, which was subsequently modified by the Boundary Treaty of September 2, 1914.

The occupation of the Canal Zone by the United States created a complicated and delicate situation. Panama's two principal cities, the only part of her territory which had ever been important from a commercial or political standpoint, were so close to the American communities at either end of the Canal as practically to form continuous urban areas. Both cities were completely surrounded on the land side by Canal Zone territory, until the return of the *Savanas* lands to Panama in 1914 gave Panama City an outlet through the Republic's own territory to the provinces lying east of the Canal. Many officials and employees of the United States lived in the Panaman cities, and nearly all of them visited these cities frequently to patronize shops or places of amusement. Several small communities of Panaman citizens, on the other hand, remained in the Zone until all land there was

[12] For the text of the treaty, see Appendix.
[13] *Treaties and Acts of Congress Relating to the Panama Canal*, p. 30.

taken for Canal purposes about 1914. The United States used the port of Colon at the beginning for importing supplies for the Canal, whereas on the other hand Panama City depended to a great extent for its connection with the outside world upon the Panama Railroad, which had passed into the hands of the United States. As owner of the railroad, the United States had acquired property rights to practically all of the land in the city of Colon and to much valuable real estate in Panama City.

It was inevitable under such circumstances that many difficult questions should arise between the two Governments. When the problems which have given rise to controversies are discussed below, it should be borne in mind that the inevitable differences of opinion which have occurred in this complicated situation have seldom affected the close and mutually helpful coöperation between the Panaman authorities and the Zone government, especially in such matters as sanitation, street construction and maintenance and public works. The relations between the two Governments have in general been far more friendly than a perusal of the published diplomatic correspondence would appear to indicate.

THE TAFT AGREEMENT

The first serious controversy between the two Governments involved the interpretation of the Canal Treaty. An Executive Order, issued by President Roosevelt on June 24, 1904, opened the Canal Zone to commerce and provided for the establishment of United States customhouses at Ancon and Cristobal, the ports at either end of the Canal; and at the same time authorized the Governor of the Canal Zone to enter into a tentative agreement for reciprocal trade relations and uniform tariff rates with the Republic of Panama.[14] The Government of Panama

[14] For the text of this order and the correspondence which followed, see *Foreign Relations, 1904,* p. 585 ff.

had apparently been prepared to enter into such an agreement, for the National Assembly, on June 6, had authorized the President to enter into negotiations for this purpose, and the President, as late as July 17, had informed the Governor of the Canal Zone that he had been authorized "to reduce or increase our duties and taxes according with the rates which your Government shall establish at the Canal Zone." [15]   On July 15, however, the Panaman Chamber of Commerce presented a memorial to the Panaman Government asserting that the Zone had been granted to the United States only for Canal purposes and not for the establishment of ports, custom-houses, and tariffs and alleging that the establishment of customhouses would ruin the trade of Panama.   On July 25, the American Minister reported that the President had protested against the action of the United States, and that there was "much agitation of the subject in Panama."

In a note dated August 11, 1904, the Panaman Minister at Washington set forth the point of view which his Government has maintained down to the present day.[16] He maintained that the Canal Treaty did not make the United States the sovereign of the Canal Zone, and that Panama, in specifically accepting limitations upon her own action in the Zone, as in agreeing under Article X not to levy taxes on Canal material, and in Article XII to permit free access to the lands of the Canal of employees and workmen, showed that she retained such sovereign rights as were not specifically granted.   He pointed also to the provisions of Article XIII, permitting the United States to import material for the Canal into the Zone free of duty as showing that Panama retained her fiscal sovereignty over the Zone.   He denied, therefore, the right of the United States to set up its own ports or to establish customs houses, and he objected to the estab-

15 *Ibid.*, p. 622-3.
16 *Ibid.*, p. 598.

lishment of post offices using American stamps for foreign mail. The Minister stated that the policy being pursued by the United States would mean the ruin of Panama's commerce and of the government finances.

Secretary Hay's reply, dated October 24, 1904,[17] set forth very fully the views of the United States regarding the exercise of sovereign rights in the Canal Zone. Mr. Hay emphasized the fact that Article III granted to the United States all of the rights which it would have if it were the sovereign of the Zone, to the entire exclusion of the exercise of such rights by Panama. He argued that the phrase "for the construction, maintenance, operation, sanitation and protection of said Canal" indicated the purpose of the grant of sovereign rights but did not limit its exercise; and he explained the provisions of Articles IX, X, XII and XIII by the fact that many employees of the Canal resided, and much Canal property was situated, in the cities of Panama and Colon at the time when the Treaty was signed, and that steamers coming to the Atlantic coast of Panama with Canal material used the port of Colon. This made the provisions exempting Canal employees and property from taxation and assuring free access to the lands and workshops of the Canal necessary. Mr. Hay further argued that some of the provisions pointed to by the Panaman Minister as providing for the exercise of authority by Panama in the Canal Zone referred solely to acts to be performed outside of the Zone in the territory of Panama and pointed to the wording of Articles IX, XII and XIII in justification of this point of view. He also pointed out that official acts of the executive, legislative and judicial authorities in Panama had explicitly recognized the cession of the Zone to the United States, and referred especially to the law of June 6, authorizing the President to enter into a tariff agreement with the United States.

[17] *Ibid.*, p. 613.

The Government of the United States continued to maintain the legal position assumed in Mr. Hay's note, and has in fact maintained this position down to the present day, but it nevertheless realized that an inconsiderate exercise of its authority in the Zone would work a great hardship to Panama. When the Secretary of War, Mr. Taft, visited the Isthmus in November 1904, therefore, he arranged a series of conferences with the Panaman authorities and the authorities of the Canal Zone, at which a *modus vivendi* satisfactory to both parties was worked out. This arrangement, which is known as the Taft Agreement, was made public on December 3, 1904, in the form of an Executive Order issued by Mr. Taft under authority from the President of the United States after its text had been formally approved by the President of Panama.[18]

The Order provided that no goods were to be imported through Ancon and Cristobal except supplies for the Canal or for the use of officials and employees of the United States, goods in transit for destinations outside of the Isthmus, and fuel to be sold to seagoing vessels. In return Panama was to reduce certain customs duties and consular fees, to maintain her constitutional prohibition of official monopolies, so far as the importation and sale of merchandise was concerned, and to permit the free importation through Panaman ports of goods destined for the Canal Zone. The Order also provided that vessels entered or cleared at Panama or Colon might use dockage facilities at the Zone ports and vice versa, and that vessels entered or cleared at Panama were to have the free use of the anchorage now in Zone waters which seagoing vessels touching at Panama had commonly used in the past. No charges were to be made on goods or persons crossing the line between Panama and the Canal Zone. The Zone post offices were to use surcharged Panaman

[18] *Ibid.*, p. 640, 643.

stamps, purchased by the United States at 40 per cent of their face value. This Executive Order, with several supplementary Orders, was given the force of law so far as the United States was concerned by the Panama Canal Act of 1912.

The Taft Agreement had been intended to serve only as a *modus vivendi* while the Canal was under construction. It remained in effect, however, for some years after the Canal was opened to commerce in 1914, and even after its formal abrogation on June 1, 1924, the rules and practices established under it were continued temporarily so far as commercial operations in the Canal Zone were concerned, pending the negotiation of a new treaty.[19]

THE COMMISSARY QUESTION

The Taft Agreement and the policy followed by the United States since its formal abrogation did much to protect the merchants of Panama, who would have been practically ruined if the Canal Zone, into which goods could be imported free of duty from the United States, had been thrown open to commerce without restrictions. Except for a few farmers cultivating small tracts of land under licenses, residence in the Zone has been restricted to officers and employees of the United States or of enterprises closely connected with the operation of the Canal. The United States Government has maintained commissaries to supply goods of all descriptions to the Canal force, but it has not permitted the general public to trade in them. Private business enterprises, except in a few special cases, have not been permitted in the Zone. On the other hand, facilities have been extended to private merchants residing in Panama for making sales to vessels transiting the Canal, although these merchants have found it difficult to compete with the Canal storehouses

[19] State Department Press Release, May 28, 1924.

and commissaries which are also engaged in this business.

The restrictions which the United States has accepted in the exercise of what it considered its treaty rights have not, however, gone far enough to satisfy the Government and the merchants of Panama. Panama has contended that there is no justification for the sale of tobacco or luxuries in the commissaries, even though the supply of staple necessities to the Canal force might be justified. She has pointed out that it is impossible with the best of intentions to prevent the smuggling of such articles into Panama. Objections have also been made to the sale by the Canal of supplies for ships passing through. While the American authorities have endeavored so far as possible to prevent the misuse of the commissary privilege, they have insisted that neither treaty provisions nor considerations of fair play required the United States to abandon its policy of furnishing supplies to its employees in the Canal Zone at reasonable prices.[20]

THE TREATY OF 1926

A Convention to replace the Taft Agreement and to adjust several other outstanding questions between the two Governments was signed on July 28, 1926.[21] This treaty would have perpetuated the restrictions which the United States had already imposed upon itself with regard to commercial activities in the Canal Zone. Except for sales to ships, articles imported by the United States into the Zone were to be sold only to its own officers and employees and to contractors working for the Canal Zone and their employees. The United States reserved, however, the right to permit the establishment of bonded warehouses. It agreed to assist Panama to prevent the smuggling into

[20] For a brief discussion of the Commissary question, see *Panama and the United States*, Foreign Policy Association Report, January 20, 1932.

[21] The text of the Treaty is printed in the *Congressional Record*, Vol. 68, Pt. 2, p. 1846.

the Republic of goods purchased in the commissaries. It also agreed that no new private business enterprises should be established in the Canal Zone with the exception of bonded warehouses, and with the further exception of enterprises directly connected with the operation of the Canal, such as cable companies, oil companies, and ship agencies. Residence on the Zone was to be restricted to officers and employees of the United States, contractors working for the Canal and their employees, and settlers farming small patches of land. There was to be reciprocal free importation of goods from Panama into the Canal Zone and from the Canal Zone into Panama, with the exception of goods from the commissaries which might be found in the possession of persons other than employees of the United States. There was likewise to be free passage of persons, with the exception of immigrants to Panama. The United States agreed to give Panama space in the Zone ports for the establishment of custom-houses.

Panama agreed in the treaty to cede to the United States as part of the Canal Zone an area in Colon which was already owned by the Panama Railroad Company and which was being used for Canal purposes. In return, the United States agreed to cede to Panama a strip of territory on the borders of Colon and also to assist in the construction of a road across the Isthmus by continuing the existing road from Panama as far as Alajuela and furnishing up to $1,250,000 toward the cost of a road from Alajuela to Colon and Porto Bello. It also agreed to construct a bridge or a ferry across the Canal and to assist Panama in constructing roads on the Pacific side to the east and west of Panama City.

The treaty provided that the owners of private lands taken in the future for Canal purposes should receive their value at the time when the land was taken rather than the value as of 1903. Although the United States for many years had usually fixed the price of land taken by amicable agreement with the owners in order to avoid the hardship entailed by strict application of the rule of the 1903 treaty, this new provision was an important safeguard for Panaman interests.

Other provisions of the treaty dealt with the passage of intoxicating liquors through the Canal Zone to points in Panama, the continuance of the existing American control of sanitation in Panama City and Colon, coöperation between the two Governments in the control of radio communication and commercial aviation, and the use of Panaman silver currency as legal tender in the Canal Zone. Article XI, which became important because of its subsequent effect on Panaman public opinion, provided that Panama would coöperate with the United States in the defense of the Canal and would consider herself in a state of war whenever the United States should be engaged in war, turning over to the United States complete control of aviation and radio communication throughout her territory if the United States should deem necessary, and giving to the United States control of the joint military operations.

When this treaty was submitted to the Panaman Congress for ratification, it encountered very strong opposition, inspired largely by the political opponents of the Government which had signed it. Much misleading propaganda was circulated with regard to the possible effects of Article XI, despite the announcement that this article had been proposed by the Panaman commissioners themselves. There was a much stronger objection to the cession of territory in the city of Colon, a provision which was highly distasteful to the Panaman Government itself and had been accepted only in order to obtain the advantages granted to Panama by other articles of the treaty. After much acrimonious discussion, the Panaman Congress declined to ratify the treaty and requested the Government to undertake new negotiations. Efforts to conclude a new agreement satisfactory to both parties have thus far been unsuccessful.

SANITATION AND PROTECTION OF THE CANAL

The Canal Treaty had contained special provisions for the sanitation and protection of the proposed waterway, because it had been evident that an especially close cooperation between the two Governments would be necessary for these purposes.

None of the problems involved in the construction of the Canal was more important than the establishment of sanitary conditions which would make it possible for the officials and employees engaged in the work to live safely in the Canal Zone, and which would prevent the waterway from being a focus of infection when it was opened to commerce. From the days when shipmasters coming to the great Fair at Porto Bello had frequently lost from one-third to one-half of their men during their visit, the Isthmus had been notoriously unhealthful for foreigners. Yellow fever alone is estimated to have killed two thousand white employees of the French Canal Company from 1881 to 1889, in a force averaging about sixteen hundred.[22] Fortunately for the success of the American enterprise, the work of Walter Reed and his associates at Habana had shown how yellow fever was transmitted and how it could be eliminated, and similar progress had been made in the control of malaria and other tropical diseases.

The Canal Treaty, in Article VII, had authorized the United States to construct and operate works of sanitation such as sewers and water supply systems in the cities of Panama and Colon, to prescribe sanitary ordinances for these cities, and to enforce such ordinances itself if the local municipal authorities should fail to do so. In January

[22] W. P. Chamberlain, *Twenty-five Years of American Medical Activity on the Isthmus of Panama*, p. 7.

1905, when the outbreak of yellow fever had made
it imperative to take adequate preventive measures without loss of time, the Panaman Government asked the
Canal authorities to take over immeditaely the enforcement of the recently drafted sanitary ordinance.[23] The
public health work in Panama City and Colon has ever
since been carried on under the direction of the Health
Officer of the Canal. Yellow fever has been practically
unknown on the Isthmus since 1905,[24] and malaria and
other tropical diseases, at least in the two Panaman cities
and in the settled portions of the Zone, have been brought
under effective control.

This work has involved the expenditure of large sums of
money and the vigilant enforcement of stringent sanitary
regulations, but it has transformed what was formerly
one of the most unhealthful districts in the world into a
place where natives and foreigners alike can live in
safety. Dr. William C. Gorgas, who had had charge
of sanitation in Habana under the Military Government of
Cuba, was Health Officer of the Canal for many years during the construction period.

The treaty of 1903 granted to the United States the
right to protect and fortify the Canal and to take over
such lands outside of the Zone as might be necessary for
this purpose. It also provided that Panama would sell
or lease to the United States the lands necessary for the
establishment of naval or coaling stations on either side
of the Isthmus.[25] The American Government was thus
given full authority to defend the Canal both against attacks by foreign enemies and against violations of its neutrality. The protection of the Canal, which involves also
the protection of Panama itself, has required certain limitations upon Panama's freedom of action with respect to
matters of military importance. In general, Panama has

[23] *Foreign Relations, 1905*, p. 707.
[24] Chamberlain, *op. cit.*, p. 14.
[25] See Articles II, III, XXIII and XXV.

willingly coöperated in measures for the defense of the Canal by affording facilities for the maneuvers of American troops in Panama territory, by coördinating her road construction program with that of the authorities in the Canal Zone, and in other respects.

A problem not foreseen by the treaty arose with the development of the wireless telegraph. In April 1914, the American Minister was instructed to point out to the Panaman Government the desirability of an agreement which would prevent the establishment of stations which might interfere with the system of wireless communication established by the United States for Canal purposes. The Minister was instructed to say that the United States believed that it would be authorized under the Canal Treaty to take over and control such stations if necessary, but that such procedure seemed undesirable because it would cause delay and friction.[26] After some negotiation, the President of Panama issued the following decree:

. . . It is decreed: From this date the radio-telegraphic stations fixed and movable and everything relating to wireless communications in the territory and territorial waters of Panama shall be under the complete and permanent control of the United States of America; and to attain that end said Government will take the measures which it deems necessary.

Several radio stations were subsequently established by the United States in remote districts of Panama where they would be useful not only for Canal purposes but more especially as a means of enabling the Panaman Government to maintain communication with its local officials.

With the development of modern commercial broadcasting, the problem of radio control became more complex. The treaty signed in 1926 dealt with this subject, but the refusal of the Panaman Congress to ratify the treaty left matters as they were. The situation was presumably further complicated by Panama's action in

[26] *Foreign Relations, 1914,* p. 1042.

abrogating the decree of 1914 by a new decree issued December 29, 1930.[27] Recent press reports have stated that the whole question of radio control is again under discussion between the two Governments.[28]

The development of commercial aviation also raised questions of the greatest importance to the defense of the Canal. While the United States could of course control flying in or across the Canal Zone, an inconsiderate exercise of this control would have prevented the establishment of air mail and passenger communication between Panama's principal cities and the outside world. This matter, like the question of radio communication, would have been satisfactorily settled if the treaty of 1926 had been ratified. It became urgent in 1928, when several companies sought permission to establish air services across the Isthmus or between Panama and foreign countries, and early in 1929 it was finally dealt with by an arrangement which took the form of executive orders issued by the two Governments. The President of the United States laid down regulations to govern aviation in the Canal Zone on February 18, 1929,[29] and on May 4 of the same year, the President of Panama established very similar rules to govern flying within the Republic. Aërial navigation by privately owned airships in Panama was placed under the control of a board on which the Governor of the Panama Canal, the Major General commanding the Panama Canal Department, and the senior officer of the United States Navy on the Isthmus, with three Panaman citizens, serve as members.[30]

BOUNDARY QUESTIONS

Article I of the Canal Treaty provides that "the United States guarantees and will maintain the independence of

[27] Panama, *Gaceta Oficial*, August 2, 1933.
[28] *New York Herald-Tribune*, August 20, 1933.
[29] Executive Order No. 5047, February 18, 1929.
[30] Panama, *Gaceta Oficial*, June 17, 1929; *Panama Star and Herald*, May 7, 1929.

the Republic of Panama." This provision has not been interpreted in practice as implying any right to interfere in the conduct of Panama's normal relations with other countries, but with respect to Panama's boundaries the United States has considered that the guaranty required it to "advise itself as to the extent of the sovereignty of the Republic of Panama and hence of the territorial limits of Panama." [31] This has involved a rather active participation in the Republic's territorial disputes with her neighbors.

A provision for the settlement of the boundary with Colombia was included, as we have already seen, in the unratified tripartite treaties of 1909. When the treaties failed of ratification, the question was of course left unsettled. In the treaty between the United States and Colombia ratified in 1922, however, in which Colombia's recognition of Panama's independence had been obtained, the United States had recognized Colombia's claim to a line based on a law which had fixed the boundaries of the State of Panama in 1855, and had furthermore undertaken to bring about the resumption of diplomatic relations between the two countries in order that a definite agreement on the line might be reached. On May 8, 1924, a meeting between the Colombian and Panaman Ministers at Washington was arranged through the good offices of Secretary Hughes, at which the Panaman Minister was informed of the recognition of his country's independence by Colombia and an exchange of diplomatic representatives was arranged.[32] On August 20, 1924, a treaty was signed under which a boundary line was definitely agreed upon.[33]

The boundary with Costa Rica gave more trouble. A long standing controversy between that country and Colombia had been submitted to arbitration by the President of the French Republic under treaties signed in 1880,

[31] Secretary Hughes' note of March 15, 1921, to Panama made public by the Department of State on March 17.
[32] State Department Press Release of May 8, 1924.
[33] League of Nations *Treaty Series*, 1925, Vol. XXXIII, p. 168.

1886 and 1896, but it had proved impossible to agree upon the execution of the award which President Loubet rendered in 1900 because the arbiter had apparently based his decision upon a misunderstanding of the geographical features of the region involved. A treaty establishing a definite line had been signed in 1905, but had not been ratified by Costa Rica. The Porras-Anderson Convention, signed in 1910 through the good offices of the United States, had submitted the interpretation of the Loubet award to arbitration by the Chief Justice of the United States Supreme Court, so far as the northern end of the line was concerned, and had at the same time established a definite boundary between the two countries on the Pacific side.[34] Chief Justice White's decision was rendered on February 12, 1914. Finding that the spur of mountains fixed upon as the boundary by President Loubet did not in fact exist, he drew a line which seemed to him most in accord with the "correct interpretation and true intention" of the former award, favoring in the main the contentions of Costa Rica.[35]

Panama refused to accept the award, on the ground that the arbiter had exceeded his powers and had not drawn the line within the confines of the territory in dispute, as the treaty of 1910 required. She continued to exercise jurisdiction over a small area on the Pacific Coast, on the Costa Rican side of the line recognized in the Porras-Anderson Treaty, maintaining that this treaty had ceased to be effective with the failure of the arbitration and that the *status quo* agreed upon in 1880 should be continued pending a final settlement. She pointed out that Costa Rica was at the same time continuing to occupy

[34] For the text of the Porras-Anderson Treaty and the correspondence which led up to its signature, see *Foreign Relations, 1910*, p. 772–822. The text of the Treaty is on p. 820. Further correspondence is printed in *Foreign Relations, 1911*, p. 674–7.

[35] *Foreign Relations, 1914*, p. 993–1028, contains the correspondence regarding the White award and the attitude assumed by Panama. The text of the White award begins on p. 1000.

territory on the Atlantic side which was claimed by Panama under the Loubet award. Although the Government of the United States, at the request of Costa Rica, urged Panama in April 1915 to accept the award, the latter refused to do so without compensation.[36]

Thus matters remained until 1921, when Costa Rica, after the failure of further diplomatic representations, sent troops to occupy the Coto region on the Pacific side, claimed by her under the Porras-Anderson Treaty but still held by Panama. Her forces were routed with heavy losses by an expedition composed largely of the Panama City police force, but a new army was sent into Panaman territory on the Atlantic side of the Isthmus, and military operations on a large scale were apparently imminent when the United States interposed and persuaded Costa Rica to withdraw her troops to permit an orderly settlement of the question.[37]

On March 15, 1921, in response to a request from the Government of Panama for a statement of the views of the United States as to its obligations toward Panama under Article I of the Canal Treaty in a situation such as that created by Costa Rica's attack, Mr. Hughes set forth the position of the United States in a lengthy note which read in part as follows:

By Article I of the Hay-Bunau Varilla Treaty, it is provided that the Government of the United States "guarantees and will maintain the independence of the Republic of Panama." The Government of the United States fully recognizes the obligation thus assumed, and its recent communications to the Governments of Panama and Costa Rica have been dictated not only by its manifest interest in the maintenance of peace but by its recognition of its duty in the circumstances disclosed. The Government of Panama cannot fail to realize that in order that the Government of the United States may fully perform its obligation under the treaty it must advise itself as to the extent of the sovereignty of the Republic of Panama and hence of the territorial limits

[36] *Foreign Relations, 1915*, p. 1131–1155.
[37] State Department Press Release, March 7, 1921.

of Panama. It follows that the Government of the United States deems it necessary to inquire fully into the merits of a controversy which relates to the boundary of the Republic of Panama. This Government has no doubt that the Government of Panama will also recognize that there is implicit in the provisions of the Hay-Bunau Varilla Treaty an undertaking on the part of Panama to observe faithfully its international obligations. The guaranty given to the Republic of Panama by the United States is obviously conditioned upon that performance.

It appears that the question which has been raised by the Government of Panama with respect to the boundary between Panama and Costa Rica has two aspects: (1) with respect to what may be termed the Pacific side of the Cordillera, and (2) with respect to the Atlantic side. The Government of the United States deems it to be beyond controversy that the boundary line on the Pacific side was determined by the arbitral award of His Excellency, the President of the French Republic, on the 11th of September, 1900. The line on the Pacific side, as thus determined, was unequivocally accepted by both the Republic of Panama and the Republic of Costa Rica in the Porras-Anderson Treaty of March 17, 1910. In Article I of that treaty it is stated that the Republic of Panama and the Republic of Costa Rica "consider that the boundary between their respective territories designated by the arbitral award of His Excellency the President of the French Republic, the 11th of September, 1900, is clear and indisputable in the region of the Pacific from Punta Burica to a point beyond Cerro Pando on the Central Cordillera near the 9th degree of north latitude."

Notwithstanding this fact the Government of Panama apparently has taken no steps to fulfill its obligation to recognize the territory on the Costa Rican side of that line as subject to the jurisdiction of the Government of Costa Rica but has continued to exercise jurisdiction over the territory beyond that boundary until the present time. It is to be observed that it is in that territory, belonging to Costa Rica, that Coto is situated. Because of the obligations and special interests of the Government of the United States, because of the obligations on the part of Panama, and because of the earnest desire of this Government that the Government of Panama shall maintain the most friendly relations with its neighbors in order that its own welfare and prosperity may be enhanced and that its territorial and political integrity may be free from attack, this Government considers it to be an unavoidable duty to request the Government of

Panama at once to take steps to confirm the boundary line from Punta Burica to a point in the central Cordillera north of Cerro Pando, near the ninth degree of north latitude, by relinquishing its jurisdiction over the territory on the Costa Rican side of that line, as defined by the Loubet award, and by transferring such jurisdiction to the Government of Costa Rica in an orderly manner.

Mr. Hughes went on to examine in detail Panama's objections to the White award, and stated that it was the opinion of the United States Government that the award was valid and binding upon Panama. He therefore urged the Panaman Government "in the most friendly, but most earnest manner" promptly to conclude arrangements with Costa Rica for the demarcation of the boundary line on the Atlantic side.

As Panama maintained the position which she had already assumed, Mr. Hughes reviewed the legal aspects of the entire boundary question in a note delivered on May 2, again expressing the belief that Panama's continued occupation of the Coto region was unjustifiable and that the White award was valid.

The Government of the United States [he said in conclusion] feels compelled to state that it expects the Government of Panama to take steps promptly to transfer the exercise of jurisdiction from the territory awarded to Costa Rica by the Loubet award, at present occupied by the civil authorities of the Government of Panama, in an orderly manner, to the Government of Costa Rica. Unless such steps are taken within a reasonable time, the Government of the United States will find itself compelled to proceed in the manner which may be requisite in order that it may assure itself that the exercise of jurisdiction is appropriately transferred and that the boundary line on the Pacific side, as defined in the Loubet award, and on the Atlantic side, as determined by the award of the Chief Justice of the United States, is physically laid down in the manner provided in Articles II and VII of the Porras-Anderson Treaty.

On August 18, after further exchanges of communications, the Government of Panama was informed that the reasonable time mentioned in Mr. Hughes' note of May 2 had elapsed and that the United States saw no reason why the Government of Costa Rica should not at once assume jurisdiction over the Coto region.[38] The dispatch of an American warship to Panama helped to make it clear that no armed resistance by the latter would be permitted, and the territory in question was consequently transferred to Costa Rican jurisdiction. There was much bitter feeling in Panama, both in government circles and among the people as a whole.

On August 24, 1921, the Department of State announced that the Chief Justice had appointed two engineers to lay down on the ground the boundary established by the White Award. This action suggested that the United States perhaps intended that these engineers should proceed with the work in coöperation with those appointed by Costa Rica even though Panama should persist in her refusal to recognize the award, but as a matter of fact the survey of the boundary has never been effected. For several years negotiations have been carried on intermittently between Panama and Costa Rica in an effort to find a basis for an amicable settlement, but no results have thus far been attained.

Maintenance of Order in Panama

By Article VII of the Canal Treaty, the United States was granted the "right and authority" to maintain "public order in the cities of Panama and Colon and the territories and harbors adjacent thereto in case the Republic of Panama should not be, in the judgment of the United States, able to maintain such order." Article 136 of the Panaman Constitution went further, providing that: [39]

[38] The notes of March 15, May 2, August 18, 1921, were made public in press releases by the Department of State.

[39] An English translation of the Panaman Constitution, from which the above is quoted, was transmitted by the President of the United States to the Senate on March 16, 1904, and printed in 58th Congress, 2nd Session, Senate Document No. 208.

The Government of the United States of America may intervene in any part of the Republic of Panama to reëstablish public peace and constitutional order in the event of their being disturbed, provided that that nation shall, by public treaty, assume or have assumed the obligation of guaranteeing the independence and sovereignty of the Republic.

The United States has on several occasions been called upon to take action under these provisions, not so much by actual military intervention, although such intervention has sometimes occurred, as by extending assistance in other ways. In the early years of the Republic, especially, the good offices of the American Government were instrumental on several occasions in settling political problems which seemed likely to produce disorder or revolution. As early as 1904, a dangerous situation arose when the Panaman Army, under the same commander who had assured the support of the local garrison to the revolutionists in November of the preceding year, was suspected of plotting to overthrow the President. The American Minister's strong moral support, and the threat to use American troops if need arose, made it possible for the local government to disband the disaffected troops.[40]

In the following year, when opposition leaders inquired what action the United States would take to assure the freedom of the congressional elections, the American Minister was instructed to inform both the Panaman Government and its opponents that the United States did not guarantee public order or assure the constitutional succession of the public powers in Panama.

The Government of the United States [wrote Mr. Root], while guaranteeing the independence of the Republic of Panama, does not purpose to interfere with that independence.

It was made clear, however, that the United States would if necessary exercise its treaty rights to maintain order in Panama City, Colon and the Canal Zone.[41]

[40] *Foreign Relations*, 1904, p. 647–651.
[41] *Ibid.*, 1905, p. 719.

The position of the United States was set forth some-
what more fully a few months later in a letter which Mr.
Root addressed to Mr. Taft, then Secretary of War, on
February 21, 1906, and in an instruction sent by the
Secretary of War to the Governor of the Canal Zone on
April 26 of the same year.   Mr. Root in his letter emphasized the fact that the conduct of elections and the maintenance of order were primarily the responsibility of the
Government of Panama, but he went on to say that any
disturbance of the peace which would imperil the interests
of the United States and which the Panaman Government
was unable or unwilling to suppress, would clearly justify
American intervention.   The instructions sent to the
Governor of the Canal made it clear that such intervention might take place in any part of the Republic in case
of necessity.[42]   Both communications were made public
at the time in the press of Panama, and on December 23,
1927, Secretary of State Kellogg announced that the
policy therein set forth was still the policy of the United
States Government.[43]

American Assistance in Elections

During the municipal elections which took place on
June 24, 1906, four persons were killed and twelve others
wounded.   It was feared that still more serious disorders
would occur during the congressional elections scheduled
for the next week.   The American Minister, therefore,
interposed his good offices at the last moment to bring
about an agreement on a compromise slate, and the voting
passed off peacefully.[44]

A more critical situation presented itself during the
presidential election of 1908.   President Amador was

[42] Foreign Relations, 1906, p. 1203–1207.
[43] Department of State Press Release, January 4, 1928.
[44] The Panaman Minister referred to this event in a note addressed to the
Department of State, May 6, 1912; Foreign Relations, 1912, p. 1140.

actively supporting his Minister of Foreign Affairs, Señor Ricardo Arias, against José Domingo Obaldía, who had been nominated by the Liberal and Conservative parties. The opposition was convinced that the election would not be free and fair without outside help, and events which occurred during the campaign seemed to bear out this belief. As the result of a conference between President Amador and Secretary Taft, who happened to be visiting the Isthmus, the Panaman Government finally agreed to invite the United States Government to appoint representatives on a commission to hear complaints without however taking the direction of the election out of the hands of the regular electoral authorities. The Government candidate withdrew from the contest shortly before the voting occurred, and Señor Obaldía was consequently elected without further difficulties.

There was again American supervision in the presidential election of 1912. Pablo Arosemena, who had become acting President after the death of Señor Obaldía in 1910, was supporting Señor Pedro A. Díaz against the candidate of the Liberal Party, Dr. Belisario Porras. The situation was complicated by the fact that the opposition, through its majority in Congress, had been able to obtain control of the electoral boards and was thus in a position to offset by fraudulent practices the intimidation and coercion which the Administration might be able to exert through the police. Both political factions urged that the United States take action to assure a proper election, and a formal request to this effect was received in May from the Panaman Government.[45] On this occasion a more complete supervision was undertaken, under the direction of a committee consisting of the American Minister, the Governor of the Panama Canal, and Colonel Greene of the United States Army, with more than two hundred assistants. There was at least one representative

[45] *Foreign Relations, 1912,* p. 1139.

of the committee in each of the sixty-one electoral districts, and the supervisors were given authority not only to see that the election was properly conducted but also that order was maintained and that there was no intimidation. The committee's efforts to prevent improper use of the police led to friction with the officials of the Government, and on July 12, after their party had been defeated in the municipal elections held a few days before, the supporters of Señor Díaz withdrew his candidacy, alleging that they had not received fair treatment from the representatives of the United States.[46] Señor Porras was therefore elected.

When President Porras' term was expiring in 1916, he refused to consider any foreign assistance in the election of his successor. His candidate, Señor Valdés, was successful without serious difficulty, although the opposition party, which had unsuccessfully requested American supervision, asserted that fraud and violence had been practiced. President Valdés died on June 3, 1918. Ciro Urriola, who succeeded him, had been elected as *designado,* or Vice-President, for a term which would expire on October 1, and a new *designado,* who would automatically become acting president, would normally be chosen by the Congress which was to be elected on July 7. On June 20, however, Señor Urriola issued a decree postponing the congressional elections, and the municipal elections scheduled for June 30, until after a new electoral law should have taken effect in the following year.

The opposition party, which controlled the electoral machinery as the Porras faction had in 1912, protested vehemently against this decree, and threatened to proceed with the elections on the dates set by law. It seemed clear that serious disorder might occur in Panama City and Colon if this threat were carried out. The United States Government, consequently, suggested to President

<hr />

[46] *Ibid.,* p. 1159.

Urriola that the decree be withdrawn, stating that its constitutionality seemed very doubtful. A few days later, partly because of the tenseness of the political situation and partly because of conditions affecting the welfare of the large force of American troops stationed on the Isthmus during the World War, the United States took over for a brief period the actual policing of Panama City and Colon. On July 2 President Urriola withdrew the decree. He had already permitted the municipal elections to take place, under orders issued at the last moment, and these had resulted in a victory for the administration. He now joined with the opposition in requesting American supervision in the congressional elections, and the United States Government consented to undertake such supervision even though the time remaining was obviously too short for the organization of adequate machinery for this purpose. Its most effective assistance took place after the election, when an advisory commission composed of high officials of the Canal Zone assisted in adjusting disputes arising from decisions of the Panaman electoral boards. The result was a victory for the government party, and Dr. Porras was chosen by the new Congress as *designado* and acting President for the period 1918–20. He was thereafter again elected, with little opposition, President for the term 1920–24.

Panaman elections have not been supervised by the United States since 1918. It will be noted that the American Government acted in 1908, 1912 and 1918 only at the formal request of the Panaman Government and of all political factions. In 1928, Dr. Porras, who had broken with Señor Chiari and was supporting the presidential candidacy of Dr. Jorge Boyd, requested American supervision, but without success.[47]

President Rodolfo Chiari, who became President through the support of Dr. Porras in 1924, was able at the end

[47] Department of State Press Release, July 27, 1928.

of his term to bring about the election of Señor Florencio Harmodio Arosemena for the term 1928–32. On the early morning of January 2, 1931, however, a group of revolutionists suddenly seized control of Panama City. A change of government in apparent compliance with the constitution was made possible by the action of the Supreme Court, which declared void a recent election of *designados* to the presidency, thus leaving as first *designado* Dr. Ricardo Alfaro, the Panaman Minister at Washington, who had been elected in 1928 and who was acceptable to the revolutionary party. To provide for the interval before Dr. Alfaro could reach Panama, Dr. Harmodio Arias, one of the leaders of the revolution, was appointed Minister of Government so that he might legally take over the executive power when President Arosemena resigned. Order was thus promptly restored, and without the intervention of the United States, although several police and one American newspaper man had been killed in street fighting during the earlier stages of the movement. The Department of State announced on January 16 that the American Minister had been instructed to attend President Alfaro's inauguration and to carry on normal diplomatic relations with his Government.[48]

POLICE QUESTIONS

Some of the most serious disagreements between the two Governments during the construction period arose from complaints against the Panaman police force. In July 1906 for example, officers from an American warship were clubbed by the police at Colon. Two years later, one of two sailors from the U.S.S. *Buffalo* who had been wounded in an encounter with the police was allowed to die from neglect at the police station. Indemnities were paid by the Panaman Government in each case, but only

[48] Department of State, *Press Releases*, January 16, 1931, p. 33.

after prolonged diplomatic negotiations.   On July 4, 1912, two Americans were killed and about sixteen others wounded in a riot in the red-light district of Panama, and in February 1915 several Americans were injured in another disturbance in the same district.   A much more serious affair occurred in April 1915 when the police opened fire with rifles on American soldiers during a street fight after a baseball game in Colon and killed a corporal who was on duty leading a patrol.   The American soldiers and civilians involved were of course not without blame in each of these disturbances, but the fatalities and bloodshed seem to have been due chiefly to the lack of discipline and the animosity toward American soldiers displayed by the Panaman police.   It was noted that the great majority of the casualities were always on the American side.[49]   The failure of the Panaman Government and its courts to punish the police officers who appeared to be responsible was especially aggravating to the American authorities, and it was not until several years later that indemnities for those who had been injured in these affairs were obtained as the result of arbitration.[50]

On at least two occasions during this period, the United States threatened to take over the policing of Panama City and Colon under Article VII of the Canal Treaty if conditions did not improve.[51]   In October 1915 the American Legation was instructed to request that the Panaman police be deprived of the high-powered rifles, the reckless use of which in the narrow, closely built up streets of the Panaman capital had been responsible for most of the casulties which had occurred.   This request

---

[49] A great volume of correspondence regarding these affairs will be found in *Foreign Relations* from 1906 on.

[50] The amount of the indemnity due for the 1912 riot was submitted to arbitration by the Dutch Minister at Washington, who rendered his award on October 20, 1916. See *Foreign Relations, 1916*, p. 918. Other claims were settled by the General Claims Commission which completed its work on June 30, 1933 (Department of State, *Press Releases*, p. 8).

[51] *Foreign Relations, 1909*, p. 488; *Ibid.*, 1915, p. 1210.

was complied with in May of the following year "under protest and because Panama is unable to resist," after energetic representations by the American Legation.[52] There appear to have been no serious clashes between American soldiers and the Panama police since that time.

In 1910, and again in 1913, the Panama Government had asked the United States to nominate American officers to reorganize and train the police force, but in each case the officer nominated had encountered so much indifference on the part of the local authorities and actual hostility on the part of the police as to make his services of no value. In 1917, however, the Panama Government entered into a contract with Colonel A. R. Lamb, of the Washington Metropolitan Police, to serve as instructor of the Panaman force, and in 1919 Colonel Lamb was appointed as Inspector General of Police under a law of reorganization drawn up with the aid of the Canal authorities. Organization and discipline were subsequently very greatly improved until the Panaman police force compared very favorably with those of any of the neighboring countries. Colonel Lamb served in Panama for several years, although the powers at first conferred upon him were substantially reduced after 1922.

The United States has very rarely actually intervened under Article VII of the Canal Treaty to maintain order in Panama City or Colon. In 1918, as we have already seen, American troops assumed the policing of the two cities for a short time, partly because of the imminent probability of political disturbances and partly because the inefficiency of the local police and their failure to control vice and drug-selling had created a situation harmful to the welfare of the large bodies of American troops stationed on the Isthmus during the war. In 1925 disturbances growing out of a rent-payers' strike led the Government formally to request the United States to

[52] *Ibid.*, 1916, p. 942.

assume police control of Panama City, and American troops remained there for nine days until order had been restored.

From 1918 to 1920, American troops were stationed in Chiriqui Province, in the western part of the Republic. Sent there originally to assist in the 1918 election, a small detachment remained to protect American lives and property which were endangered by the lawless conditions of the province and the failure of the local authorities to protect foreign interests. They were withdrawn after certain reforms had been effected.

PANAMA's FINANCIAL ADMINISTRATION

The Canal Treaty, unlike the Permanent Treaty with Cuba or the later treaties with the Dominican Republic and with Haiti, contained no provision specifically relating to Panama's public finances. It did however provide that the United States should pay Panama $250,000 annually in gold coin, beginning nine years after the ratification of the Treaty, and also a lump sum of $10,000,000 at the time of ratification. Article 138 of the Panaman Constitution set aside $6,000,000 of this latter sum to be invested in securities bearing a fixed rate of interest "in order to secure for posterity a part of the pecuniary advantages derived from the negotiations for the construction of the interoceanic canal." The greater part of the remainder was appropriated in 1904 for a long list of public works in all of the provinces of the Republic. Both the treaty annuity and the income from the constitutional fund, which is invested in first mortgages on real estate in New York City, have been pledged from time to time with the acquiescence of the United States as security for loans for public improvements.

Shortly after the outbreak of the World War, the Panaman Government found itself involved in increasingly acute financial difficulties. The Government had borrowed repeatedly to cover deficits in the budget and had also permitted the growth of a large floating debt, much of which was owed to the Panama Canal for services of various kinds. The appointment of a foreign financial adviser was discussed, but was disapproved in 1917 by the Panama Congress. At the end of the following year, however, a law was enacted to authorize the appointment of a "fiscal agent," who might be either a native or a foreigner, and who would be selected with the aid of the good offices of the Government of the United States. This official was to investigate the situation of the treasury and to advise the Secretary of the Treasury regarding needed fiscal legislation. He was also to have supervision over the accounting system, with the very important power of disapproving orders of payment when they were not in accord with the law or when other improprieties existed. His decisions in such cases were subject to the approval of the Executive Power and to final review by the Supreme Court.[53]

Mr. Addison T. Ruan was appointed Fiscal Agent in January 1919 under a two-year contract which was subsequently renewed for a second two-year period. With his aid, the Government effected important financial reforms, and was able not only to pay the floating debt but to accumulate a $3,000,000 surplus which made possible the beginning of an ambitious road construction program. Mr. Ruan's successors were Mr. W. W. Warwick, 1923–5, and Mr. Floyd Baldwin, who has held the position since 1925. The situation of the Fiscal Agent in Panama is entirely different from that of American officials serving under treaties in certain other countries. His powers are defined solely by Panaman law, and his decisions can be overruled by the Panaman authorities. His presence does not diminish the responsibility of the President and the Congress in the field of fiscal policy.

[53] *Leyes expedidas por la Asamblea Nacional de Panama . . . 1918–9*, p. 38.

CHAPTER III

RELATIONS WITH THE DOMINICAN REPUBLIC

Early History

No other Latin American country has suffered more than the Dominican Republic from internal disorder, financial exploitation and foreign intervention. Santo Domingo City was the first center of European power in the New World, but the colony of which it was the capital was to a great extent abandoned after the discovery of richer territories in Mexico and Peru, and the few Spanish families which remained suffered much during the European wars of the eighteenth century from attacks by the more numerous and wealthier French colonists who had taken possession of the western end of the island. Between 1801 and 1809, the Spanish settlements were successively conquered by Toussaint L'Ouverture, occupied by French troops, and reconquered by Spain. In November 1821 the Dominicans revolted from Spain and hoisted the flag of Colombia, but three months later their territory was overrun by Haitian troops and annexed to the neighboring Republic. A revolt in 1844, at a time when the Haitian Government was occupied by revolutionary disturbances at home, established the independence of the Dominican Republic. Haitian efforts at reconquest were defeated by the tenacious resistance of the Dominicans, and by emphatic diplomatic representations from the United States, France and Great Britain, but it was not until 1855 that the last Haitian invasion was repulsed.

Even during the wars with Haiti, there was almost continual civil strife within the Republic, between factions headed by Pedro Santana and Buenaventura Baez.   To obtain protection from Haiti and support against enemies at home, each of these leaders repeatedly sought to establish some form of foreign protectorate.   Proposals were made at different times to France, Spain and the United States, but the two former states presumably had little desire to test the efficacy of the Monroe Doctrine, and the slavery question was an obstacle to any connection with the United States.   Early in 1861, however, when it was clear that the approaching Civil War would tie the hands of the American Government, Santana succeeded in effecting the annexation of the Republic by Spain.   Discouraged by continual Dominican revolts and by the heavy losses among the Spanish troops from yellow fever, and realizing that the United States would soon be in a position to demand "dangerous explanations," [1] Spain abandoned the colony in 1865.

A few years later Santana's rival, Baez, sought to annex the Republic to the United States.   A treaty for this purpose, and another treaty providing for the lease of Samaná Bay, were signed in 1869, but were rejected by the United States Senate.   President Grant supported the Baez Government with American naval forces for a short period while efforts were made to obtain approval for a new arrangement, but the opposition in the Senate and the revelation of certain unsavory financial operations which discredited the whole project finally led to its abandonment.

There was a period of renewed internal disorder until Ulises Heureaux came into power in 1882 and established a brutal and despotic régime which lasted until his death in 1899.   During this period, the suppression of disorder

[1] This was the expression used in the preamble of the project of law presented by the Spanish Government to the Cortes. Quoted in Welles, *Naboth's Vineyard*, Vol. I, p. 288.

and the expenditure of funds borrowed abroad made it possible for the Republic to enjoy the first relative prosperity in its troubled history. Heureaux's financial operations, however, were a source of future trouble.

HEUREAUX AND THE SAN DOMINGO IMPROVEMENT COMPANY

In 1869 the Dominican Government had contracted the so-called Hartmont loan. From the sale of bonds to a face value of £757,700 the Government was to have received only £320,000 under the terms of the contract, but it received in fact only £38,000, the greater part of the remainder having been misapplied by the promoters or lost through failure to dispose of the bonds. The loan had gone into default in 1872. Heureaux adjusted the claims of the bondholders from the proceeds of a new loan obtained in 1888 from the firm of Westendorp in Amsterdam, and a second loan, for the construction of a railway from Puerto Plata to Santiago, was obtained from the same bankers in 1890. Both loans went into default in 1892.

In the following year the interests of the Dutch firm were turned over to an American corporation known as the San Domingo Improvement Company. The outstanding bonds were refunded by a new issue to the amount of £2,035,000 at 4½ per cent, and the collection of customs duties was placed in the hands of the Improvement Company to secure the payment of interest and amortization. The contract provided that the company, in case of default, might ask the Dutch, Belgian, British, French and American Governments to appoint members of a financial mission to control the customs.

The San Domingo Improvement Company now became the adviser and partner of Heureaux in a series of financial operations which soon created a foreign debt entirely beyond the Government's capacity to pay. Through its subsidiary corporations, it bought and sold the Government's bonds, conducted construction work on the Central Dominican Railway, supervised the collection of customs duties, and generally acted as the Republic's fiscal agent. In 1895, when a dispute between the President and the Banque Nationale, a French corporation, led the French Government to present a large claim and to support it by a naval demonstration, the company purchased the control of the bank. The whole foreign debt was again refunded in 1897, after the Government had found itself unable to meet interest charges on the outstanding bonds which had been issued with the company's aid in various foreign countries in 1893, 1894 and 1895. A new unified loan of £4,236,750 was created, of which a portion with a coupon rate of 4 per cent was sold to the public at 66.[2]

FOREIGN INTERVENTION

The new bonds were already in default when Heureaux was assassinated in 1899 and a faction bitterly opposed to the Improvement Company came into power. In 1901, after proposals for a new adjustment had failed because the bondholders opposed a further reduction in their claims, the Government removed the agents of the Improvement Company from the customhouses. This led to diplomatic intervention by several foreign governments on behalf of the bondholders. The Dominican Government was forced to sign an agreement with French and Belgian bondholders in 1901, under which a specific mortgage on the customs revenues at Santo Domingo City and Macorís was created for the latter's benefit, and in

[2] A concise account of the Dominican Republic's early financial history is given in the Annual Reports of the Council of the Corporation of Foreign Bondholders in London. See also John Bassett Moore's report to the President of the United States in 1905, reprinted in *Foreign Relations, 1905*, p. 344–9.

July 1903 the German, Italian and Spanish Governments compelled the negotiation of diplomatic protocols providing for the payment of specific monthly sums to their nationals. In May 1904 the Italian Government demanded and obtained a new agreement, hypothecating 10 per cent of all customs revenues and creating a specific lien on those at Samaná for the benefit of Italian claimants.[3]

In the meantime, the United States had intervened diplomatically on behalf of the Improvement Company, and a protocol was signed by the two Governments on January 31, 1904, providing that the company should withdraw from the Republic, transferring to the Government its interests in the Central Dominican Railway and the National Bank in return for a total payment of $4,500,-000. The company had originally claimed $11,000,000. The terms on which the payment was to be made were submitted to an arbitral commission.[4]

The commission rendered its award on July 14, 1904. The $4,500,000 was to be paid in monthly instalments of $37,500 during the first two years and $41,666.66 thereafter, and the customs revenues from the Republic's northern ports, including especially Puerto Plata, Sánchez, Samaná and Monte Cristi, were assigned as special security for these payments. If the Financial Agent appointed for the purpose by the United States should fail at any time to receive a payment when due, he was to be authorized to take over the actual collection of the customs, first at Puerto Plata and subsequently, if necessary, at the other northern ports. He was also to act as Financial Adviser of the Government in all matters affecting its ability to pay the award.[5] Since the Dominican Government failed to make the first payment due

---

[3] *Foreign Relations, 1905*, p. 387.
[4] *Foreign Relations, 1904*, p. 270.
[5] *Ibid.*, p. 274.

under the award, and in fact indicated a willingness to have the customhouses placed under immediate American control,[6] the Financial Agent took over the collection of customs at Puerto Plata in October 1904.

THE MODUS VIVENDI OF 1905

In September 1904 the American Minister estimated that the total debt of the Dominican Republic was more than $32,000,000, of which two-thirds was owed to European creditors. Fixed charges on the funded debt alone amounted to $1,700,000, as against the Government's total annual income of $1,850,000.[7] Continual civil war since the death of Heureaux had made an already disastrous financial situation almost hopeless. Since the Government had failed to carry out the agreements made with its European creditors between 1901 and 1904, it was in constant dread lest the states which had compelled it to sign these contracts should seize by force the customhouses which had been assigned as security. Several of these had already protested against the Improvement Company award, and the taking over of the customhouse at Puerto Plata by the United States, as a violation of their own rights. As President Roosevelt said in his Annual Message of 1905:

There was imminent danger of foreign intervention. The previous rulers of Santo Domingo had recklessly incurred debts and owing to her internal disorders she had ceased to be able to provide means of paying the debts. The patience of her foreign creditors had become exhausted, and at least two foreign nations were on the point of intervention, and were only prevented from intervening by the unofficial assurance of this Government that it would itself strive to help Santo Domingo in her hour of need. In the case of one of these nations, only the actual opening of negotiations to this end by our Government prevented the seizure of territory in Santo Domingo by a European power.

[6] *Ibid.*, p. 280–283.
[7] *Foreign Relations, 1905*, p. 302.

The negotiations to which the President referred were opened on December 30, 1904, when Secretary Hay sent the following telegram to Mr. Thomas C. Dawson, the American Minister at Santo Domingo: [8]

Confidential.   You will sound the President of Santo Domingo, discreetly but earnestly and in a perfectly friendly spirit, touching the disquieting situation which is developing owing to the pressure of other Governments having arbitral awards in their favor and who regard our award as conflicting with their rights. Already one European government strongly intimates that it may resort to occupation of some Dominican customs ports to secure its own payment.   There appears to be a concert among them.   You will ascertain whether the Government of Santo Domingo would be disposed to request the United States to take charge of the collection of duties and effect an equitable distribution of the assigned quotas among the Dominican Government and the several claimants.   We have grounds to think that such arrangement would satisfy the other powers, besides serving as a practical guaranty of the peace of Santo Domingo from external influence or internal disturbances.

Carlos Morales, who had obtained a precarious hold on the presidency a few months earlier, was entirely willing to place the customhouses under American control.   He had in fact informally suggested such action in the spring of 1904, believing that revolutionary movements might be discouraged if insurgent leaders could no longer obtain the customs revenues at ports which they might seize.[9] The negotiations proceeded rapidly, despite some opposition from the Cabinet and from public opinion, and despite what appeared to be an effort, made through the medium of the Spanish Chargé d'Affaires, to persuade the Government to turn to Germany rather than to the United States for assistance [10]; and on February 7, 1905, a treaty was signed by which the United States undertook to attempt the adjustment of all the financial obligations of the

[8] *Ibid.*, p. 299.
[9] *Ibid.*, p. 300.
[10] *Foreign Relations, 1906*, p. 596.

Dominican Republic and to assume the collection of all the customs revenues.

In presenting this treaty to the United States Senate, President Roosevelt made a very important statement of his views on the responsibility of the United States Government in the Caribbean:

It has for some time been obvious [he said] that those who profit by the Monroe Doctrine must accept certain responsibilities along with the rights which it confers; and that the same statement applies to those who uphold the doctrine. It cannot be too often and too emphatically asserted that the United States has not the slightest desire for territorial aggrandizement at the expense of any of its southern neighbors, and will not treat the Monroe Doctrine as an excuse for such aggrandizement on its part. We do not propose to take any part of Santo Domingo, or exercise any other control over the island save what is necessary to its financial rehabilitation in connection with the collection of revenue, part of which will be turned over to the Government to meet the necessary expense of running it, and part of which will be distributed pro rata among the creditors of the Republic upon a basis of absolute equity. The justification for the United States taking this burden and incurring this responsibility is to be found in the fact that it is incompatible with international equity for the United States to refuse to allow other powers to take the only means at their disposal of satisfying the claims of their creditors and yet to refuse, itself, to take any such steps.

Mr. Roosevelt also pointed out that any state which intervened to compel the Dominican Government to meet its debts would be entitled to preferential payment under the recent decision of The Hague Tribunal in the Venezuela case. The interests of American creditors would thus be sacrificed if other states acted and the United States did not. The other states, furthermore, could obtain payment only by taking over the customhouses for an indefinite period, and

the United States Government could not interfere to prevent such seizure and occupation of Dominican territory without either itself proposing some feasible alternative in the way of action, or else virtually saying to European governments that they would not be allowed to collect their claims. This would be an unfortunate attitude for the Government of the United States to be forced to maintain at present. It cannot with propriety say that it will protect its own citizens and interests, on the one hand, and yet on the other hand refuse to allow other governments to protect their citizens and interests.[11]

When the United States Senate adjourned in March without taking action on the treaty, there was again serious danger of European intervention. The internal political situation also became acute, because it appeared that the administration's effort to obtain financial relief had failed. Minister Dawson therefore approached the creditors and found that all of them, with the exception of the Improvement Company, were willing to accept a *modus vivendi* under which the customs would be collected by American officials and 55 per cent of the proceeds would be held in trust in New York pending a final adjustment of the debt. President Morales approved such an arrangement by decree on March 31, and Colonel George R. Colton was nominated by the President of the United States to take over the Customs Receivership. All payments to creditors were temporarily suspended, while Professor Jacob H. Hollander was appointed to investigate the Republic's public debt.[12] The arrangement was not acceptable to the Improvement Company, which represented not only the principal American but also the largest British creditors, but when the British Chargé d'Affaires at Washington requested assurances that the interests of British bondholders under the company's award would not be prejudiced, he was informed that the President of the United States could not at that time recognize any special rights and privi-

[11] *Foreign Relations, 1905,* p. 334 *ff.*
[12] The correspondence regarding the *modus vivendi* will be found in *Foreign Relations, 1905,* p. 357 *ff.*

leges of the Improvement Company over other creditors.[13]

The *modus vivendi* brought about a definite improvement in the Republic's financial situation, for the Receivership increased receipts to a point where the treasury
received more from the 45 per cent allotted to the Government than it had previously received from the entire customs revenue. It also improved political conditions, although a new revolt at the end of 1905 led to
the fall of President Morales and the accession to power
of Ramon Cáceres, one of the ablest rulers in the Republic's history, who remained in the Presidency until his
assassination in 1911.

THE TREATY OF 1907

Since the United States Senate was unwilling to ratify
the 1905 Treaty, Federico Velásquez, the Minister of
Finance, was sent to Washington in June 1906 to work
out an agreement with the creditors which might serve
as a basis for a new arrangement. With the aid of Professor Hollander and of the Department of State, he
obtained the assent of a substantial proportion of the
creditors to the settlement of their claims at from 10
to 90 per cent of their face value, and made arrangements with Kuhn, Loeb and Company of New York for
a loan to provide the necessary funds.[14] On February 8,
1907, he signed a new treaty with the United States.
This agreement differed from that signed in 1905 mainly
in that it simply committed the United States to aid in
carrying out arrangements already effected by direct negotiations between the Dominican Republic and its creditors on the one side and between the Republic and Ameri-

[13] *Ibid.*, p. 374, 377.
[14] Extracts from the Annual Report of the Dominican Minister of Foreign
Relations, giving an account of Señor Velásquez' mission, are printed in
Foreign Relations, 1907, Vol. I, p. 354 *ff.*

can bankers on the other, instead of obligating the United States itself to attempt the adjustment of the Dominican debt. It was promptly ratified by the United States Senate.

Under the new treaty the President of the United States was to appoint a General Receiver of Dominican Customs with the necessary assistants and employees. Payments of interest and sinking fund on the bonds issued under the plan of adjustment were to be made by the Receiver before paying any of the customs receipts to the Dominican Government. The Dominican Government promised full protection to the Receivership, and the Government of the United States was to "give to the General Receiver and his assistants such protection as it may find to be requisite for the performance of their duties." Until the whole amount of the bonds issued under the treaty had been paid, the Dominican Government was not to increase its public debt except by previous agreement with the Government of the United States, and a similar agreement was to be necessary for the modification of the import duties.[15]

The treaty went into effect on July 8, 1907, and on August 1, Mr. William E. Pulliam, who had recently replaced Colonel Colton at the head of the Receivership under the *modus vivendi*, was appointed General Receiver of Customs. The service was placed by executive order under the Bureau of Insular Affairs in the War Department, thus assuring a proper supervision over accounts and personnel.[16]

On September 16, 1907, the Dominican Congress approved a law authorizing the proposed loan. An issue of $20,000,000 in fifty-year, 5 per cent bonds made possible the adjustment of nearly the whole of the public

[15] For the text of the Treaty see Appendix, *infra*, p. 283.
[16] Executive Order of July 25, 1907. See *Foreign Relations, 1907*, Vol. I, p. 317.

debt, which had been estimated a short time before at more than $30,000,000, and left a small balance for the purchase of certain onerous concessions granted by previous administrations and for the construction of public works. Approximately $4,000,000 in cash which had been impounded under the *modus vivendi* was also available for these latter purposes.

POLITICAL EVENTS, 1907–1913

Before the customs were placed under foreign control, the lack of means of communication and the existence of a large number of ports each serving its own isolated district had made it easy for revolutionary leaders to provide themselves with funds by seizing one or more customhouses. Local leaders whom the Government was unable or disinclined to subdue had often exploited one or more ports for their own personal benefit by agreement with the central authorities. Under the new treaty, the traditional method of financing revolts was no longer available, and the entire product of the customs revenues, after the expenses of collection and the service of the debt, went into the national treasury. The establishment of a customs receivership thus appeared to be a remedy not only for financial ills but also for internal political disorder.

After the assassination of President Cáceres in November 1911, however, it became clear that a part at least of the apparent improvement in political conditions had been due to the presence of a strong Chief Executive. The death of Cáceres left the military control of the capital in the hands of Alfredo Victoria, the commander of the local garrison. When this officer compelled the Congress to elect his uncle, Eladio Victoria, as President for a six-year term beginning in 1912, other political leaders started revolts in several sections of the Republic, and conditions became so disturbed, especially along the Haitian border, where the Haitian Government was actively assisting some of the revolutionary leaders, that the customs service was compelled to abandon several of its frontier ports.[17]

In September two American commissioners, Mr. W. T. S. Doyle, the Chief of the Latin American Division of the Department of State, and General McIntyre, the Chief of the Bureau of Insular Affairs, were sent to Santo Domingo to endeavor to reëstablish peace. The warship on which they travelled carried 750 marines under whose protection the closed customhouses were to be reopened and protected if such action should seem necessary. The commissioners persuaded President Victoria to dismiss his nephews, the Minister of War and the Commander of the Army, against whom the revolution was especially directed, and to announce that he would himself retire in 1914 at the end of the term for which President Cáceres had been elected.[18] Both the commissioners and the revolutionists, however, felt that the President was not acting in good faith; and on November 25, Victoria was forced to resign, apparently by a threat that he would receive no further money from the customs if he remained in power.[19] A few days later the Congress unanimously elected Monsignor Nouel, the Archbishop of Santo Domingo, as Provisional President for two years.

On the day when the commissioners were appointed, the Department of State had also acted to prevent further conflicts with Haiti along the frontier. The controversy over the boundary between the two countries, which dated back to colonial times, had become acute when the Dominican Government attempted to build a road in the disputed territory in 1910, and in January 1911 the United States had proffered its good offices to reach a settlement.

[17] *Foreign Relations, 1912*, p. 366.
[18] For these negotiations, see *Foreign Relations, 1912*, p. 366 *ff.*
[19] *Ibid.*, p. 376.

Both sides accepted American mediation, but no result was reached in the conferences which were subsequently held in Washington. Meanwhile there had been further incidents, and the uncertainty about the location of the line had facilitated the operations of the revolutionists, especially as they were apparently receiving aid from officials in Haiti. It had also made much more difficult the prevention of smuggling by the American customs authorities. On September 24, 1912, therefore, the Haitian and Dominican Governments were informed that the United States had decided to fix a *de facto* line, without prejudice to the rights of either party, and to instruct the General Receiver to see that the line was respected by means of a border patrol. Both Governments seem to have acquiesced in this action, although perhaps with some reluctance.[20]

Despite the moral support which he received from the United States, President Nouel found his position intolerable. The more important factional leaders refrained for a time from open revolt, but they gave the new administration no effective assistance except when they could thereby obtain political or pecuniary concessions. Their demands and intrigues made the proper conduct of government practically impossible. The Archbishop was repeatedly dissuaded from resigning only by urgent personal appeals from President Taft and President Wilson, and in March 1913 he finally refused to continue in office and embarked for Europe.

When the Congress met to elect a new president, there was a prolonged contest between the leaders of the three principal political parties, General Horacio Vásquez, Ex-President Juan Isidro Jiménez and Don Federico Velásquez. A compromise after two weeks of futile balloting resulted in the election of José Bordas Valdés as Provisional President for one year. For some months the country was

[20] *Foreign Relations, 1911*, p. 151–167;—*1912*, p. 340–349, 368, 380–387.

relatively quiet, in spite of the dissensions between various factions which wished to dominate the administration, but in September Governor Céspedes of Puerto Plata, a supporter of General Vásquez, began a new revolt.

Mr. Bryan, who had by this time become Secretary of State, adopted a policy somewhat different from that of his predecessor. The American Chargé d'Affaires was told to inform Governor Céspedes of "the profound displeasure felt by this Government at his pernicious revolutionary activity, for which this Government will not fail to fix the responsibility," [21] and Mr. Sullivan, the newly appointed American Minister, subsequently informed both sides, in writing, that "revolution would never again bring a government into power" in Santo Domingo, and promised the revolutionists that the United States would see that free and fair elections were held if they laid down their arms.[22] A peace agreement which left Bordas in control was finally signed as the result of the Minister's efforts. The election of a constitutional convention, which was held later in the year, was partially supervised by American agents, despite objections from the Dominican Government.

THE WILSON PLAN

The outcome of the revolt had been a victory not so much for President Bordas as for a group of military leaders who controlled his army. The most important of these was Desiderio Arias, who had been a disturbing factor in Dominican politics for several years. He had been the chief leader of the revolt against the Victoria Government in 1912, and had remained in military control of a large section of the country under President

[21] *Foreign Relations, 1913,* p. 425.

The account which follows of political conditions in 1913, 1914, and 1915 is based mainly on correspondence published in *Foreign Relations* for those years.

[22] *Ibid.,* p. 432.

Nouel. His insubordination and financial exactions had been one of the principal factors in forcing the Archbishop to resign. The revolt of September 1913 had been chiefly a protest against the power which he exercised under President Bordas, and its failure left the President to a great extent in his hands.

Bordas became involved in new difficulties early in 1914, when it became evident that he wished to remain in the presidency. In February his impeachment by Congress was prevented only by the interposition of the American Minister.[23] In March he was compelled to break with Arias when the latter demanded the vice-presidency and a payment of $300,000 in cash as the price of his continued support,[24] and then started a revolt. In the meantime the presidential elections, which should have been held within one year after Bordas' inauguration on April 14, 1913, had been delayed by the failure of the Congress to pass necessary legislation. The legality of the President's remaining in office thus became doubtful, and the suspicion that he was purposely prolonging his tenure caused many other political leaders to support the movement against him. The civil war thus continued during June and July, extending into new areas, with increasing danger to foreign lives and property, as time passed.

On July 29, the President of the United States asked that hostilities be suspended to afford an opportunity to present a plan for the restoration of peace. A general armistice for fifteen days was signed at Puerto Plata on August 6, and on August 15 two new commissioners, Ex-Governor Fort of New Jersey, and Mr. Charles Cogswell Smith, sailed for Santo Domingo on an American warship. They bore with them the "Wilson Plan," which read as follows:

The Government of the United States desires nothing for itself from the Dominican Republic and no concessions or ad-

[23] *Foreign Relations, 1914*, p. 205.
[24] *Ibid.*, p. 214.

vantages for its citizens which are not accorded citizens of other countries. It desires only to prove its sincere and disinterested friendship for the republic and its people and to fulfill its responsibilities as the friend to whom in such crises as the present all the world looks to guide Santo Domingo out of its difficulties.

It, therefore, makes the following earnest representations not only to the existing *de facto* Government of the Dominican Republic, but also to all who are in any way responsible for the present posture of affairs there:

I. It warns everyone concerned that it is absolutely imperative that the present hostilities should cease and that all who are concerned in them should disperse to their several homes, disbanding the existing armed forces and returning to the peaceful occupations upon which the welfare of the people of the republic depends. This is necessary, and necessary at once. Nothing can be successfully accomplished until this is done.

II. It is also necessary that there should be an immediate reconstitution of political authority in the republic. To this end the Government of the United States very solemnly advises all concerned with the public affairs of the republic to adopt the following plan:

(1) Let all those who have any pretensions to be chosen President of the Republic and who can make any sufficient show of exercising a recognized leadership and having an acknowledged following agree upon some responsible and representative man to act as Provisional President of the Republic, it being understood that Mr. Bordas will relinquish his present position and authority. If these candidates can agree in this matter, the Government of the United States will recognize and support the man of their choice as Provisional President. If they cannot agree, the Government of the United States will itself name a Provisional President, sustain him in the assumption of office, and support him in the exercise of his temporary authority. The Provisional President will not be a candidate for President.

(2) At the earliest feasible date after the establishment and recognition of the Provisional Government thus established let elections for a regular President and Congress be held under the authority and direction of the Provisional President, who will, it must of course be understood, exercise during his tenure of office the full powers of President of the Republic; but let it be understood that the Government of the United

States will send representatives of its own choosing to observe the election throughout the republic and that it will expect those observers not only to be accorded a courteous welcome but also to be accorded the freest opportunities to observe the circumstances and processes of the election.

(3) Let it be understood that if the United States Government is satisfied that these elections have been free and fair and carried out under conditions which enable the people of the republic to express their real choice, it will recognize the President and Congress thus chosen as the legitimate and constitutional Government of the Republic and will support them in the exercise of their functions and authority in every way it can. If it should not be satisfied that elections of the right kind have been held, let it be understood that another election will be held at which the mistakes observed will be corrected.

III. A regular and constitutional government having thus been set up, the Government of the United States would feel at liberty thereafter to insist that revolutionary movements cease and that all subsequent changes in the Government of the Republic be effected by the peaceful processes provided in the Dominican Constitution. By no other course can the Government of the United States fulfill its treaty obligations with Santo Domingo or its tacitly conceded obligations as the nearest friend of Santo Domingo in her relations with the rest of the world.

A telegram which had been sent to the commissioners by the Secretary of State on August 13 read: [25]

You are instructed to observe and follow out with utmost care plan which has been presented you by the Secretary of State. No opportunity for argument should be given to any person or faction. It is desired that you present plan and see that it is complied with.

Within a few days after the arrival of the commission, the plan had been accepted. Dr. Ramón Baez, selected by agreement between the principal political leaders, was inaugurated as Provisional President on August 28. Arias had not been included in the conferences and had in fact continued his military operations in the North, but he

[25] Both the Wilson Plan and the telegram referred to will be found *ibid.*, p. 247.

agreed to recognize the authority of the new administration after the United States Government had proposed that American marines should assist in arresting him. The ensuing presidential election, which was "observed" by representatives of the commission, gave Juan Isidro Jiménez a small majority over Horacio Vásquez, who was his chief opponent.

Negotiations with the Jiménez Administration

When the new President was inaugurated on December 5, 1914, the United States renewed efforts which it had already made during the Bordas administration to obtain the acceptance of reforms by which it hoped that conditions in the Dominican Republic could be definitely stabilized. Financial difficulties had materially contributed to the weakness of the four administrations which had been in power since 1912, even though special arrangements had been made to permit advances from the customs receipts in excess of amounts which the Government would have received under a strict interpretation of the treaty; and the expenditure of all available funds for military purposes had resulted in the accumulation of a large floating debt in damage claims, unpaid salaries and sums due to local business houses.

This was regarded as a violation of the Dominican Government's obligation under the treaty of 1907 to make no increases in its indebtedness without the consent of the President of the United States. Since there appeared to be no way to prevent continued increase of claims against the Government except by seeing that the expenditures were kept within proper bounds and that funds were not wasted or misapplied, President Bordas had been persuaded in May 1914 to agree to the appointment of a "Financial Expert" with power to control expenditures, and Mr. Charles M. Johnston had been installed in this position on June 17. The Dominican Congress, however, had refused to regularize his position by law, thus making his tenure of office very uncertain. Assurances that the office would be placed on a definite legal basis appear to have been obtained from President Jiménez before his inauguration.[26] Soon afterward, much more extensive reforms were proposed. On December 14, 1914, the American Minister was instructed to urge the new President to issue decrees placing the collection of the internal revenues as well as the customs under the Receivership; definitely recognizing Mr. Johnston as Comptroller, with power to prepare the budget and to countersign all payments; amending the contract of the Director General of Public Works, who was an American, so as to give him a more definite tenure and greater authority over his subordinate personnel; and sharply reducing military expenses. In connection with the last reform proposed, Mr. Bryan indicated that the United States Government would be prepared to assist in reorganizing the police or creating a constabulary with a view to the complete abolition of the existing army.[27] It was later suggested that wireless communication and the land telegraph and telephone systems also be placed under the control of an engineer designated by the United States.[28]

Although President Jiménez showed himself unwilling to accept the reforms thus proposed, Mr. Johnston continued to act as Comptroller, and his efforts to restrict expenditures led to much friction with the Dominican officials. Mr. Johnston's position was one of the matters which were taken up with the Department of State in May 1915 by a Special Commission which the Dominican Government sent to Washington. This commission obtained from the American Government an agreement that

---

[26] In this connection, see *Foreign Relations, 1915*, p. 323.
[27] *Foreign Relations, 1914*, p. 260.
[28] *Foreign Relations, 1915*, p. 297.

Mr. Johnston should serve henceforth as an employee of the Receivership and purely in an advisory capacity, upon the understanding that the Dominican Government would itself take the necessary measures to keep its expenditures within its revenues. The duties of the Receivership were thus extended to include giving advice on financial subjects, such as the settlement of claims and debts, the establishment of an accounting system, and the balancing of the budget, but any effective control over expenditures was discontinued.[29]

The commission also took up a dispute which had arisen with regard to the appointment of the lesser customs officials. The Department of State had always maintained that the Treaty gave the President of the United States the power to appoint all customs officials, but a provisional agreement had been made in 1907 under which the Dominican Government was permitted to name collectors and other employees, with the exception of the highest officials of the service, so long as the appointments were acceptable to the General Receiver and the appointees were removed at his request. Difficulties arose early in 1915 when the Dominican Government attempted to remove several employees for purely political reasons. Efforts to settle these difficulties with the commission were not entirely successful, but the commissioners were assured that the General Receiver would consult the Dominican Government before making appointments and would not name an employee against whom the Government had any well-founded objection.[30]

Meanwhile political conditions in Santo Domingo showed little improvement. The President's advanced age and feeble health made it very difficult for him to deal with the intrigues of his political opponents and the insubordination of his own followers. Frequent revolts by

[29] *Ibid.*, p. 311.
[30] *Ibid.*, p. 302.

local military chiefs were checked only by the grant of road-building contracts or other favors which simply encouraged other leaders to blackmail the Government in the same way, and there was more than a suspicion that the President's own military supporters were not averse to the country's continuing in a state of turmoil because of the excuses thus afforded for expenditures by the army. Arias, who had been made Minister of War, was again in control of the military forces, and his support was retained only at the cost of disastrous financial and political concessions.

The Government of the United States had repeatedly endeavored to bring about more orderly conditions both by public threats and exhortations and by offers of definite military assistance. On January 12, 1915, upon being informed that the Government wished because of its political difficulties to delay consideration of the measures which the United States Government had recently proposed, the following instruction was sent to the American Legation: [31]

You may say to President Jiménez that this Government will support him to the fullest extent in the suppression of any insurrection against his Government. The election having been held and a Government chosen by the people having been established, no more revolutions will be permitted. You may notify both Horacio Vásquez and Arias that they will be held personally responsible if they attempt to embarrass the Government. The people of Santo Domingo will be given an opportunity to develop the resources of their country in peace. Their revenues will no longer be absorbed by graft or wasted in insurrections. This Government meant what it said when it sent a commission there with a proposal looking to permanent peace and it will live up to the promises it has made. Reasonable delay in carrying out the proposed reforms is not objectionable but the changes advised are the reforms necessary for the honest and efficient administration of the Government and the early and proper development of the country. There should be no unnecessary

[31] *Ibid.*, p. 279.

delay therefore in putting them into operation. Keep us advised. A naval force will be sent whenever necessary.

A still more emphatic declaration that President Jiménez would receive from the United States "any assistance that will be necessary to compel respect for his administration . . . whether the attacks made upon him are direct, or indirect, open, or in secret" was made by Mr. Bryan on April 9, when a plot to have the President impeached by Congress was reported.[32] On several occasions, the American Government indicated its willingness to suppress disorders with its own troops if the President should so request, but Jiménez was clearly reluctant to ask for such assistance.

When Mr. W. W. Russell was reappointed as American Minister in August 1915 he was instructed to insist upon a sufficient extension of American control to assure the maintenance of peace and to prevent the further accumulation of unauthorized indebtedness. If possible he was to obtain a new treaty which would achieve this purpose, but if this proved impossible he was to take the position that the United States possessed sufficient authority under the existing treaty to name a financial adviser and to create an adequate police force. The Minister found that there was little probability that the Dominican Congress would approve such a treaty as was proposed. On November 19, therefore, he presented a note reviewing at great length the difficulties which had arisen between the two Governments and stating: [33]

My Government therefore has decided that the American-Dominican Convention of 1907 gives it the right:—

A. To compel the observance of Article III by insisting upon the immediate appointment of a financial adviser to the Dominican Republic who shall be appointed by the President of the Dominican Republic upon designation of the President of the United States, and who shall be attached to the Ministry of

[32] *Ibid.*, p. 283.
[33] *Ibid.*, p. 333.

Finance to give effect to whose proposals and labors the Minister will lend all efficient aid. . . . (Here followed a detailed description of the powers to be given to the Financial Adviser, which included full authority to control expenditures.)

B. To provide for the free course of the customs and prevent factional strife and disturbances by the creation of a constabulary, which the Dominican Government obligates itself, for the preservation of domestic peace, security of individual rights and the full observance of the provisions of the convention, to create without delay and maintain. This constabulary shall be organized and commanded by an American to be appointed, as "Director of Constabulary," by the President of the Dominican Republic, upon nomination of the President of the United States. In like manner there shall be appointed to the constabulary such other American officers as the director of constabulary shall consider requisite . . .

The Dominican Government declined to acquiesce in the proposals thus made, defending the course which it had thus far pursued and emphasizing the efforts which the Jiménez administration had made to restore order. Despite the terms in which the demands of the United States had been formulated, no further action of importance seems to have been taken for some months.

American Intervention

The beginning of the series of events which led to the downfall of the Jiménez administration and the military intervention of the United States was tersely described by the American Minister in a telegraphic report to the Department of State on April 15, 1916: [34]

Great excitement here yesterday. Commander of fort and chief of republican guard made prisoners in the country place of the President. Desiderio Arias objected to this method of removing his friends, entered fort and took command as Minister of War; sent for me last night to explain his attitude saying that he was not in rebellion against the President but that this coup, initiated by Minister of the Interior, was sure

[34] *Foreign Relations, 1916*, p. 221.

to cause trouble and he took this step to preserve order.   Members of all opposition parties flocked to Arias and offered services with the exception of Velásquez faction.   *Castine* in port.

RUSSELL.

Arias controlled Santo Domingo City, but he did not have the support of the entire army.   President Jiménez, who had left the capital, was able to muster a considerable force of troops loyal to himself; and while Arias proceeded to have the Congress impeach the President, the latter moved forward to attack the city.   The United States had offered active military support in suppressing Arias' revolt, and the President appears at first to have expressed a wish that American marines should retake the capital. Subsequently, however, he declined to accept such assistance, and resigned rather than continue the struggle. The executive power passed into the hands of his cabinet, pending the election of a new President by the Congress. Arias, however, remained in military control, and was apparently in a position to dominate any action which the Congress might take.   In the meantime several American naval vessels, under the command of Admiral Caperton, had been sent to Dominican ports.

On May 13 the American Minister and Admiral Caperton informed Arias that the city would be occupied and his forces disarmed by American troops if he did not evacuate the forts and surrender his arms and ammunition by 6 A.M. on the next day.   Before that hour arrived, Arias had withdrawn into the interior with his army, and when the American marines entered the city in the morning they encountered no opposition.   There was, however, as the Minister reported, "considerable anti-American sentiment." [35]   Marines were subsequently landed in Puerto Plata and Monte Cristi, and during June and July they were sent to several of the more important towns in the interior.   Admiral Caperton announced in a proclamation

[35] *Ibid.*, p. 227.

issued in June that the American troops would remain "until all revolutionary movements have been stamped out and until such reforms as are deemed necessary to insure the future welfare of the country have been initiated and are in effective operation." [36]

Although the constitutional authority of the Council of Ministers to exercise the executive power seemed somewhat doubtful, the American authorities at Santo Domingo were unwilling to have the Congress choose a provisional president because they feared that Arias would be able to obtain the election of one of his friends.[37] The complete elimination of Arias was now one of the chief objectives of American policy. Mr. Russell endeavored therefore to dissuade the Congress from acting for the time being, but his efforts were only partly successful, for by June 11 a bill naming Federico Henríquez y Carvajal, the Chief Justice of the Supreme Court, had passed the Chamber of Deputies and two readings in the Senate. Dr. Henríquez, however, insisted that his name be withdrawn. Further action was delayed by disagreements between the two houses and by the clumsiness of the procedure prescribed by the Constitution, but on July 25 Dr. Francisco Henríquez y Carvajal, a brother of the Chief Justice, was elected Provisional President for five months. The new President was a physician and also a distinguished jurist, who had taken little part in recent political events.

In the meantime, the Receivership, under orders from Washington, had not only reëstablished the comptrollership but had taken control of the internal revenue collections. It thus put into effect by its own action the system of financial administration which the United States

---

[36] *Ibid.*, p. 231.

[37] The account which follows of events leading up to the establishment of the Military Government is based in part upon the rather incomplete correspondence published in *Foreign Relations*, and in part on the very full statement in Sumner Welles, *Naboth's Vineyard*, and the well-documented statement of the Dominican side of the story in Max Henríquez Ureña, *Los Yanquis en Santo Domingo*.

had heretofore sought to obtain by agreement. The Council of Ministers made a vigorous but ineffective protest. On August 18 the Receivership took a still more radical step when it announced publicly that all payments to the Dominican Government would be suspended until a complete understanding was reached regarding the interpretation of the 1907 treaty.[38] The new President, who had assumed office only a few days before but had not been recognized by the United States, was thus placed in a seemingly impossible position.

President Henríquez indicated that he was prepared to accept the status quo with which he was confronted in the financial administration and to avail himself of American assistance in reorganizing the financial services, but he insisted that he was unable for constitutional reasons to meet the demands of the United States in their fullest extent. On September 20, however, he submitted a draft treaty conceding practically all of the demands regarding financial control and promising military reforms which in his opinion would have eliminated many of the worst abuses existing under previous administrations. This was not acceptable to the United States because it did not definitely provide for the control of the military forces by American officers. He subsequently indicated that he would consider the employment of foreign military instructors under contracts, and he and his advisers appear to have felt that there was still a prospect of an agreement when Minister Russell went to Washington in October for a conference with the State Department.[39] Negotiations were then necessarily suspended because the Legation was left without even a Chargé d'Affaires.

The terms of several members of the Dominican Congress were to expire on November 28, 1916, and their

[38] The text of the announcement is given, in Spanish, in Henríquez Ureña, *op. cit.*, p. 129.

[39] *Ibid.*, p. 145–151.

successors must be elected, under the Constitution, by electoral colleges which had been chosen several years before for a six-year term. As it was known that these colleges were to a great extent controlled by friends of Arias, some of the other political leaders were reluctant to have the elections take place. The President, however, appears to have been informed that the United States might make the absence of a Congress after November 28 the excuse for establishing a military government,[40] and he therefore issued a decree on November 14, calling for elections by those colleges which had not already acted of their own accord.

This proved to be an unfortunate step, for it convinced the Department of State that it would have to deal with a Dominican Government dominated by Arias if the elections were permitted to take place. On November 22 Secretary Lansing expressed this fear in a letter to President Wilson, pointing out also that the Henríquez Government had refused to agree to the reforms which the United States considered essential and that the suspension of payments was creating an intolerable situation for which the American Government could not long continue to assume responsibility. Mr. Lansing recommended that the Dominican Republic be placed immediately under military occupation and submitted the draft of a proclamation to be issued by Captain Harry S. Knapp, who had just been placed in command of the American naval forces. The President replied on November 26: [41]

It is with the deepest reluctance that I approve and authorize the course here proposed, but I am convinced that it is the least of the evils in sight in this very perplexing situation. I therefore authorize you to issue the necessary instructions in the premises.

I have stricken out the sentence in the proposed proclamation which authorizes the commanding officer to remove judges and

[40] *Ibid.*, p. 170.
[41] *Foreign Relations, 1916*, p. 242.

others in certain circumstances. It may be necessary to resort to such extreme measures, but I do not deem it wise to put so arbitrary an announcement in the proclamation itself.

On November 29 Captain Knapp issued the proclamation. After referring to the increase of indebtedness in violation of Article III of the 1907 treaty, the refusal of the Dominican authorities to accept the reforms proposed by the United States, and the continuance of internal disorders in the Republic, Captain Knapp declared and announced: [42]

. . . that the Republic of Santo Domingo is hereby placed in a state of Military Occupation by the forces under my command, and is made subject to Military Government and to the exercise of military law applicable to such occupation.

This military occupation is undertaken with no immediate or ulterior object of destroying the sovereignty of the Republic of Santo Domingo, but, on the contrary, is designed to give aid to that country in returning to a condition of internal order that will enable it to observe the terms of the treaty aforesaid, and the obligations resting upon it as one of the family of nations.

Dominican statutes, therefore, will continue in effect in so far as they do not conflict with the objects of the Occupation or necessary regulations established thereunder, and their lawful administration will continue in the hands of such duly authorized Dominican officials as may be necessary, all under the oversight and control of the United States Forces exercising Military Government.

The ordinary administration of justice, both in civil and criminal matters, through the regularly constituted Dominican courts will not be interfered with by the Military Government herein established; but cases to which a member of the United States forces in Occupation is a party, or in which are involved contempt or defiance of the authority of the Military Government, will be tried by tribunals set up by the Military Government.

All revenue accruing to the Dominican Government, including revenues hitherto accrued and unpaid—whether from customs duties under the terms of the Treaty concluded on February 8,

[42] *Ibid.*, p. 246.

1907, the Receivership established by which remains in effect, or from internal revenue—shall be paid to the Military Government herein established, which will, in trust for the Republic of Santo Domingo, hold such revenue and will make all the proper legal disbursements therefrom necessary for the administration of the Dominican Government, and for the purposes of the Occupation. . . .

At the same time orders were issued forbidding the possession of firearms and explosives by individuals and establishing a strict censorship of the press, the telegraph and the mails.[43] The American officials at once assumed control, and Dr. Henríquez left the country.

THE MILITARY GOVERNMENT

Captain Knapp's proclamation had contemplated the continued functioning of the existing administrative organization under the general control of the military government. The American officials had apparently hoped for the coöperation at least of the members of the cabinet, but they soon found that the existing ministers had completely abandoned their offices and that it would be impossible to persuade other properly qualified Dominicans to replace them. American naval officers were therefore placed in charge of the executive departments, with a few American assistants; but the great majority of the Dominican officials, including judges, provincial governors and municipal authorities, remained in office.

As the terms of a portion of the members of the Congress had expired, and it was considered inadvisable to hold new elections, the Military Governor exercised the legislative power throughout the existence of the occupation, and promulgated a number of laws of great importance. He was regarded by the United States as acting for and on behalf of the Dominican Government, and in

43 Henríquez Ureña, *op. cit.*, p. 180–182.

a sense as a trustee.[44] He thus administered all branches of the Government as though he were the legitimate president of the Dominican Republic, and even exchanged diplomatic correspondence with the Government of the United States regarding questions where an agreement tween the two Governments was required by the Treaty of 1907.

One of the first tasks of the Military Government was the establishment of order. In a few places, bands of armed men had resisted the American invasion, but were soon overcome. It was difficult to suppress the banditry which had flourished during the disturbed conditions of the past five years, and which now assumed in some districts the character of a patriotic movement. Extensive military operations were necessary during 1917 and 1918 in Seibo and Macorís provinces, but in general the country enjoyed a tranquillity and order which it had not known for many years. The civilian population was so far as possible disarmed, and a Dominican constabulary was organized by American officers. This force, under the command of Dominicans who received their training during the occupation, still exists.

The finances of the Government were also put in order. As in Cuba, the high price of sugar during the war brought prosperity, and there was a notable improvement in the revenues. Current indebtedness was paid, and a considerable surplus was made available for public works. The claims which had accumulated since the general settlement under the 1907 treaty, amounting to nearly $15,000,000, were examined and adjudicated by a commission of three Dominicans and two Americans appointed on June 26, 1917, by the Military Governor.[45] In payment of the awards, bonds to the amount of slightly over $4,000,000 were issued to the claimants in 1918.

[44] For a discussion of the theoretical position of the Military Governor, see the memorandum published in *Foreign Relations, 1918,* p. 382–389.
[45] *Foreign Relations, 1917,* p. 721.

The Military Government also embarked on an ambitious program for the improvement of economic and social conditions. Roads were built in all sections of the Republic, bringing important sections of the interior within a few hours of the capital by automobile instead of several days by horseback, and greatly encouraging production and commerce. The school system was completely reorganized, with the aid of a commission of prominent Dominicans, and the number of children enrolled was increased from 18,000 to nearly 100,000, with a 100 per cent improvement in the average daily attendance. The public health work was also reorganized and much was accomplished toward the improvement of sanitary conditions.[46]

Material benefits, however, did little to reconcile the Dominicans to foreign rule. Despite the enthusiasm and disinterestedness with which the American officials devoted themselves to the program for the rehabilitation of the country, there was a deep-seated hostility to foreign domination. The unfortunate events which inevitably occur under military rule, and the inevitable friction arising from differences in race and language, and too often from tactlessness or lack of patience, made the situation worse. The Dominican political leaders were naturally especially bitter in their opposition, and the mistakes which were inevitably made by naval officers who were striving to discharge tasks for which they were in some cases not fitted either by training or temperament afforded much opportunity for just or unjust criticism. Discontent grew more pronounced when the prosperity of the war years gave way to the economic depression of 1920.

[46] Reports by the Military Governor of his work during the first two years are printed in *Foreign Relations, 1917* and *1918.* A more concise statement is contained in a pamphlet entitled *Santo Domingo, Its Past and Its Present Condition,* published by the Military Government on January 1, 1920. For other discussions, see Welles, *op. cit.,* Knight, *The Americans in Santo Domingo,* and especially Professor Carl Kelsey's report, *The American Intervention in Haiti and the Dominican Republic,* published by the American Academy of Political and Social Science, March 1922.

The Reëstablishment of the Dominican Government

In December 1920 President Wilson directed the Military Governor to issue a proclamation declaring that the Government of the United States believed that the time had arrived when it might "inaugurate the simple processes of its rapid withdrawal from the responsibilities assumed in connection with Dominican affairs." To this end a commission of representative Dominicans, with an American technical adviser, was to be appointed to formulate amendments to the Constitution and a general revision of the laws of the Republic, including especially the electoral law. The commission, which consisted of seven of the most distinguished citizens of the Republic, was organized and started work two months later.[47]

A second proclamation, issued on June 14, 1921, set forth in more detail the procedure which the United States proposed to follow, and stated that the American troops might be withdrawn within eight months if adequate coöperation were received from the Dominican people. Elections were to be held within one month to choose the electoral colleges which under the Dominican Constitution must select the members of Congress and the President. The Congress was to be constituted as soon as possible in order that it might approve a Convention of Evacuation ratifying all acts of the Military Government, giving the General Receiver of Customs a right to collect a portion of the internal revenues if necessary to meet the service of the foreign debt, and providing for an American military mission to complete the training of the Dominican constabulary. After the convention had been approved by Congress, the electoral colleges would be permitted to choose a President to whom the Military Governor would transfer his authority.

[47] The proclamations of December 1920, June 1921, and March 1922 were published in the form of press releases by the Department of State.

Although the proposed Convention of Evacuation implied less American control in financial and military affairs than did the reforms demanded by the Department of State before the intervention, the Dominican political leaders strongly objected to its provisions and refused to advise their followers to participate in the elections to be held under the proclamation. The Military Governor was therefore compelled to postpone the elections. During the following months the American representatives at Santo Domingo made several unsuccessful efforts to reach an agreement with the Dominican leaders. Even the proposal to withdraw the provision for a military mission, upon the understanding that a small force of marines would remain in the Republic until the new government was able to insure the maintenance of order with its own forces, was not accepted. The Dominican leaders insisted upon complete and unconditional evacuation, to which the American Government was not prepared to agree.

The uncertainty regarding the duration of the Military Government made worse the economic crisis which had overtaken the Dominican Republic, like other sugar-producing countries, in 1920. Due in part to the decrease in revenues, and in part also to well-meant but ill-advised efforts to assist the Dominican farmers to obtain better prices for their crops, the Government found itself in a desperate financial situation. A road construction program, which the Military Governor wished to carry out before withdrawing from the country, had been suspended, throwing many laborers out of work. A foreign loan appeared to offer the only solution, but it was obviously impossible to obtain such a loan until the political question had been settled one way or the other. On March 6, 1922, therefore, the Military Governor issued a new proclamation, withdrawing those of December 1920 and June 1921, and stating that the Military Government would remain in the Dominican Republic until its public works program had been carried out and until the training of the constabulary had been completed. A loan of $6,700,000 was soon afterward obtained in New York.

Negotiations for the withdrawal of the Military Government were nevertheless almost immediately resumed. Dr. Francisco Peynado, a prominent Dominican lawyer, visited Washington in the spring of 1922 to discuss the situation informally with the Department of State. He was subsequently joined by General Horacio Vásquez and Señores Federico Velásquez and Elías Brache. These leaders, who represented nearly all of the Dominican parties, agreed to accept a convention ratifying all contracts made by the Military Government and all executive orders and other acts which had levied taxes, authorized expenditures or established rights on behalf of third persons. This did not of course imply that such executive orders could not subsequently be modified, like any other law, by appropriate legal procedure. They insisted, on the other hand, that elections for a constitutional government be held under a Dominican provisional administration rather than under the Military Government, and that all American troops be withdrawn when the constitutional government was inaugurated.[48]

An agreement on this basis was reached in June 1922.[49] While the Military Governor was to remain in Santo Domingo for the time being, he was to delegate the greater part of his authority to a Provisional President and Cabinet selected by a commission composed of the four leaders who had negotiated the plan and Archbishop Nouel. The Military Governor was to retain a measure of military and financial control, but the American troops were to be concentrated in not more than three places unless disturbances arose which the Dominican constabulary could

---

[48] The best available account of the negotiations leading up to the evacuation of the Dominican Republic is that of Welles, in his *Naboth's Vineyard*, Vol. II.

[49] The text of this agreement was also issued as a press release.

not suppress. A new electoral law and other necessary internal reforms were to be promulgated by the Provisional President, and subsequently confirmed by an elected Congress and a constitutional convention; and the new convention with the United States was thereafter to be negotiated by the Provisional President and approved by Congress, which was at the same time to pass a law specifically validating the acts of the Military Government independently of the convention. Subsequently, a constitutional President was to be elected and inaugurated and the American forces were to be withdrawn.

The President of the United States designated Mr. Sumner Welles, former chief of the Latin American Division in the State Department, as Commissioner in the Dominican Republic to assist in carrying out the plan of evacuation. On October 21, 1922, Juan Bautista Vicini Burgos was installed as Provisional President, with a Cabinet selected by agreement between the party leaders. The execution of the plan presented many difficulties, for the coöperation which had at first existed between the different political groups gave way to intense rivalry as the time for the election approached. The efforts of the various factions to obtain an advantage over their opponents made it necessary at one time entirely to suspend the electoral procedure and to revise the electoral law. Finally, however, the preliminary steps were carried out, and in March 1924 General Horacio Vásquez, who had figured so prominently in Dominican politics for a generation, was elected as constitutional President. He was inaugurated in July 1924 and the Military Government came to an end.[50]

The Convention of Ratification, which was signed on June 12, 1924, listed in detail the specific executive orders, resolutions, administrative regulations and contracts of the

[50] Welles, *op. cit.*, gives a detailed account of the delays caused by political rivalry.

Military Government which were recognized as valid, and which were to remain in effect until abrogated by legislative action. It provided that no subsequent act of the Dominican Republic should affect the validity or security of rights acquired under these executive orders, contracts, et cetera, and that controversies which might arise in this connection should be settled by arbitration if justice could not be obtained in the Dominican courts. The bond issues of 1918 and 1922 were specifically recognized as legal, binding and irrevocable obligations of the Republic; and it was agreed that the treaty of 1907 should remain in force during the life of these bond issues and that the duties of the General Receiver should be extended to include the application of the revenues pledged for their service.[51]

EVENTS SINCE 1924

Conditions in Santo Domingo after the withdrawal of the Military Government were very different from those which had existed before 1916. General Vásquez, the new President, enjoyed much genuine popularity and personal prestige, and public opinion opposed revolutionary activities which might lead to a new intervention. In the National Army, as the constabulary which had been organized under the Military Government was now called, the President had a well disciplined and equipped force which was greatly aided in the maintenance of order by the newly constructed highways. Financial conditions were on the whole good, and the country was wealthier than ever before because of the development of the sugar industry.

President Vásquez substantially increased the foreign debt, first by an issue of $3,300,000 in 1926,[52] mainly for the purchase of electric light plants at Puerto Plata and

---

[51] For the text of the Convention, see Appendix, *infra*, p. 286.

[52] This was the balance of a $10,000,000 loan authorized in 1922 under the Military Government, of which the $6,700,000 above referred to was the first installment. The whole loan had been validated by the Convention of Ratification.

Santiago, and subsequently by two issues of $5,000,000 each in 1927 and 1928, for the construction of various public works. In order to permit the issue of new loans under more advantageous conditions, the 1907 treaty was replaced by a new convention, very similar in its terms, signed December 27, 1924.[53]

Although the Republic's revenues were far greater than ever before, reaching more than $15,000,000 in 1927 and 1929, expenditures had also increased, and the prospect for the future became unfavorable when the decline in sugar prices began. Early in 1929, therefore, President Vásquez invited General Charles G. Dawes to organize a financial commission [54]

to recommend methods of improvement in the system of economic and financial administrative organization, both national and municipal, for the installation of a scientific budget system and for an efficient method whereby the Government may control all of its expenditures.

After three weeks' study of the situation, the commission presented drafts of a budget law, a general accounting law, a law of finance, a law for public improvements, a law for the reorganization of the government departments, and a civil service law, all of which were promptly enacted by the Dominican Congress. Some of them were subsequently put into execution with the assistance of American experts but others were never enforced.[55]

The constitutional amendments adopted in 1924 had provided for a presidential term of four years. President Vásquez, however, had been elected, though not inaugurated, before the new Constitution went into effect, and he served a six-year term as provided in the Constitution of 1908. As the time approached for a new election,

[53] For the text of the Treaty, see Appendix, *infra*, p. 290.
[54] *Report of the Dominican Economic Commission* (Chicago, Lakeside Press, 1929).
[55] Dominican Republic, Report of the Special Emergency Agent for the period, October 23, 1931, to December 31, 1932, p. 37–8.

the President and the Vice President were candidates for a second term, while the various opposition groups united to support Federico Velásquez for President and Rafael Estrella Ureña for Vice President. Late in 1929, General Vásquez became dangerously ill and was forced to go to the United States for treatment, leaving the administration in the hands of Vice President Alfonseca. The enmities already existing between some of his principal supporters and especially between the Vice President and General Rafael Trujillo, the commander of the army, became more pronounced in his absence, and were only patched up on the surface when the President returned and assumed the direction of his campaign for reëlection in January 1930.

In the meantime the opposition had been loudly demanding the abrogation of certain changes which had been made in the electoral law of 1924, asserting that these changes gave too much control to the President. A commission was appointed to recommend further amendments, but its report, which was rendered on January 10, 1930, fell far short of meeting the opposition leaders' demands. Some of the latter, therefore, were led to consider an attempt at revolution without waiting for the election. They were encouraged by the rivalries which the President's obviously feeble health had inspired in his own party and by the attitude of General Trujillo, who felt that the President and his advisers were endeavoring to displace him as head of the army.

On February 23, 1930, a group led by Estrella Ureña seized the fortress at Santiago, where a large quantity of arms and ammunition is said to have been left practically unguarded. Equipping a volunteer force with these supplies, the revolutionists marched on the capital. The army stood aside, and the President was powerless to resist. Through the mediation of the American Legation, Estrella Ureña was appointed Minister of the Interior, and assumed charge of the Executive Power on March 3, after the resignation of the President and the Vice President. As the change had been made in accord with the provisions of the Constitution, the United States continued diplomatic relations with the Government, without raising any question of recognition.[56]

When the elections were held on May 16, General Trujillo, whose control over the army had not been affected by the revolution, was the sole candidate, as his opponents had withdrawn two days earlier charging intimidation and fraud. The new President was inaugurated on August 16, 1930, for a four-year term. He faced a far more difficult situation than his predecessor, for the political unrest which affected other Latin American countries during the depression was evident in Santo Domingo also, and he was compelled to suppress several small armed revolts during the first two years of his administration. More recently, however, political conditions appear to have improved.

The depression also unfavorably affected the Government's financial situation. Revenues fell off from more than $15,000,000 in 1929 to less than $10,000,000 in 1930, and to $7,311,417 in 1931.[57] At the same time the amount which the Government was required to pay for the service of its foreign debt was very greatly increased because heavy sinking fund payments became due in 1930 under the loan contracts. An unusually destructive hurricane which destroyed a large part of Santo Domingo City on September 3, 1930, also caused heavy extraordinary expenditures. It soon became evident that the essential expenses of running the administration could not be paid if the full debt service were continued.

[56] Press releases describing the progress of the revolt and the action taken by the American representatives were issued by the Department of State, Feb. 25, 26, 27, and 28, and March 1, 1930; *Press Releases*, March 1, 1930, p. 91–3.

[57] Report of the Special Emergency Agent, 1931–2, p. 50.

On October 23, 1931, therefore, the payment of the sinking fund on the foreign debt was suspended by law. To make this possible without requesting the General Receiver of Customs to assume responsibility for action contrary to the provisions of the treaty under which he had been appointed, the customhouses at Santo Domingo, San Pedro de Macorís, and Puerto Plata were removed from his control by Presidential decree and placed under a Special Emergency Agent. This official was to pay from the collections at these ports such sums as might be necessary, in addition to collections by the General Receiver, to continue interest payments on the debt, and was to pay to the Government not over $125,000 each month, turning over any balance to the General Receiver of Customs for sinking fund purposes.[58]   Mr. William E. Dunn, an American, who had already been acting as Financial Adviser to the Government under contract, was appointed as Special Emergency Agent. The Department of State raised no objection to the Government's action, although it was admittedly a violation both of the loan contracts and of the Convention with the United States.[59]

While operating under the Emergency Law, the Government has endeavored to effect financial reforms which would improve the general situation of its treasury. A law passed April 26, 1932, provided for the reorganization of the Internal Revenue Service under the technical supervision of the Special Emergency Agent, and Mr. Fred Rickards was engaged as technical adviser for this work. On May 16, 1932, the Special Emergency Agent was authorized to assume the additional duties of Director of the Budget. A Budget Committee was subsequently appointed to assist him, and it is stated that the measures thus adopted resulted in closing the year 1932 without

[58] For the text of the Emergency Law, see *ibid.*, p. 25.

[59] Department of State press release of Nov. 11, 1931, *Press Releases*, Nov. 14, 1931, p. 454.

a deficit.[60]   A satisfactory final adjustment of the Republic's financial problems, however, can hardly be hoped for until conditions in the sugar industry improve or until other products are developed to give renewed life to agriculture and industry.[61]

[60] Report of the Special Emergency Agent, 1931–2, p. 16.
[61] In 1933 Mr. Dunn was succeeded as Special Emergency Agent by Mr. Oliver P. Newman.

CHAPTER IV

THE AMERICAN INTERVENTION IN HAITI

HAITI BEFORE 1915

During the eighteenth century the French colony of Saint Domingue was the richest and the most prosperous of the European possessions in the West Indies. Upon its great plantations, operated by slave labor, was produced an important fraction of the world's sugar supply, besides great amounts of indigo, cacao, cotton and other tropical products. This wealth was concentrated, however, in a relatively few hands, and many of those who owned property lived in Paris and left the management of their affairs to overseers. Out of a population of more than half a million, there were only 32,000 whites and 24,000 colored freedmen. The rest were Negro slaves working under conditions so destructive of life and so unfavorable for reproduction as to require the constant replenishment of the supply by new importations from Africa. Among the whites, there were rivalries and hatreds between the official class, the creole aristocracy, and the poorer Frenchmen,—the *petits blancs*. All of the whites were set apart by rigid caste distinctions from the free Negroes and mulattoes, although many of these had been educated abroad and owned plantations and slaves.[1]

[1] The classic description of the French colony before the revolution is that of Moreau de St. Méry, *Déscription . . . de la Partie Française de l'Isle de St. Domingue*, 2 vols., Philadelphia, 1798. An excellent description is also given in T. Lothrop Stoddard's *French Revolution in San Domingo*, Boston, 1914. Stoddard's book is the leading authority on the events of the revolution in Haiti.

The natural enmities between the different elements in the ruling class found expression in armed strife when the mother country's control became less effective at the time of the French Revolution. Each faction attempted to take advantage of events in France to improve its own position. The mulattoes, exasperated by the white colonists' violent opposition to the States-General's ineffective efforts to remove the restrictions against them, organized a revolt which was cruelly suppressed. A Negro uprising in the rich Plaine du Nord destroyed many lives and much property. France's enemies, Spain and England, occupied portions of the colony. Their troops were eventually driven out by a Negro leader, Toussaint L'Ouverture, who had formerly served in the Spanish army but who went over to the French in 1794 and soon after became the real ruler not only of the French but also of the Spanish end of the island.

In December 1801, when a temporary peace with England freed his hands in Europe, Napoleon sent a large army which defeated the Negro leaders and regained control of the colony. Toussaint was arrested, by treachery, and sent to die in a French prison. Yellow fever, however, almost wiped out the French forces. A new revolt compelled the evacuation of the island in November 1803, and on January 1, 1804, the independence of the Republic of Haiti was formally proclaimed. Those whites who had not already fled were systematically exterminated. During the long period of almost continuous civil strife, marked by appalling cruelty and excesses on both sides, the towns had been burned, the sugar mills had been destroyed, and even the fine residences of the French proprietors had been torn down stone by stone.

Dessalines, who had led the final revolt, later proclaimed himself Emperor of Haiti, and ruled until his assassination in 1806. The former colony was then divided for a time between Henri Christophe's kingdom in the north and a Republic under Pétion, a mulatto leader, in the south, but it was reunited after Christophe's suicide in 1820. For the next ninety-five years, Haiti led a troubled existence, disturbed by revolutions at home, by wars with the neighboring Dominican Republic, and by frequent military demonstrations by foreign powers to obtain redress for real or alleged injuries suffered by their nationals.[2]

Although the overwhelming numerical predominance of the pure-blooded African element always made the Negro military leaders a powerful political factor, and frequently enabled them to rise to supreme power, the Republic was really ruled, during much of this period, by a small mulatto aristocracy living in the principal towns. There was an impassable gulf between this class and the peasants, who cultivated their small garden patches in the plains or the hills and whose very language, a primitive patois of French-African-Spanish origin, was different from that of the French speaking *élite*. Descended for the most part from slaves who at the time of the French Revolution had but recently been imported from Africa, the peasants had inherited none of the European traditions which were the basis of the culture of the townspeople. To them, the Government was merely an alien force, oppressing and exploiting those who could not keep out of reach of the petty military despots who represented it in each locality. They knew nothing of political affairs and for the most part participated in the civil wars only when forcibly impressed as soldiers by one side or the other. Entirely illiterate, they naturally had no conception of the meaning of the ballot. As this class comprised at least ninety per cent of the population, it was obvious that real republican institutions could not exist.

The *élite*, on the other hand, naturally came to regard

[2] One of the best accounts of Haitian history between 1804 and 1915 will be found in H. P. Davis, *Black Democracy*, New York, 1929.

the Government as the patrimony of their own class. They alone possessed the education and the intelligence which were required in official positions. The Negro military chiefs who generally occupied the Presidency were compelled to rely upon them for the greater part of the work of administration. As the native business men found themselves unable to compete with German and other foreign merchants who appeared in increasing numbers with the development of commerce, and who derived great advantages from the protection afforded by their own Governments, the Haitian upper class were forced more and more to depend upon the public treasury for their livelihood. The condition of the country and the lack of capital made it impossible for those who owned land to develop it, and agriculture remained almost exclusively in the hands of the peasants. The ruling class had little interest in the construction of roads or the improvement of conditions in the rural districts, and the revenues were expended almost entirely for the benefit of the city population.

At the end of the nineteenth century, political conditions in Haiti appeared to have become somewhat more stable, and successful revolts were less frequent. There had been a series of strong presidents, and high coffee prices,—for coffee was by this time the one important export crop,— had brought a measure of prosperity. Unfortunately, however, a new period of disorder began about 1908, with the increasing frequency of the so-called *caco* revolutions. The *cacos* were turbulent, adventure-loving peasants living in the wild mountain country along the northern part of the eastern frontier. Under chiefs who were virtually professional revolutionists, they supported any political leader who wished to purchase their services, and retired to their homes, ready for a new revolt, after the government had been overthrown. The administrations established by their aid at Port-au-Prince had no forces with which to combat them after the *caco* armies had been disbanded and paid off. Revolutions consequently succeeded one another with increasing frequency, and between August 1911 and July 1915 there were six Presidents, none of whom served so much as a year. During the latter part of this period, new Presidents barely established themselves in office before they were compelled to flee at the approach of the same *caco* forces which had placed them there.

THE FRENCH LOANS

The apparent approach of a state of virtual anarchy in Haiti necessarily caused concern to the Government of the United States. American interests in the Republic were relatively unimportant, but there were a considerable number of French and German merchants, and the Haitian Government, like the Dominican Republic in 1905, was heavily in debt to European creditors. Bond issues of 26,000,000 and 50,000,000 francs respectively had been sold in France in 1875 and 1896, in each case on terms far from advantageous to the Haitian Government, and in 1910 a further loan of 65,000,000 francs for the purpose of funding the internal debt and retiring depreciated paper currency was contracted for with American, French and German bankers. At the same time, the bankers interested established the Banque Nationale, which, though a privately owned institution, was to act as the Government's treasury and to receive and have custody of all Government funds. This bank also enjoyed the sole right of note issue and was intrusted with the execution of the contemplated currency reform. Besides the external debt, there was a large internal and floating debt, the amount of which increased rapidly after 1912 with successive issues of bonds to pay the expenses of the revolutions. These bonds went largely into the hands of local German merchants, who were accused of financing several of the revolutionary movements in order to obtain favors of various sorts from the incoming governments.

Each of Haiti's numerous debts was secured by a specific "affectation" of customs duties, and the Bank was authorized to pay over to the creditors the money derived from each item of pledged revenues, delivering to the Government only the balance remaining after the requirements of the debt service had been met. Since the Government had pledged practically every source of income, no funds would have been available for current expenses if the Bank had not advanced a fixed sum each month for this purpose under the so-called Budget Convention, recouping itself at the end of the fiscal year from the surplus remaining in the treasury after other obligations had been discharged.

CONTROVERSY WITH THE BANK

In 1914 a serious controversy arose between the Government and the Bank. The American Minister reported on June 9, that the Bank intended to refuse to renew the Budget Convention for the coming year, and that it hoped by this action to compel the Government to seek financial aid which would result in the establishment of American customs control.[3] The Bank did, in fact, refuse to advance further funds in August, asserting that the continual revolutionary disturbances had so affected the Government's revenue that no funds would remain at the end of the fiscal year for the repayment of approximately $1,500,000 which had already been advanced.[4] This placed the Government in a desperate financial situation and in fact contributed to its defeat by a revolution in which its own unpaid soldiers and former partisans took an active part. The new administration, despite the protests of the Bank and a formal statement by the United

[3] *Foreign Relations, 1914,* p. 345.
[4] *Ibid.,* p. 353; *Foreign Relations, 1915,* p. 497.

States Government that it would not recognize the legality of the proposed issue, proceeded to put into circulation a large amount of new paper money.[5] It also attempted to obtain possession of the large fund belonging to the Government but held by the Bank under the 1910 loan contract to be used in retiring the outstanding paper currency, but the greater part of this fund was sent to New York on an American warship in December 1914 at the request of the Bank. A few days later some $66,000 in cash was forcibly taken by the Government from the Bank.[6]

Under a decree issued in January 1915 the Government took the treasury service away from the Bank and provided that customs duties should be paid in the future to local merchants, to be disbursed without the Bank's intervention.[7] This constituted not only a violation of the contract with the Bank but also a violation of the Government's obligations toward all of its creditors, making inevitable a default on the foreign debt as soon as the funds already collected by the Bank for the benefit of the creditors should be exhausted. The Government of the United States protested repeatedly against these violations of the Bank's concession, but the Haitian Government maintained that the Bank as a French corporation was not entitled to any diplomatic support from the United States and insisted further that it was willing to arbitrate all questions pending with the Bank in accordance with provisions in its concession.

CONTROVERSY WITH THE NATIONAL RAILROAD COMPANY

A dispute had also arisen between the Government and the National Railroad Company. This American corporation had undertaken to build a railroad from Cap Haitien

[5] *Foreign Relations, 1914,* p. 373.
[6] *Foreign Relations, 1915,* p. 501.
[7] *Ibid.,* p. 510 ff.

to Port-au-Prince, on condition that the Government guarantee bonds to the amount of $20,000 per kilometer to defray the cost. A few sections of the line completed before 1914 had been accepted by the Government, although only after a controversy regarding the character of the work done, and bonds to the amount of about $3,500,000 had been sold, mostly in France. In August 1914 the Government had failed to make good its guaranty of interest on these bonds and informed the company of its intention to seize the railroad line on the ground that the work had not progressed so fast as the contract required. A stay in the foreclosure proceedings was obtained through the good offices of the Department of State and negotiations for a settlement of the dispute continued without concrete results between the Government, the Department of State and the company until after the American intervention.[8]

POLICY OF THE UNITED STATES

It has frequently been stated that the United States intervened in Haiti in 1915 for the benefit of the American interests in the National Bank and the National Railroad. This explanation is at best only partly correct. The persons who directed the Bank and the Railroad were active in attempting to bring about intervention, and their complaints doubtless played a part in persuading the American Government that conditions in Haiti were becoming intolerable, but there were other considerations apart from the desire to safeguard these relatively unimportant American investments which played a far more influential part in shaping the policy of the United States. The published correspondence between the Department of State and the American Legation at Port-au-Prince in 1914–15,

[8] The correspondence regarding the controversy with the National Railroad is published in *Foreign Relations, 1915*, p. 538 *ff.*, and *Foreign Relations, 1916*, p. 368 *ff.*

shows that the Wilson administration was endeavoring to put an end to revolutionary conditions in Haiti as part of a broad, somewhat idealistic program for the establishment of stable government throughout the Caribbean region. It was substantially the same policy as that followed in dealing with the Dominican Republic. In Haiti, as in the other Caribbean countries, the United States feared that a continuance of disorder would lead to complications with European states. Various foreign governments had repeatedly landed marines to protect their nationals during disturbances at Port-au-Prince and Cap Haitien and there was apprehension that they might eventually take more active steps, especially if there should be a default on the foreign debt. Several efforts had been made by German interests to establish coaling stations at the Mole St. Nicholas, a peninsula dominating the principal trade route between New York and Panama, and both the French and the German Governments had officially expressed to the United States a feeling that they had special interests in Haiti and that they should participate in any financial control which might be established. In reply to the German Government, Mr. Bryan wrote on September 16, 1914: [9]

. . . the Government of the United States is well known to have taken for many years and without variation of policy the position that neither foreign influence nor interest proceeding from outside the American hemisphere could, with the consent of the United States, be so broadened or extended as to constitute a control, either wholly or in part, of the government or administration of any independent American state.

On July 2, 1914, the American Minister at Port-au-Prince had been instructed to sound out the Haitian Government regarding its willingness to enter into a treaty

[9] For the French attitude, see *Foreign Relations, 1915*, p. 514. The German demand for participation and Mr. Bryan's reply were quoted in Mr. Lansing's letter to Senator McCormick, printed as an appendix to the Senate Committee's report on Haiti, Senate Report No. 794, 67th Congress, 2nd Session. The same letter discusses the question of the Mole St. Nicholas.

giving the United States control over the Haitian customs.[10] Negotiations had hardly been begun, however, before a new revolution occurred. The Department of State had apparently been prepared to uphold by force President Zamor, with whom it had been negotiating, in order to bring about not only the signature of the desired treaty but also an agreement similar to that recently effected in the Dominican Republic for the holding of an election under American supervision. The Government fell so suddenly, however, that there was no opportunity for such action.[11]

On November 12, 1914, two days after the inauguration of President Théodore, the American Minister was instructed to inform him that he would be recognized when a commission had been named with full powers to negotiate with the United States (1) a convention providing for the establishment of customs control, (2) a settlement of questions affecting the National Railway and the National Bank, (3) an agreement by Haiti to give full protection to all foreign interests in Haiti, and (4) a pledge never to lease any Haitian territory to any European government for use as a naval or coaling station. The Department subsequently added to these conditions a requirement that a protocol be signed for the arbitration of pending American claims.[12] President Théodore, however, declined to accept the proposed customs control and the American Minister was instructed that the Government of the United States had no desire to assume any responsibility in connection with Haiti's fiscal system except in accord with the wishes of the Haitian Government and that he was not, therefore, to press the matter.[13] Renewed revolutionary activity soon interrupted the negotiations again. Mr. Bryan, nevertheless, continued his effort to

[10] *Foreign Relations, 1914*, p. 347.
[11] *Ibid.*, p. 355.
[12] *Ibid.*, p. 359–60.
[13] *Ibid.*, p. 367.

apply in Haiti the same policy which had been followed with apparent if not lasting success in the Dominican Republic. In November 1914 he had sent to the American Legation a copy of the so-called Wilson Plan, with the suggestion that it might serve as a basis for the establishment of peaceful conditions in Haiti,[14] and on February 20, 1915, he informed the Legation that President Wilson was sending to Haiti the same commissioners,—Ex-Governor Fort and Mr. Smith,—who had recently established peace in the neighboring Republic.[15] The commissioners arrived just after the proclamation of Guillaume Sam, Théodore's successor, and they returned to Washington ten days later, apparently without having carried on any important negotiations with the Haitian Government. Mr. Paul Fuller, who was sent to Port-au-Prince about two months later to make a new effort to negotiate a treaty, appears to have accomplished equally little.[16] It was clear by July 1915 that no Haitian Government would be likely to accept the measure of control which the Department of State considered necessary for the establishment of political and financial stability.

THE AMERICAN INTERVENTION

Guillaume Sam had been proclaimed President on March 4, 1915. A new revolution began almost immediately in the north, and a large number of persons suspected of complicity, including many members of prominent families, were imprisoned in the penitentiary at Port-au-Prince. On July 27, when an uprising occurred in this city, 167 of these prisoners were massacred by order of the commander of the prison, who subsequently fled to

[14] *Ibid.*, p. 357.

[15] *Foreign Relations, 1915*, p. 464.

[16] Little correspondence about the Fort-Smith mission and none about Mr. Fuller's mission has been published by the United States Government. Brief statements will be found in A. C. Millspaugh, *Haiti under American Control, 1915–1930*, Boston, World Peace Foundation, 1931, p. 30–32, and in *The American Occupation of Haiti*, Foreign Policy Association Information Service, 1929.

the Dominican Legation but was found there by a mob and killed. On the following day a mob invaded the French Legation, where the President had taken refuge, dragged him out of his hiding place, and literally tore him to pieces in the streets. There was a complete disappearance of constituted authority at Port-au-Prince, for the revolutionary army was still in the north. A self-appointed revolutionary committee assumed authority in the city but was unable to control either the disorganized soldiers or the hysterical populace, and there was intense apprehension for the safety of foreigners. It was under these conditions that Admiral Caperton landed marines and assumed control. He at once began the disarmament of the Haitian forces, and order was gradually established.[17]

When the Haitian Congress assembled, under the protection of the American marines, the American Chargé d'Affaires and Admiral Caperton were instructed to make the following declaration: [18]

First: Let Congress understand that the Government of the United States intends to uphold it, but that it can not recognize action which does not establish in charge of Haitian affairs those whose abilities and dispositions give assurances of putting an end to factional disorders.

Second: In order that no misunderstanding can possibly occur after election, it should be made perfectly clear to candidates as soon as possible and in advance of their election, that the United States expects to be intrusted with the practical control of the customs, and such financial control over the affairs of the Republic of Haiti as the United States may deem necessary for an efficient administration.

The Government of the United States considers it its duty to support a constitutional government. It means to assist in the establishing of such a government, and to support it as long as necessity may require. It has no design upon the political or territorial integrity of Haiti; on the contrary, what has been done, as well as what will be done, is conceived in an

[17] For a vivid description of the events immediately preceding the American intervention see Chargé d'Affaires Davis' account in *Foreign Relations, 1916*, p. 311.

[18] *Foreign Relations, 1915*, p. 479.

effort to aid the people of Haiti in establishing a stable government and in maintaining domestic peace throughout the Republic.

Two days later, M. Sudre Dartiguenave was elected President of the Republic by 94 out of 116 votes. Dartiguenave was apparently the candidate preferred by the American officials at Port-au-Prince, who had been holding frequent conferences with members of Congress and with aspirants to the presidency in an effort to reach an understanding regarding the future relations between Haiti and the United States, and he doubtless owed his election largely to this preference. Admiral Caperton later testified, however, that no bargain of any kind had been made with Dartiguenave before his election, and that no pressure in his favor had been brought to bear upon any member of Congress.[19]

Although the American forces occupied and maintained order in Port-au-Prince and subsequently extended their control to other coast towns, there was still much disorder and pillage in the interior. There was also much opposition to the American intervention in the capital itself, and this feeling became more intense at the end of August and the beginning of September, when Admiral Caperton took over several of the Haitian customhouses, to prevent the revenues from falling into unauthorized hands, and also to provide funds for public works for the relief of unemployment.[20] On September 3, therefore, the American naval authorities proclaimed martial law in Port-au-Prince and its adjacent territory.

In the meantime the treaty negotiations had begun. Admiral Caperton had informed the Navy Department

[19] Millspaugh, *op. cit.*, p. 41, quotes the statement which Admiral Caperton made before the Senate Committee in 1921. The statement, with a mass of other testimony and information regarding events in Haiti before 1922 are published in: *Inquiry into Occupation and Administration of Haiti and Santo Domingo, Hearings before a Select Committee on Haiti and Santo Domingo,* U. S. Senate, 67th Congress, 1st Session.

[20] *Foreign Relations,* 1915, p. 434, 518.

on August 7 that M. Dartiguenave, then President of the Senate, had stated in the presence of members of Congress "that Haiti must and will accede gladly to any terms proposed by the United States." He said that the Haitian leaders were ready to cede the Mole St. Nicholas and to give the United States the right to intervene in Haiti's affairs and the control of the customhouses, begging, however, "to avoid as far as possible humiliation." "They insist," reported the Admiral, "that no government can stand except through protection of the United States. Without this protection, there would be nothing but anarchy in Haiti, according to their statements. Most Haitians now fear that the Americans will withdraw their troops." [21]

The Treaty of 1915

On August 12, the day of the presidential election, the Chargé d'Affaires was instructed to submit to the new Government a treaty generally similar to those formerly proposed but with additional paragraphs providing for the establishment of a constabulary under American control, and for the coöperation of the United States in "the sanitation and public improvement of the Republic." No request was made for the cession of the Mole St. Nicholas. The Chargé was at first instructed to obtain the approval of this treaty without modification by the Haitian Congress in advance of its signature, but this proved impracticable and several changes in the treaty were in fact made to meet objections raised by the Haitian Government. A final agreement was not reached, however, until after the Department of State had threatened to consider the establishing of a military government or permitting the control to pass to another political faction. [22]

The treaty was signed on September 16, and was promptly ratified by the Chamber of Deputies. When the

[21] *Ibid.*, p. 431.
[22] *Ibid.*, p. 437.

Haitian Senate delayed action, Admiral Caperton was instructed on November 10 to make the following statement to the President and his Cabinet: [23]

I have the honor to inform the President of Haiti and the members of his Cabinet that I am personally gratified that public sentiment continues favorable to the treaty, that there is a strong demand from all classes for immediate ratification, and that treaty will be ratified Thursday.

I am sure that you, gentlemen, will understand my sentiment in this matter and I am confident if the treaty fails of ratification that my Government has the intention to retain control in Haiti until the desired end is accomplished and that it will forthwith proceed to the complete pacification of Haiti so as to insure internal tranquillity necessary to such development of the country and its industry as will afford relief to the starving populace now unemployed. Meanwhile the present Government will be supported in the effort to secure stable conditions and lasting peace in Haiti whereas those offering opposition can only expect such treatment as their conduct merits.

The United States Government is particularly anxious for immediate ratification by the present Senate of this treaty, which was drawn up with the full intention of employing as many Haitians as possible to aid in giving effect to its provisions, so that suffering may be relieved at the earliest possible date.

Rumors of bribery to defeat the treaty are rife but are not believed. However, should they prove true those who accept or give bribes will be vigorously prosecuted.

On the following day the treaty was ratified. It was subsequently revealed that Admiral Caperton had informed one of his subordinates that the negotiation of the treaty had been facilitated "by exercising military pressure at propitious moments," but Admiral Caperton testified before a Senate Committee that he thought that this had referred to measures which he had taken "to quiet the *cacos* and keep them from intimidating the members of Congress and the Senate," and that "there was no actual military movement made against the Congress." [24]

[23] *Ibid.*, p. 458.
[24] Millspaugh, *op. cit.*, p. 54. Millspaugh's book is the best existing account of events in Haiti since the American intervention.

In this connection, it is interesting to note that President Dartiguenave, in a proclamation issued a few days after the ratification of the treaty, praised the action taken by Congress and said: [25]

. . . Without entering into a discussion of facts anterior to the coming of the Americans, remember that in a moment of our supreme despair the powerful and generous nation of North America saw our unhappiness, took pity on us and came in the name of humanity and universal fraternity to offer us the hand of friendship and of succor. Was it necessary to repel, even under a disguised form, as several people of the type of many of my predecessors seem to think, this friendly aid?

Being persuaded of the loyalty of the Government of the United States and convinced that its people, who by means of their works have become so great as to become our ideal, desire fully to guide us in the route which centuries of civilization have made, which we, unhappy slaves of false reasoning brought about by jealous prejudices, have never tried to find, I have not a second of hesitation. . . .

You have not been strangers to the struggle brought about by diversity of opinion whereby people opposed to the convention struggled against the Government to prevent its acceptance. We have defended it foot by foot and have guaranteed its various clauses in order to overcome the imminent peril with which lack of reflection and blindness was liable to threaten our national sovereignty. And who can deny that the formal refusal to accept the convention would have been the destruction of our independence? . . . In the future the people will see that we have done the best thing and that we have acted for love of country. . . .

The treaty provided that the Government of the United States would, "by its good offices, aid the Haitian Government in the proper and efficient development of its agricultural, mineral and commercial resources, and in the establishment of the finances of Haiti on a firm and solid basis." The President of Haiti, upon nomination by the President of the United States, was to appoint a General Receiver to collect all customs duties and a

[25] *Foreign Relations, 1915*, p. 459.

Financial Adviser who should "devise an adequate system of public accounting, aid in increasing the revenues and adjusting them to the expenses, inquire into the validity of the debts of the Republic, enlighten both Governments with reference to all eventual debts, recommend improved methods of collecting and applying the revenues, and make such other recommendations to the Minister of Finance as may be deemed necessary for the welfare and prosperity of Haiti." Haiti was not to increase its public debt nor to reduce the customs duties except by previous agreement with the President of the United States. A constabulary was to be organized and officered by Americans appointed upon the nomination of the President of the United States, and measures for the sanitation and public improvement of the Republic were to be carried out under the supervision of engineers appointed in the same manner. A protocol was to be executed for the settlement of all pending foreign claims. Articles XI and XIV provided: [26]

Article XI. The Government of Haiti agrees not to surrender any of the territory of the Republic of Haiti by sale, lease, or otherwise, or jurisdiction over such territory, to any foreign government or power, nor to enter into any treaty or contract with any foreign power or powers that will impair or tend to impair the independence of Haiti.

Article XIV. The high contracting parties shall have authority to take such steps as may be necessary to insure the complete attainment of any of the objects comprehended in this treaty; and, should the necessity occur, the United States will lend an efficient aid for the preservation of Haitian independence and the maintenance of a government adequate for the protection of life, property and individual liberty.

A *modus vivendi* signed on November 29 provided that the treaty should go into effect provisionally, pending its ratification by the United States Senate.[27] Naval and

[26] For the text of the Treaty see Appendix, *infra*, p. 297.
[27] For the text, see *Foreign Relations, 1915*, p. 460.

marine officers were appointed temporarily to act as Financial Adviser, General Receiver, Chief of the Constabulary and engineers in charge of public works and sanitation. The organization of the constabulary began at once. During the following year, executive agreements were signed fixing the salaries of the various American officials to be employed under the treaty, and providing in detail for the organization of the constabulary. After the exchange of ratifications on May 3, 1916, civilians were appointed as General Receiver and Deputy General Receiver and as Financial Adviser, and naval and marine officers were definitively appointed as heads of the other treaty services. A law enacted by the United States Congress in June 1916 authorized the detail of such officers for duty with the Haitian Government.

The treaty had been made originally for a period of ten years, but Article XVI had provided:

The present treaty shall remain in full force and virtue for the term of ten years, to be counted from the day of exchange of ratifications, and further for another term of ten years if, for specific reasons presented by either of the high contracting parties, the purpose of this treaty has not been fully accomplished. . . .

It early became apparent that the flotation of a foreign loan for the refunding of the public debt and the economic rehabilitation of the Republic would be impossible if American control of Haiti's finances were continued for only ten years. On March 1, 1917, the Haitian Government had requested the good offices of the United States in obtaining such a loan, and on March 28, 1917, an Additional Act was signed, fixing the duration of the original agreement at twenty years. In view of the provisions of Article XVI, quoted above, it was not considered necessary to submit this Act to the United States Senate.[28]

[28] For the text see Appendix, *infra,* p. 298.

The Constitution of 1918

President Dartiguenave suggested early in 1916 that the Haitian constitution should be revised in such a way as to bring it more into conformity with the state of affairs created by the treaty. The United States Government took an active interest in the proposed revision and especially in the elimination of the prohibition against foreign land ownership, which had formed a part of earlier Haitian constitutions, for it was believed that the economic development of the Republic would be impossible so long as foreign interests could not purchase real estate. A draft of a new constitution was therefore discussed in detail by the American authorities, both civil and military, with President Dartiguenave. It also received careful consideration by the State and Navy Departments in Washington. President Dartiguenave, however, had been unable to obtain the coöperation of the Congress, in which was vested authority to amend the constitution. Before the legislative body met for its session in April 1916 it was evident that there would be a majority opposed to the administration. The President, therefore, arbitrarily dissolved the Senate and summoned the Chamber of Deputies as a constituent assembly. The Chamber, however, refused to function in this capacity, and a new Congress chosen in January 1917 showed itself equally unwilling to adopt the President's views. In order to prevent the approval of a constitution differing from that on which he had agreed with the American authorities, the President dissolved the Congress on June 19. He was supported in this action by the American military authorities, and the order of dissolution was delivered by Major Butler, the Chief of the Constabulary.

The revised Constitution was subsequently put into effect by plebiscite held on June 12, 1918. The popular vote was, of course, a mere form although not more so,

perhaps, than previous elections which had been held in
Haiti. The large majority by which the constitution
was approved was undoubtedly due chiefly to the fact
that the American constabulary officers were instructed
frankly to advocate its adoption.

The new Constitution permitted foreigners residing in
Haiti to own land for residential, agricultural, commercial, industrial or educational purposes. It also ratified and validated all acts of the military occupation and
of the Haitian Government prior to its adoption. Among
its most important provisions were transitory Articles
C and D: [29]

Article C. The first election of members of the legislative
body after the adoption of the present Constitution shall take
place on January 10 of an even-numbered year.
The year shall be fixed by a decree of the President of the
Republic published at least three months before the meeting
of the primary assemblies.
The session of the legislative body then elected shall convene
on the constitutional date immediately following the first
election.
Article D. A Council of State, created in accordance with the
same principles as those of the decree of April 5, 1916, and
composed of 21 members distributed among the different departments, shall exercise the legislative power until the legislative body is constituted, on which date the Council of State
shall cease to exist.

Under these provisions, President Dartiguenave and his
successor, President Borno, governed the Republic for
twelve years without the assistance of an elected Congress.
The control over legislation exerted by the President
through the appointed Council of State naturally facilitated the adoption of measures agreed upon by the two
Governments for the realization of the purposes of the
treaty. A closer coöperation was possible than could

[29] An English translation of the Constitution is printed in *Foreign Relations, 1918*, p. 487.

have existed if there had been a Congress independent of the Executive, but the arrangement eventually led, as we shall see, to complaints of dictatorship in Haiti and severe criticism.

AMERICAN CONTROL OVER FINANCES AND LEGISLATION

Meanwhile, the Financial Adviser and the General Receiver had established an effective control over Haiti's finances. The Government of the United States had insisted upon the deposit of all Haitian funds, including those derived from the internal revenue as well as from the customs, to the credit of the General Receiver, and it had also insisted that the Haitian Government consult with and accept the advice of the Financial Adviser in formulating its budget. The control already exercised by the Financial Adviser over expenditures was made definite and permanent by an agreement effected December 3, 1918, under which every order of payment issued by the Minister of Finance must be approved by the Financial Adviser before being honored by the Bank.

An agreement reached on August 24, 1918, through an exchange of notes, provided that "every project of law bearing upon one of the objects of the treaty will be, before being presented to the legislative power of Haiti, communicated to the representative of the United States for the information of this Government and, if necessary, for a discussion between the two governments." [30]

The United States had insisted upon these grants of authority as necessary for the execution of the purposes of the Treaty and had found justification for demanding them in the rather broad language of that document. The Haitian Government, on the other hand, had resisted, though unsuccessfully, what it considered an extension of the powers granted to the United States. A serious

[30] These agreements are referred to in Millspaugh, *op. cit.*, p. 77 (footnote) and p. 78.

dispute arose in 1920, when the Council of State enacted
several laws to which the American authorities had objected, while at the same time declining to approve certain
measures which the Financial Adviser had advocated.
The American Minister informed the Haitian Government that the legislation just enacted would not be recognized by the United States and demanded its repeal.
When this demand was not complied with, the Financial
Adviser informed the Haitian Government that Article
V of the Treaty would for the time being be strictly construed so that all funds would be set aside for the payment
of Haiti's creditors, leaving nothing for the payment of
the salaries of government officials. The payment of
salaries was resumed, however, after an appeal by the
Haitian Government to the Department of State, and the
objectionable measures were subsequently modified in such
a way as to meet the American Government's views.[31]

THE PROTOCOL OF 1919

All payments on Haiti's foreign debt had been suspended by the American authorities after the intervention. The Republic was already in arrears before 1915
on the amortization of the 1875 and 1896 bonds, as well
as on the service of the National Railroad Bonds, and the
removal of the treasury service from the National Bank
in February of that year had put an end to the accumulation of funds for the debt service. After the intervention, the Government's income had been so affected by
internal disorder and administrative disorganization that
an early resumption of payments was out of the question.
Besides the funded debt, the Government owed large
sums to native and foreign claimants. In several cases it
had been compelled by diplomatic or military pressure
before 1915 to recognize these obligations or to agree

[31] *Ibid.*, p. 77–81.

to arbitrate the amount, but it was obvious that it could not pay them as conditions stood. To both the Haitian and the American authorities, a large foreign loan seemed the only solution.

In accord with Article XII of the treaty of 1915, a protocol for the settlement of all pending claims and also for the flotation of a foreign loan was signed on October 3, 1919. With certain specified exceptions, the claims were to be passed upon by a commission of which one member was to be nominated by the Haitian Minister of Finance, another by the Secretary of State of the United States, and a third, who should be neither a Haitian nor an American, by the Financial Adviser. To pay the awards of the commission, and in general "to establish the finances of Haiti on a firm and solid basis," the Protocol provided for the issue of a $40,000,000 loan, payable in thirty years, and secured by a first charge on the internal revenues and a charge second only to the expenses of collection on the customs duties. It was agreed that American control of the "collection and allocation" of the hypothecated revenues would be provided for during the life of the loan after the expiration of the treaty of 1915 for the protection of the bondholders.[32]

Unsatisfactory conditions in the bond market, and differences of opinion between the Haitian Government and the Financial Adviser delayed the flotation of the proposed loan for more than two years. The full service of the bonds of 1875, 1896 and 1910 was, however, resumed in 1920.

THE BANK AND THE CURRENCY REFORM

In the meantime an effort had been made to settle the outstanding questions between the Government and the National Bank. Admiral Caperton had caused the treas-

[32] For the text of the Protocol, see Appendix, *infra*, p. 299.

ury service to be returned to the Bank on August 9, 1915, and on July 10, 1916, an agreement was signed by which the Haitian Government recognized the Bank's contractual rights and the latter agreed to make the Government a loan of $500,000.[33] The long discussed currency reform was put into effect in 1919, when the Haitian gourde was definitely stabilized at twenty cents United States currency under a plan worked out with the Bank by the Financial Adviser. In the following year, the National City Bank of New York purchased the sole control of the National Bank of Haiti. In connection with this purchase, the Department of State insisted upon a revision of the Bank's concession to eliminate many provisions which were considered objectionable or unfair.

The Caco Revolt

Order was established throughout the Republic without great difficulty soon after the intervention, but in 1918 an insurrection began in the same region where *caco* bands had been recruited in former times. While this outbreak was fomented and supported by disaffected Haitian politicians, its chief cause seems to have been the revival of the *corvée*, an old Haitian law under which each inhabitant was compelled to work for a given period on the roads. A few of the American constabulary officers who directed road construction showed little tact or discretion in exacting labor from the inhabitants, and the abuses which occurred aroused deep resentment among the peasant population. Even after orders were issued for the suspension of the *corvée* system, it appears to have continued for some months in the section around Hinche and Maissade where the outbreak occurred. The situation soon became so serious that the American marines were compelled to take the field, and the revolt was not

[33] *Foreign Relations, 1916*, p. 358.

entirely suppressed until after two years of military operations, in which some 1,500 Haitians lost their lives.[34]

During the *caco* revolt, many charges of cruelty and improper conduct were made against the marines and the American officers in the constabulary. These charges intensified the criticism which certain elements of American public opinion had from the first directed against the American occupation of Haiti and the Dominican Republic, and they led the United States Senate, in 1921, to appoint a committee to report upon the whole problem. Under the chairmanship of Senator Medill McCormick, this committee visited both Republics and took a great mass of testimony. It submitted its report on Haiti on April 20, 1922.[35]

The Senate Committee's Report

The committee condemned the abuses in the *corvée* which had helped to bring on the *caco* revolt. With regard to the more serious charges against the marines, it found that *caco* prisoners had been illegally executed in a few cases, of which approximately ten were fairly well substantiated. It also found that isolated acts of cruelty had apparently occurred, although such acts had in no case been approved or tolerated by the higher American authorities. In general, however, the accusations against the American military forces appeared to be based merely on rumor or hearsay, and in many cases there was a strong suspicion that they had simply been manufactured by persons in Haiti who sympathized with the *caco* revolt. Referring presumably to the American critics of the American occupation, the committee condemned "the process by which biased or interested individuals and

[34] This was the estimate of the Senate Committee, *Inquiry into Occupation and Administration of Haiti and the Dominican Republic*, Report, p. 14, 67th Congress, 2nd Session, Senate Report 794.

[35] This is the Report cited in the preceding footnote.

committees and propagandists have seized on isolated instances, or have adopted as true any rumor however vile or baseless in an effort to bring into general disrepute the whole American naval force in Haiti." In general, the committee expressed "its admiration for the manner in which our men accomplished their dangerous and delicate task."

The committee also gave consideration to broader questions of policy. While it took note of the great benefits which had been conferred on the people of Haiti by the establishment of peace and order, the improvement of sanitary conditions in the cities, the construction of roads, the stabilization of the currency, and the resumption of the payment of the debt service and of government salaries, it indicated that there had been a "failure to develop a definite and constructive policy under the Treaty or to centralize in some degree responsibility for the conduct of American officers and officials," and also that there had been a "failure of the Departments in Washington to appreciate the importance of selecting for service in Haiti, whether in civil or military capacities, men who were sympathetic to the Haitians and able to maintain cordial personal and official relations with them." The committee felt "that the American people will not consider their duty under the treaty discharged if, in addition to what has been accomplished, there are not placed within the reach of the Haitian masses, justice, schools, and agricultural instruction." It therefore recommended the sending to Haiti of a commission comprising a commercial adviser, an expert in tropical agriculture and an educator like Dr. Moton of Tuskegee. With regard to the continuance of the military occupation, the committee felt that "drastic reduction of the marine force, or its early withdrawal, would certainly be followed by a recurrence of brigandage and by the organization of revolutionary bands."

APPOINTMENT OF AN AMERICAN HIGH COMMISSIONER

In accord with a recommendation made informally by the committee before the submission of the report, Brigadier General John H. Russell was appointed as American High Commissioner in Haiti in February 1922, to act as the diplomatic representative of the United States, with the rank of Ambassador, and to supervise and direct the work of the treaty officials. As senior officer present, he also exercised authority over the Marine Brigade. Except in questions affecting the internal administration of the military forces, he received all of his instructions from the Department of State. His appointment greatly increased the effectiveness of the treaty services by making possible the coördination of all their activities and the elimination of overlapping and friction.

A few months after General Russell's appointment, the Haitian Council of State, disregarding President Dartiguenave's efforts on behalf of another candidate, elected M. Louis Borno as President of the Republic. The American authorities did nothing to influence the action of the Council of State in this matter, and some of them, in fact, regarded M. Borno's election with apprehension because he had tenaciously upheld the Haitian Government's point of view in controversies which had arisen during the period of his service as Minister of Foreign Affairs under the preceding administration. Immediately after his inauguration, the new President indicated that he intended to abandon the policy of obstruction which his predecessor had sometimes seemed inclined to follow and to coöperate frankly and effectively with the High Commissioner and the treaty officials.

Under the régime established by the treaty, it had been possible for either the Haitian or the American authorities to prevent action on projects falling within the purposes of the treaty, but it had not been possible for either without the other's coöperation to accomplish anything of constructive importance. Distrust and differences of opinion had too often delayed action on the most urgent and necessary projects, and obstructive tactics on the part of the Haitian authorities had been encouraged by the fact that the American officials too often worked at cross purposes with one another. With an attitude of coöperation on the part of President Borno and with the centralization of American policy, it was possible to adopt and to carry out a broad program for the realization of the main purposes of the treaty. In the formulation of this program, President Borno played a more active and influential part than has perhaps been generally recognized. He was by no means subservient to the American officials and in many cases refused to act upon their advice or insisted upon the adoption of his own point of view. Serious conflicts were avoided, however, by the tact and statesmanship which both the President and the High Commissioner showed in dealing with controversial questions.

THE LOAN OF 1922

The first important act of the new Government was the approval of the proposed foreign loan. It had been decided that the $40,000,000 of bonds authorized by the protocol of 1919 would be divided into series, to be issued as needed. The first of these, Series A, to the amount of $16,000,000, was placed in New York in 1922. By calling for bids, the very favorable price of 92.137 for the 30 year 6 per cent bonds was obtained from the National City Company of New York. The proceeds of the loan made possible the payment in cash of the outstanding French bonds and of many other obligations of the Government, and left a substantial balance for public works and other productive purposes. Series B, to the amount of $4,234,041.94, was subsequently issued to claimants who had received awards from the Claims Commission created under the protocol of 1919. Series C was issued in 1923 to retire the National Railroad bonds, after the holders of the latter had agreed to accept an exchange at the rate of $75 in the new bonds for $100 of the old. The amount of the new issue was $2,660,000. This arrangement materially diminished the amount which the Government would otherwise have had to pay under its guaranty of the railway bonds, and was thus highly profitable to the Haitian treasury. At the same time, the French bondholders agreed to surrender a portion of the interest due on the old bonds to be used for new construction. The principal problems still outstanding between the Government and the Railroad Company were settled under this arrangement, although a new concession, which the arrangement contemplated, was not finally approved by the Haitian Government until 1932.

THE WORK OF THE TREATY SERVICES, 1923–1929

With the refunding of the foreign debt it was possible to effect a complete reform in Haiti's financial administration. The combination of the offices of Financial Adviser and General Receiver in January 1924 made for increased efficiency and a better organization, and the elimination of the "affectations" on separate items of revenue permitted a much needed reform of the customs tariff and the introduction of better methods of accounting and of handling funds. Under a law passed by the Council of State on June 6, 1924, the collection of the internal revenues was intrusted to a bureau headed by an American responsible to the General Receiver. Receipts from the internal taxes substantially increased thereafter, even though a projected thoroughgoing reform of the internal revenue system was delayed. Since customs receipts also increased, the Government had ample funds, not only for its current expenses but for public improvements, and it was able to accumulate a cash surplus which amounted to more than $4,000,000 on September 30, 1929.[36] It was this surplus which enabled the Haitian Government to maintain its essential public services and at the same time to continue payments on the foreign debt during the depression.

After the suppression of the *caco* revolt, the United States Marine Brigade took no active part in the maintenance of order or in political matters. The trial of Haitians by American military courts, which had been a source of irritation in the early years of the occupation, was practically discontinued. The marines were concentrated at Port-au-Prince and Cap Haitien. The Haitian constabulary, now completely organized, and with a constantly increasing number of Haitian officers, maintained order throughout the country and provided a security for life and property which the Republic had not hitherto known.

The six years from 1923 to 1929 saw notable progress in what the treaty of 1915 referred to as "the sanitation and public improvement of the Republic." Easy and rapid communication with all sections of the country was afforded by a system of inexpensively constructed automobile roads, upon which great numbers of cheap motor busses were soon operating; and many of the more remote districts were opened up by the improvement of the trails used by the peasants. The Public Works Service, which was responsible for the construction and maintenance of the highways, also rehabilitated several old French irrigation systems which had become useless except in so far as the peasants of each locality had been able by their own efforts to maintain them. The construction of needed public buildings and the beautification of the

[36] Eighth Annual Report of the American High Commissioner at Port-au-Prince, p. 55.

cities were other aspects of the work of this department.[37]

Of still more importance, perhaps, from the standpoint of its effect on the daily life of the people, was the work of the Public Health Service. At the time of the intervention, a very large proportion of the population had been more or less incapacitated by yaws, malaria and other diseases, and medical assistance, outside of the largest towns, was literally unobtainable. The American naval doctors attached to the Public Health Service reached and cured great numbers of sufferers in the country districts through rural clinics which were held at stated intervals in a large number of villages. The extent of the work performed by these free clinics may be gathered from the fact that they gave 1,341,000 treatments during the year 1929.[38] Equally effective work was done in the Haitian towns, where street cleaning, mosquito control measures and the establishment of a good water supply prevented the spread of many formerly prevalent diseases. Modern hospitals were also established in the more important towns, and such services as prenatal clinics and the medical inspection of school children were developed. All of this was accomplished with the coöperation of the Haitian physicians. There was perhaps a more general appreciation and less criticism of the work of the Public Health Service than of any other phase of the work undertaken by the American treaty officials.

The improvement of the physical conditions under which the Haitian people lived was only one phase of the task which the High Commissioner and his associates wished to accomplish. The American authorities felt that the masses of the population must not only be brought to a higher standard of living but must also be better

[37] The work of the treaty services between 1922 and 1929 is described in detail in the Reports of the American High Commissioner at Port-au-Prince, which were published annually during this period by the Department of State.

[38] *Report of High Commissioner, 1929*, p. 34.

fitted in other respects to discharge the duties of citizen-
ship if the conditions which had brought on the American
intervention were to be permanently eliminated.

Government stabilization [wrote the High Commissioner, in
1926] must come from the development of Haiti's economic
resources through agricultural and industrial education.[39]

A new treaty service, the *Service Technique de l'Agriculture et de l'Enseignement Professionel,* was therefore established in 1924, under an agreement between the two Governments signed in the previous year. Its duty was to
create a system of vocational and agricultural instruction
and also to promote the agricultural development of the
Republic.

The work of the *Service Technique* was in the main educational.   A Central School of Agriculture was established
near Port-au-Prince to train Haitians to participate in
the various phases of its program and especially to train
teachers for the rural farm schools, through which it was
hoped to give the children of the country districts a rudi-
mentary education as well as a knowledge of improved
methods of cultivation.   Several experiment stations were
also established to explore the possibility of developing
new crops, and a small amount of work, limited by lack
of funds and personnel, was done directly with Haitian
farmers.   At the same time, several hundred boys and
girls were given vocational training in the cities.   The
program was an exceedingly ambitious one, and it absorbed a considerable part of Haiti's revenues for some
years.   The concrete results, however, up to the time
when the American officials were withdrawn, were not
correspondingly great.   Although several new agricultural
enterprises were established, mainly with foreign capital,
agricultural production showed no appreciable increase
during the period of the American Occupation.   It must

[39] *Report of High Commissioner, 1925,* p. 6.

be realized, however, that no very notable achievement beyond the preliminary work of organization and the training of Haitian personnel, could reasonably have been expected within the short time that the service was in existence.

The task of the *Service Technique* was, in fact, more difficult than that of the other treaty services. Americans who had had similar experience in other countries were available for the work of the financial service, and the Navy and Marine Corps had provided trained officers for the constabulary and the Public Works and Public Health Services. It was not so easy to find Americans who combined technical training in agriculture or industrial education with the peculiar qualifications needed for work in Haiti, and the fact that many of the Americans who were selected did not speak French greatly handicapped their teaching work. The development of an adequate Haitian personnel was still more difficult. Since it was impracticable for financial reasons, as well as inadvisable for reasons of policy, to employ a large number of American teachers, no considerable part of the population could possibly be reached by educational work until Haitian teachers had been trained. Since practically none of the peasant class had sufficient education to serve as a foundation for the training at the Central School, the required Haitian personnel could be obtained only from among the *élite* who, as a class, had never had any interest in agriculture and who were greatly handicapped in dealing with the peasants by barriers of caste prejudice and suspicion. The work of the rural farm schools was therefore carried on under great difficulties, although sixty-five of these schools had been established by the end of 1929.[40]

DISCONTENT WITH THE AMERICAN OCCUPATION

Despite the material benefits brought to the country

[40] *Report of High Commissioner, 1929,* p. 39.

by the American intervention, there was much discontent among the only class of the Haitian people which was able to give expression to its sentiments and desires. The peasants, who had benefited most from the establishment of peace and the other work of the treaty services, were hardly able even to comprehend what had occurred. Many of the *élite*, on the other hand, actually found their situation more difficult than before 1915. With the establishment of strict control over government funds and the expenditure of the revenues on public works and other constructive enterprises rather than for the sole benefit of the ruling class, it was no longer possible for the majority of this class to expect to obtain a living from the Government. They could not, unfortunately, derive much benefit from the development of commerce, which was largely in foreign hands, and they were unfitted by temperament and tradition for any participation in new agricultural enterprises which might otherwise have offered an outlet for their energy. Many families who had formerly been prominent in politics were thus reduced to poverty and want.

Moreover, foreign control of important branches of the public administration was bitterly resented by many Haitians from motives of patriotism and national pride. This feeling was aggravated by occasional tactlessness on the part of individual Americans and by an intense sensitiveness which made the Haitians quick to look for any suggestion of race prejudice or of a feeling of superiority. Difficulties of this nature were inevitable under the circumstances in spite of the efforts made by the American officials to eliminate members of the treaty services who were temperamentally unfitted for their work.

Although there had been no disturbance of public order since 1920, the activities of discontented political factions and especially their use of the press had sometimes caused serious annoyance or alarm to President Borno and to the representatives of the United States. Liberty of the press had of course been unheard of before 1915, when any editor who ventured to attack the Government would have been imprisoned, if not executed. During the first years of the American intervention, seditious publications had been punished by American military courts under martial law, but this practice was discontinued in accordance with a recommendation by the Senate Committee in 1922. Thereafter the press theoretically enjoyed the broad liberty guaranteed by the Constitution of 1918, and some newspapers proceeded to attack the Haitian Government and the American officials in articles which were often so libelous and obscene that they would have led to criminal prosecution in any other country. Such articles constituted a positive danger to public order, because the more ignorant and thoughtless portion of the population was prone to regard any appearance of weakness on the part of the authorities as an invitation to revolt. The legal freedom of the press was therefore restricted by a law passed by the Council of State; and when it proved impossible to obtain convictions under this law from Haitian juries, the authorities resorted to the expedient of holding offending journalists in jail for considerable periods without trial. This exposed both the Borno administration and the American officials, who acquiesced in the practice, to severe criticism both at home and abroad.

Since the Constitution of 1918 had provided that the first election of members of Congress should occur in an even numbered year to be fixed by a decree of the President, and neither M. Borno nor his predecessor had considered it advisable to act under this provision, the legislative power and the power to elect the President of the Republic had continued to be exercised by an appointed Council of State. M. Borno had been reëlected in 1926, and when he failed to issue a call for Congressional elections in

October 1929 his opponents feared that he would attempt again to succeed himself or to bring about the election of one of his close supporters at the end of his second term in 1930. His administration had by this time become intensely unpopular among the *élite*, partly because he was unable to satisfy more than a small part of the demands of other political leaders for appointments and favors, and partly because of his policy of cooperation with the United States. This unpopularity intensified the feeling against the United States, which was regarded as responsible for maintaining the President in office.

The President's opponents found their opportunity in events which occurred at the end of October 1929 in the Central School of Agriculture. The students there had been largely supported by scholarships and nearly all of these had naturally been obtained by boys from Port-au-Prince and other towns who had the necessary scholastic qualifications. In the hope of making it possible for a few boys from the country to attend the school, it was decided to devote one-fifth of the scholarship fund to payment for practical labor on the school farm. The students left their classes in protest against this decision and the opposition leaders seized upon the "strike" as an opportunity to bring about a demonstration of hostility to the Borno Administration and to the American intervention. They succeeded in causing a sympathetic strike in the other schools and among the Haitian employees of the *Service Technique* and of some branches of the customs service. An active propaganda and a violent press campaign created much excitement in Port-au-Prince. "With the students and custom clerks of the Port-au-Prince customhouse running through the streets, the mob element, always large and dangerous by reason of the general illiteracy and low economic status of the population, began to take part. The stage was set for rioting, looting and bloodshed." [41]   On December 4 the High Commissioner found it necessary to make martial law effective so that the marines might aid the constabulary in maintaining order.   Tranquil conditions were at once reëstablished in Port-au-Prince, and the enforcement of martial law was discontinued after twelve days.

Political agitators, however, had also been at work in the country districts where some unrest already existed because of the drop in coffee prices and because of a small tax which had recently been imposed on the manufacture of rum.   Their efforts with the peasants were in the main unsuccessful, but one very unfortunate incident occurred at Cayes, where a mob of some 1500 country people attempted to invade the town and ten persons were killed in a clash with a detachment of twenty American marines.

THE FORBES COMMISSION

While these disturbances were relatively unimportant in themselves, they served their purpose by attracting unfavorable attention to the state of affairs existing in Haiti.   The President of the United States, who had already had under consideration the appointment of a commission to make a study of the whole Haitian problem, decided that an immediate investigation was necessary. On December 7, therefore, he requested the necessary authority and appropriation from Congress.   This was granted after a delay of two months, and in February the Hon. W. Cameron Forbes was appointed as chairman of the commission with Messrs. Henry P. Fletcher, Elie Vezina, James Kerney and William Allen White as the other members.   The commission proceeded at once to Port-au-Prince with instructions to make recommendations as to "when and how we are to withdraw from Haiti" and "what we shall do in the meantime." [42]   At

[41] Ibid., p. 9.
[42] See p. 1 of the Commission's Report cited in following footnote.

the same time, the President announced that he had requested Dr. Moton, the President of Tuskegee Institute, to make an investigation of the educational system of Haiti. Dr. Moton did not, however, visit Haiti until some months later.

The Forbes Commission arrived at Port-au-Prince on February 28, 1930, and spent sixteen days in the Republic. Much of this time was devoted to the political crisis. After their success in obtaining action by the United States through the strikes and riots in November and December, it was clear that the opposition might create more serious disorders if M. Borno were permitted to control the election of his successor, and it was therefore urgently necessary to devise some means within the framework of the Haitian Constitution to afford an opportunity for the election of a new President who would be satisfactory to a majority of the ruling class. With the assistance of General Russell, the commission obtained acceptance of a plan under which the Council of State was to elect a candidate satisfactory to all factions who, in turn, would hold popular elections for members of Congress. The new President was to resign when the Congress met, and his successor was to be elected by that body in accord with the Constitution, to serve the remainder of the presidential term. As the term had been fixed at six years under a constitutional amendment adopted in 1928, the President thus elected would serve until after the expiration of the Treaty of 1915.

The commission devoted the greater part of its remaining time to public hearings at which the Haitian opponents of the Borno régime and of the American intervention were given an opportunity to express their views. In the report [43] which was submitted to President Hoover immediately upon its return to Washington, it discussed all

[43] *Report of the President's Commission for the Study and Review of Conditions in the Republic of Haiti*, Washington, 1930.

phases of the Haitian problem in some detail and made a series of recommendations which were formally approved by the President of the United States. The more important of these, referred to by the commission as "sequent steps" to be taken by the United States Government, were as follows:

(1) That the President declare that the United States will approve a policy, the details of which all the United States officials in Haiti are directed to assist in working out, providing for an increasingly rapid Haitianization of the services, with the object of having Haitians experienced in every department of the Government ready to take over full responsibility at the expiration of the existing treaty;

(2) That in retaining officers now in the Haitian service, or selecting new Americans for employment therein, the utmost care be taken that only those free from strong racial antipathies should be preferred;

(3) That the United States recognize the temporary President when elected, provided the election is in accordance with the agreement reached by your commission with President Borno and the leaders representing the opposition;

(4) That the United States recognize the President elected by the new legislature, acting as a National Assembly, provided that neither force nor fraud have been used in the elections;

(5) That at the expiration of General Russell's tour of duty in Haiti, and in any such event not before the inauguration of the permanent President, the office of High Commissioner be abolished and a nonmilitary Minister appointed to take over his duties as well as those of diplomatic representative;

(6) That whether or not a certain loss of efficiency is entailed, the new Minister to Haiti be charged with the duty of carrying out the early Haitianization of the services called for in the declaration of the President of the United States above recommended;

(7) That, as the commission found the immediate withdrawal of the Marines inadvisable, it recommends their gradual withdrawal in accordance with arrangements to be made in future agreement between the two Governments;

(8) That the United States limit its intervention in Haitian affairs definitely to those activities for which provision is made

for American assistance by treaty or by specific agreement between the two Governments;

(9) That the new Minister be charged with the duty of negotiating with the Haitian Government further modifications of the existing treaty and agreements providing for less intervention in Haitian domestic affairs and defining the conditions under which the United States would lend its assistance in the restoration of order or maintenance of credit.

RELATIONS WITH THE NEW ADMINISTRATION

The plan for the change of administration was carried out without serious difficulty, although it was necessary for the United States to assume a very firm attitude at the last moment to compel respect for the agreement which had been made and for President Borno to remove several recalcitrant members of the Council of State. M. Eugène Roy, a private banker whose reputation for integrity and impartiality won him the confidence of all factions, was inaugurated as President on May 15, 1930. The Congressional elections which were held in October resulted in an overwhelming victory for the "Nationalist" or anti-Borno groups. The National Assembly was convoked in special session on November 17, to receive President Roy's resignation and to elect his successor. The choice fell upon M. Stenio Vincent, who had for many years been one of the principal leaders in the movement to bring about a withdrawal of the American occupation.

Meanwhile, General Russell had submitted his resignation as American High Commissioner, thus bringing to a close nearly eight years of devoted and effective work. He was succeeded by a civilian Minister who combined with his ordinary diplomatic duties the responsibility for the direction of the American treaty services, and who was especially charged with the negotiation of agreements providing for as rapid a withdrawal as might be practicable of all American control in Haiti's internal affairs.

Since the appointment of the High Commissioner in

1922, the training of Haitian personnel had been emphasized as one of the most important duties of the American treaty services. Haitian engineers and physicians had played an important part in the Public Works and Public Health Services, and 36.42 per cent of the officers in the Garde d'Haiti, as the constabulary was now called, were Haitians on September 30, 1929.[44] Many Haitians also held positions of importance in the financial services and in the *Service Technique,* and the subordinate personnel throughout the treaty organization was of course almost entirely native. With a few exceptions, however, the key positions in each treaty service were still occupied by Americans, and the policy pursued up to the time of the Forbes Commission's report had not contemplated any important change in this respect until the expiration of the Treaty in 1936. In the Garde, for example, it was felt that the Haitian officers, nearly all of whom had risen from the ranks, would not be properly qualified to occupy the higher positions until after a period of training comparable to that which the American officers whom they were to succeed had already had in the Marine Corps; and a somewhat similar situation existed in the other services. The American treaty officials, who felt an intense pride in the tangible accomplishments of their organizations, had been somewhat reluctant to replace highly trained American technical experts by Haitian employees until the latter had fully demonstrated their ability. Many of them had been convinced that an extension of the Treaty after 1936 would be necessary if the task undertaken by the United States in 1915 were to be satisfactorily accomplished. The American Government, however, had now decided to terminate its responsibilities in Haiti at the earliest possible date, and the Forbes Commission had recommended a rapid withdrawal of the American personnel, even at a sacrifice of efficiency.

[44] *Report of High Commissioner, 1929,* p. 17.

Headed by a group of leaders who had formerly criticized every aspect of the American intervention, the new
Administration was little disposed to coöperate in any way
with the treaty services. It had, moreover, been led by
various circumstances to expect a more complete and
immediate change in the whole relationship between the
two Governments than the Administration at Washington
had really contemplated. The misunderstandings which
thus arose were a serious obstacle to the negotiations for
an orderly withdrawal of American control from the
treaty services. Several controversies, frequently over
questions of minor importance, caused loss of valuable time
during the winter of 1930–31; and on some occasions a
serious situation might have arisen had it not been for
the statesmanship and the conciliatory spirit of President Vincent and his successive Ministers of Foreign Affairs.

Shortly after the new President's inauguration, M. H.
Pauléus Sannon, the Minister of Foreign Affairs, submitted
to the American Legation plans calling for the "Haitianization" of all of the treaty services except the Garde d'Haiti
within periods of one or two years.[45] M. Sannon indicated,
however, that his Government wished to maintain the
efficiency of the treaty services and to avail itself to the
fullest extent of the services of the Haitians who had
been trained under the American régime. He therefore
proposed to discuss the whole problem with a view of
determining upon the most satisfactory mode of procedure.

The United States could not accept that part of the
Haitian Government's plan which related to the financial
administration, because it was considered inconsistent with
existing agreements between Haiti and her foreign creditors. It will be remembered that the protocol of Octo-

[45] The Haitian Government published some information regarding the
Haitianization negotiations in its *Exposé Général de la Situation, Exercice
1930–1931.*

ber 3, 1919, had provided that American control of the "collection and allocation" of the revenues hypothecated for the service of the bonds issued thereunder would be "provided for during the life of the loan after the expiration of the . . . treaty, so as to make certain that adequate provision be made for the amortization and interest of the loan." The loan contracts contained similar provisions. Strong as was its desire to terminate completely its intervention in Haiti's internal affairs, the United States Government did not feel that it could accept any arrangement inconsistent with these agreements without a breach of faith with the bondholders. It was also felt that Haiti's interests would be better served by a program of Haitianization different in some other respects from that proposed. In accordance with M. Sannon's suggestion, therefore, the winter and spring of 1931 were devoted to a careful examination of the situation in each of the services with a view to working out a detailed, coördinated plan.

The formulation of this plan was delayed by the controversies which arose in connection with the current work of the treaty services, and also by difficulties between the President and the Congress which led to the resignation of President Vincent's first Cabinet in May 1931. M. Abel Leger succeeded M. Sannon as Minister of Foreign Affairs. In the meantime, six months' study of the problem had convinced those responsible for the direction of American policy that there was little to gain by delaying the process of Haitianization in the Public Works and Public Health Services, where there was already a group of mature and experienced Haitian employees who would probably benefit relatively little from further training in subordinate positions, or in the *Service Technique*, where conditions which had existed since the strike of 1929 made it impossible to hope for any further constructive achievement. The Haitian Government, on its side, had decided that it desired to assume full responsibility for the conduct of the treaty services at the earliest practicable date. The two Governments were still far apart in their views regarding the reorganization of the financial services and to a lesser degree in their views about the Haitianization of the Garde; but they finally concluded to sign an agreement dealing with those questions upon which an accord could be reached.

The Haitianization Agreement

The Haitianization Agreement of August 5, 1931, provided that all American officials should be withdrawn from the Public Works Service, the Public Health Service, and the *Service Technique* on October 1 of the same year, although an American Scientific Mission, composed of naval medical personnel, was to remain in control of the sanitation work and the chlorination of the water supply in Port-au-Prince and Cap Haitien, where the presence of American marines gave the United States a special interest in the maintenance of proper health conditions. The United States also consented to abrogate the agreements concluded in 1918, requiring that all projects of law be submitted to the American Legation for approval before consideration by the legislative body,—an arrangement which was no longer workable with an elected Congress,— and providing for the formal visa of the Financial Adviser on all orders of payment issued by the Minister of Finance. The Service of Payments and the auditing of expenditures remained, however, under the control of the Financial Adviser, and the Haitian Government recognized its obligation to keep its expenditures within the limits of appropriations duly authorized with the accord of the Financial Adviser and to proceed in agreement with the Financial Adviser in adopting measures affecting revenues. At the same time, the Land Title Registry Office, an important service hitherto administered by the Financial Adviser, was placed directly under the Minister of Finance.

The agreement made provision for the payment of an indemnity to the civilian American officials who were to be dismissed from their positions on such short notice. Those who had held commissions in the three services received the equivalent of nine months' salary. Nearly all of these had been drawn from the faculties of American universities, at a time when it had seemed possible to offer them assurance of a long term of employment, and they had made no arrangements to renew their academic connections at home for the coming year because they had been aware that the two Governments, until late in the spring, had been contemplating a plan of Haitianization under which their services would have been needed for at least a year to come. A smaller indemnity, varying with the amount of accrued leave to which they would normally have been entitled, was granted to American officials who had not had a permanent status.[46]

FURTHER NEGOTIATIONS 1931–32

The agreement left for future consideration several other matters which had been under discussion between the two Governments, including especially the reorganization of the Financial Service, the Haitianization of the Garde, and the withdrawal of the United States Marine Brigade. The first of these was the most difficult, because the Government of the United States, for reasons which have already been indicated, did not feel free to agree to any scheme of financial administration which was not in accord with the agreements under which Haiti's foreign loans had been contracted. The Haitian Government took a different view of its obligations under the loan contracts and the protocol of 1919, although it insisted upon its determination to maintain the service of the bonds in

[46] For the text of the Haitianization Agreement, see Appendix, *infra*, p. 303.

full. It had proposed the Haitianization of the entire Financial Service, including the Customs Administration, and the appointment of an American "fiscal agent," with general powers of inspection but no effective authority, who would provide for the service of the debt out of revenues deposited by the Haitian authorities in the National Bank. Without attempting to go into the question whether such an arrangement would afford the bondholders adequate security, in view of the difficulties which Haiti had experienced in the administration of her finances before 1915, the United States had pointed out that the arrangement was not acceptable because it radically changed the nature of the financial control which had been promised to the bondholders under the loan contracts.

The question of Haitianizing the Garde was less difficult, for much progress toward this end had already been made. The process of training and promoting Haitian officers had been pushed actively without awaiting the outcome of negotiations between the two Governments, and in December 1930 one of the five military departments into which the territory of the Republic was divided had been placed under the command of a Haitian officer. Early in 1931 President Vincent had proposed an agreement for the complete Haitianization of the Garde by December 31, 1934, but the Government of the United States had considered it inadvisable at that time to assume any definite obligation regarding the date for withdrawing all of the American officers until there had been an opportunity to observe the work of the Haitian officers who were being placed for the first time in positions of heavy responsibility, and to learn from experience whether such rapid Haitianization could safely be carried out. The United States was deeply interested in the maintenance of the efficiency of the Garde, both because of its continuing responsibilities in connection with the Republic's finances and because of its obligation under the treaty of 1915 to assist Haiti in the preservation of order. It seemed equally inadvisable to make a definite promise regarding the withdrawal of the Marine Brigade, which had now been reduced to about 800 men. It would have been contrary to the policy of the United States Government to permit its officers to serve in a force like the Garde without some backing by American troops, and the continued presence of the brigade during the period while the Garde was being reorganized under Haitian officers seemed obviously desirable for its moral effect. The technical American military occupation, however, was formally discontinued on the day when the Haitianization Agreement was signed.

The three still outstanding problems were discussed by the two Governments during the thirteen months following the signature of the Haitianization Agreement. During this period, the relations between the two Governments grew more cordial, for the Haitianization of the majority of the treaty services removed many points of friction, and a satisfactory working arrangement was established between the members of the Cabinet and the American officials who still remained. The bitterly unfriendly feeling of the Haitian *élite* appeared also to be diminishing. Under these conditions it was possible to reëxamine the entire problem in a new spirit. The settlement of two of the questions left open by the Haitianization Agreement had been made less difficult by the fact that the Haitian Garde officers were satisfactorily discharging the increasingly important duties intrusted to them, making it possible to contemplate the early withdrawal of the American officers and the Marine Brigade. The two Governments were still far apart in their points of view on the financial problems, but both showed a willingness to make substantial concessions. After M. Albert Blanchet was appointed Minister for Foreign Affairs, in July 1932, an agreement was finally worked out.

The Treaty of 1932

The treaty signed at Port-au-Prince on September 3, 1932, was intended to be a final settlement of practically all questions arising out of the American intervention of 1915.[47] The two Governments agreed to terminate as soon as possible and in an orderly manner the special situation created under the treaty of 1915, in accordance with a program which was set forth in detail. Certain articles of the former treaty, including especially that providing for American participation in the "sanitation and public improvement" of Haiti, were definitely abrogated. The provisions relating to the Garde were to be abrogated upon the complete Haitianization of that force, and those relating to the control of the Republic's finances were to be abrogated on December 31, 1934, on which date the existing system of financial administration would be superseded by a new arrangement, to remain in effect during the life of the outstanding bonds. The detailed plan for the Haitianization of the Garde and the new agreement regarding the finances were embodied in protocols attached to the treaty.

Protocol A provided that the American officers in the Garde should be replaced as rapidly as possible, in such a manner that the force should be completely commanded by Haitian officers by December 31, 1934. The withdrawal of the Marine Brigade was to begin not later than that date, and the work of the American Scientific Mission was to terminate at the same time. At the suggestion of the Haitian Government, an American military mission was to be established to complete the training of the Garde, with authority to inspect its work and to make appropriate recommendations to the commandant or to the President of the Republic, but without direct authority over the organization.

[47] The text was published Sept. 6, 1932, Department of State, *Press Releases*, Sept. 10, 1932, p. 150.

Protocol B provided that a "Fiscal Representative," appointed by the President of Haiti upon the nomination of the President of the United States, should replace the Financial Adviser-General Receiver on December 31, 1934. The new official was to collect all customs duties, with the assistance of a personnel appointed upon his recommendation by the President of Haiti. The Internal Revenue Service, on the other hand, was to be placed under a Haitian director with an exclusively Haitian personnel. The requirement of the protocol of 1919, that collection of the pledged revenues should be controlled by an official nominated by the President of the United States, was met by a provision that the Fiscal Representative should have the right to inspect the work of the Internal Revenue Service and to make recommendations for its improvement if there should be a serious decline in collections. In general, the Haitian Government was given more liberty of action in financial matters than under the treaty of 1915. It obligated itself to balance its annual budget, but it obtained the very important right to distribute available funds between the different government departments as it saw fit without foreign intervention. A pre-audit of expenditures was provided for through the Service of Payments, which was to remain under the control of the Fiscal Representative.

The new treaty was immediately submitted to the Haitian National Assembly, composed of the two houses of Congress in joint session. Although a large majority of this body had been elected in January 1932 as political supporters of the Vincent Administration, it had come into conflict with the Executive Power earlier in the year, when the President had opposed constitutional amendments to extend for four additional years the two-year terms for which the Congressmen had just been elected, to increase their salaries, and to augment the constitutional powers of Congress at the expense of the Executive.

Harmony had apparently been restored by a compromise and a change in the Cabinet, but the controversy had left a spirit of resentment which encouraged some of the President's political opponents to make the new treaty the occasion for a violent attack upon his Administration. The committee appointed to consider the treaty reported after a brief examination, during which the Minister for Foreign Affairs was given little opportunity to set forth the Government's point of view, that the new agreement increased rather than diminished the American financial control and that it made this control virtually permanent. Upon this report, the National Assembly unanimously rejected the treaty on September 15, after brief but tumultuous proceedings.

President Vincent replied to the action of Congress in a statement published on September 16. He admitted that the new treaty fell short of meeting Haiti's aspirations, but asserted that a better arrangement could not have been obtained in view of the situation created by previous events and agreements. He pointed out that the new treaty would mean the complete Haitianization of the Garde and the withdrawal of the American marines at an earlier date than could otherwise be hoped for; and that the American financial control, far from being increased, would be diminished, because the broad, general powers exercised under existing agreements would be defined and limited and Haiti would recover the control of the Internal Revenue system and the right to dispose freely of funds available for budgetary expenses. He pointed out that the duties of the Fiscal Representative under the new treaty would not continue indefinitely but would terminate automatically upon the retirement or refunding of the outstanding bonds. In conclusion, he solemnly warned Congress of the responsibility assumed by it in rejecting a treaty concluded after prolonged and difficult negotiations, which would have brought about the "methodic and definitive liquidation" of the situation created by the treaty of 1915. The Congress nevertheless closed its annual session without taking further action on the treaty.

A few days after the vote in the National Assembly, the Haitian Government inquired informally whether the Government of the United States would be disposed to make separate agreements regarding the Haitianization of the Garde and the withdrawal of the Marine Brigade and the Scientific Mission, leaving for future settlement the questions affecting the financial administration. The American Legation replied that the arrangement embodied in the treaty of September 3, which represented the logical culmination of the recommendations of the Forbes Commission, must be carried out as a whole and not piecemeal. The "freedom of action of both Governments was necessarily limited by the existence of definite obligations subscribed to by previous Governments in Haiti and the United States which must be respected and carried out"; and the Government of the United States felt that Protocol B, relating to the financial administration, contained "the maximum concessions to the point of view of the Haitian Government, considering the obligations of existing agreements assumed by both Governments." [48]

THE AGREEMENT OF 1933

In subsequent negotiations, the effort to abrogate the greater part of the treaty of 1915 was abandoned, and the questions relating to the Garde and the financial administration were settled by means of an executive agreement, which did not require ratification by the Haitian Congress. This "accord," signed on August 7, 1933, contains provisions substantially similar to those of the protocols attached to the unratified treaty, but with modifications designed to meet some of the criticisms made in Haiti

[48] Press release of Oct. 10, 1932, Department of State, *Press Releases*, Oct. 15, 1932, p. 215–23.

against the earlier agreement.[49]   The Garde is to be Haitianized on October 1, 1934, and the withdrawal of the Marine Brigade and the American Scientific Mission is to be completed within thirty days thereafter.   The new agreement makes it clear that an American Military Mission is to remain in Haiti after the withdrawal of the marines only if the President of Haiti so requests, and that it will be withdrawn if either Government so desires.

The duties of the Financial Adviser-General Receiver will be taken over on January 1, 1934, by a Fiscal Representative appointed by the President of Haiti upon the nomination of the President of the United States.   This official will direct the Customs Service and the Service of Payments, and will supervise and to some extent control the internal revenue administration.   He will also have power to see that the budget is balanced.   The number of Americans in his employ is specifically limited to eighteen.   Any controversy arising under the accord is to be submitted to arbitration if it cannot be settled through diplomatic channels.

Except for a limited control in financial matters, therefore, the American intervention in Haiti will terminate before the end of the year 1934.   The treaty of 1915 will remain in effect until May 3, 1936, but many of its provisions will henceforth be inoperative.   American participation in Haiti's financial administration will terminate with the final retirement of the outstanding bonds, which will probably take place in 1942 or 1943.

[49] For the text, see Appendix.

CHAPTER V

EFFORTS TO PROMOTE STABLE GOVERNMENT IN CENTRAL AMERICA

THE CENTRAL AMERICAN CONFERENCE OF 1907

Central America, politically and historically, includes the five small republics of Guatemala, El Salvador, Honduras, Nicaragua and Costa Rica. These countries formed an administrative unit in colonial times under the Captain General at Guatemala City, and their relations with one another have been especially close since they obtained their independence. In all of them, the population is concentrated for the most part in the fertile and relatively healthful regions on the Pacific side of the continental divide, separated from the Caribbean Sea by a formidable barrier of mountains and dense tropical jungle. They were thus to a great extent cut off from communication with the outside world until the construction of railroads to San José, Costa Rica, in 1891, and to Guatemala City, in 1908, and the opening of the Panama Canal brought their more important towns within easy reach of the United States and Europe. Isolation was one of the factors which retarded their political and economic development.

The Federal Republic of Central America, which was established soon after the declaration of independence in 1821, broke up into its component parts during the next eighteen years after a long and disastrous civil war. The central government, established first at Guatemala City and then at San Salvador, was powerless to maintain itself

against the local jealousies and the separatist spirit in the
states. Several subsequent efforts to reëstablish the
Union, the latest of which took place in 1921, were defeated by the same obstacles.

Despite their common origin, and the historical ties
which have made Central America a distinct international
community, there are decided differences, both in the racial
composition of the population and in the economic and
political conditions of the various states. In Guatemala,
which is the most populous and commercially the most
important, the great majority of the people are pure-
blooded Indians, who have retained the languages and
many of the customs of their Maya ancestors despite four
centuries of white and *mestizo* domination. In such a
country the operation of democratic institutions is of
course practically impossible. The elections are a mere
form so far as the mass of the voters is concerned, and
the government in practice is dominated by a small ruling
class, often under a strong military dictatorship. In El
Salvador, a strong military organization and the conservative influence of a wealthy white upper class have
also been factors making for stability, although the proportion of pure-blooded Indians is very much smaller
than in Guatemala and the number of *mestizos* relatively
greater. In Honduras and Nicaragua, the great mass of
the population is of mixed Spanish and Indian blood.
There has been less agricultural and commercial development in these two countries, with the result that economic and social backwardness have tended to promote
political instability. Since politics is the chief interest
of the ruling classes, there has been no strong element
primarily interested in the maintenance of peace. Revolutionary disturbances in these countries have been more
frequent and more destructive than in Guatemala and
El Salvador, because they have assumed the character of
civil wars involving a large part of the people, whereas

political movements in the latter countries have generally taken the form of *golpes de estado*, military *coups d'état* confined to the garrison towns.

Costa Rica, on the other hand, has a population predominantly of Spanish descent, made up largely of small landowners who have exerted a powerful influence in favor of stable government and against civil war. In recent years elections have been held under conditions which afforded the defeated party little excuse for a resort to arms and political disturbances have consequently been rare and for the most part unimportant. A reluctance to become involved in the international and internal wars which have afflicted the other countries has caused Costa Rica to maintain a policy of aloofness toward them.

While some of the Central American states have thus made more progress than others, all have suffered to a greater or lesser extent from internal political disorder. The maintenance of stable government in each state was made difficult not only by the factors which have worked to the same end in most of the other Latin American countries, but also by conditions peculiar to Central America. The bitter party strife which preceded the final breakup of the original Central American Federation gave rise to political friendships and enmities which crossed state lines and which assured Liberals or Conservatives in one state of sympathy and support from members of the same party in the others long after the states themselves had become separate republics. Defeated leaders were thus not only given asylum in neighboring states, but often furnished arms and money with which to make a new effort to regain control, using the territory of another state as a base of operations. The fear of attacks of this nature led the state governments to regard with distrust any administration in a neighboring state which was controlled by the opposite party, and it became not uncommon for one government to seek to overthrow a neighboring government with which it was not on good terms simply as a protective measure. This practice caused international wars as well as internal disorder.

During the latter part of the nineteenth century the Central American states began to have more contact with the outside world and to attract investments of foreign capital. American interests developed the great banana industry on the hitherto sparsely settled Caribbean coast and built railroads there and in the more thickly settled interior. European bankers made loans to each of the five governments, and considerable numbers of foreign merchants and planters established themselves in the interior of each republic. The inability of the local governments to afford adequate protection to these interests in time of civil war inevitably brought on complications with foreign powers. The external loans, some of which had been floated without any adequate consideration of the borrowing government's capacity to pay and under conditions which led to the diversion of a large part of the proceeds for purposes which to say the least were unproductive, soon went into default. The United States was affected, not only because American citizens and their interests had to be protected, but also because injuries to citizens of other countries inevitably raised questions connected with the Monroe Doctrine.

The United States attached a special importance to the maintenance of the Monroe Doctrine in Central America because Lake Nicaragua and the valley of the San Juan River offered the only practicable route other than that at Panama for the construction of a canal from the Caribbean to the Pacific. During the greater part of the nineteenth century negotiations to safeguard American interests in any waterway which might be constructed and to prevent its control by other powers were the most important duty of American diplomatic representatives in Central America; and relations with Great Britain were for a time seriously affected by the latter's activities in territory which would have commanded the canal route. Even after the construction of the Canal at Panama, the probability that a second canal will eventually become necessary has had an important influence on the relations between the United States and Nicaragua.

When President Roosevelt adopted his new Caribbean policy, which found its first expression in his action in the Dominican Republic, he naturally turned his attention to Central America. Conditions there had been unusually disorderly during the years 1906 and 1907.[1] In 1906 the United States and Mexico had jointly interposed their good offices to bring about the cessation of a war between Guatemala and El Salvador arising from the support given by the Salvadorean Minister of War to a revolution against President Estrada Cabrera of Guatemala. A truce was established at a conference on the U.S.S. *Marblehead*, and a general peace conference attended by all of the Central American Republics met at San José, Costa Rica, in the following September and adopted a series of treaties providing for the judicial settlement of international disputes and obligating each Central American state to refrain from assisting revolutionary movements against the government of another. Within a few months, however, a new war occurred between Honduras and Nicaragua. The endeavors of the other states to prevent the outbreak of hostilities failed because of the uncompromising attitude of President Zelaya of Nicaragua, and the war resulted in the victory of the Nicaraguan troops and the establishment in Honduras of a government dominated by Zelaya's influence.

Since the Governments of Guatemala and El Salvador were unwilling to permit such an extension of Zelaya's

[1] For events in Central America in 1906, 1907, and 1908 see especially the volumes of *Foreign Relations* for those years. An account will also be found in Munro, *The Five Republics of Central America* (New York, 1918), Chapter X.

power, a general war involving all four countries seemed inevitable; but the United States and Mexico again interposed their good offices and brought about a temporary settlement. Zelaya, however, continued to exercise a dominating influence in Honduras, and early in 1907 began to furnish open assistance to revolutionists who were attempting to overthrow the Government of El Salvador. Energetic diplomatic representations by the United States prevented further hostilities for the moment, and in November all of the Central American Governments were persuaded by the United States and Mexico to send representatives to a conference at Washington to consider measures which would place the relations between the five Republics on a permanently stable basis.

The conference framed a series of treaties which thenceforth became the basis of the relations of the Central American states with one another. The most important of these was the General Treaty of Peace and Amity, which provided for the maintenance of peace and the compulsory judicial settlement of all disputes. It also permanently neutralized Honduras, whose geographical position and relative weakness had often made her territory the theater of Central American conflicts. The treaty further provided that the contracting parties should not allow political leaders from a neighboring country to reside near the border of the country whose peace they might disturb, and that they should immediately bring to the capital and subject to trial anyone who should initiate or foster revolutionary movements against the government of another Central American state. Another treaty provided for the establishment of a Central American Court of Justice, which should decide all cases of every kind arising between the contracting governments. There were a number of other conventions providing for the establishment of a Central American Bureau somewhat similar in purpose to the Pan American Union, for the establishment of a pedagogical institute, and for coöperation in a number of other matters of general interest.[2]

The new treaties appeared at first to have little practical effect. Zelaya openly assisted revolutionary movements in El Salvador, and the Salvadorean and Guatemalan Governments were accused by those of Honduras and Nicaragua of aiding a revolution in Honduras in 1908. The Central American Court established a *modus vivendi* which prevented further hostilities, but really peaceful conditions could not be established so long as the rivalry between Zelaya and Estrada Cabrera, the powerful dictator of Guatemala, continued to dominate Central American politics. After the fall of Zelaya in 1909, and the civil wars which resulted in the defeat of his party in Honduras and Nicaragua in 1910 and 1912, however, Central America enjoyed several years of unusual tranquillity. The various governments generally respected their obligation to refrain from aiding revolutions against neighboring governments, and the diplomatic representations which the United States made from time to time to those which seemed remiss in exercising proper surveillance over political exiles from nearby countries was a powerful influence on the side of peace.

THE CENTRAL AMERICAN COURT

One of the weakest points in the system established by the Central American Treaties was the Court of Justice.[3] In its first case, the complaint of Honduras and Nicaragua *vs.* Guatemala and El Salvador in 1908, the Court prob-

[2] The Report of the American representative at the Conference was published by the Government Printing Office at Washington, and also in *Foreign Relations* for 1907, p. 665–727. The more important of the treaties are conveniently printed in a pamphlet issued by the World Peace Foundation in February, 1917, entitled *The New Pan Americanism,* Part III, "Central American League of Nations."

[3] For a complete history of the Central American Court of Justice, see the article by Professor Manley O. Hudson in the *American Journal of International Law,* Vol. 26, No. 4, October, 1932.

bably prevented an international war, but when it rendered its final decision its prestige suffered greatly from the fact that the judges from each of the four states interested clearly voted as the interests of their own governments dictated. The impression thus created, that the members of the Court regarded themselves rather as the political representatives of the administration appointing them than as judges removed from any national or partisan control, was strengthened in 1910 when the new administration in Nicaragua removed the judge representing that country. Despite the protests of the other judges that the Treaty established a term of five years for the members of the Court, Nicaragua compelled the Court to accept its action by withholding its contribution for the latter's expenses.

The Court was not successful in attempts at mediation in the Nicaraguan revolutions of 1910 and 1912, because in each case one or both of the contending factions refused to accept its proposals, even though the action of the Court was approved by the United States. The only other matters dealt with by the tribunal during the first eight years of its existence were a proposal that it intervene in an election in Costa Rica in 1914, when it refused to act, and four complaints by individual citizens against the governments of other Central American states. In each of these, the Court decided against the plaintiff, usually on the ground that local remedies had not been exhausted.

In 1916, Costa Rica and El Salvador complained to the Court of Nicaragua's action in entering into the Bryan-Chamorro Treaty, under which Nicaragua had granted to the United States an option for the construction of an interoceanic canal by way of the San Juan River and the privilege of establishing a naval base in the Gulf of Fonseca. Costa Rica asserted that Nicaragua had had no right to enter into the Treaty without her consent because

President Cleveland, in deciding certain disputed questions regarding the validity of a boundary treaty between the two states, had expressly stated in an award handed down in 1888 that "the Republic of Nicaragua remains bound not to make any grants for canal purposes across her territory without first asking the opinion of Costa Rica." El Salvador objected to the proposed naval base, asserting that the waters of the Gulf of Fonseca were owned jointly by the three countries bordering thereon and that Nicaragua consequently had no right to cede a portion of the Gulf to a foreign power. She also asserted that the establishment of the naval base would be a menace to her own freedom and autonomy.[4]

Both countries had protested to the United States and Nicaragua when it first became known that the Treaty was under consideration. The Department of State had replied to Costa Rica that the canal treaty merely constituted an option to construct the canal and thus could not affect Costa Rica's interests. It had also pointed out that Costa Rica, like Nicaragua, had entered into a protocol in 1900 under which both Governments agreed to negotiate with the United States regarding the construction of a canal.[5] In reply to El Salvador, it pointed to the fact that the Nicaraguan Government considered itself authorized to dispose of the territory where the proposed naval base would be established and that El Salvador's rights would in any event be safeguarded because the United States Senate had ratified the Treaty with an express proviso that nothing contained therein was intended to affect any existing right of Costa Rica, El Salvador or Honduras.

The United States had carried on negotiations with both countries during 1915 in an effort to meet their objections to the canal treaty. Costa Rica had objected

[4] The essential correspondence regarding this controversy is published in *Foreign Relations* for 1914, 1915 and 1916.

[5] The text of this protocol is reprinted in *Foreign Relations, 1916*, p. 821.

to the grant of an option as equivalent to an agreement
for the non-construction of the canal, but her spokesman
had suggested that an agreement might be reached if the
United States would undertake to begin construction, say,
within fifty years.[6] The President of El Salvador had
also informally indicated his personal willingness to consent to the establishment of a naval base in the Gulf of
Fonseca in return for assistance in economic and educational matters.[7] Negotiations with both countries came
to an end, however, when the Senate ratified the
Nicaraguan Treaty and the two Governments brought suit
against Nicaragua before the Central American Court.

Honduras had not joined in El Salvador's complaint to
the Court or in the protest to the United States. Her
Government, in fact, did not accept El Salvador's contention that the Gulf of Fonseca belonged jointly to the
three countries bordering upon it, and on September 30,
1916, she formally protested against the theory of a condominium, sending a copy of her note to the Central
American Court.[8]

The Court, however, decided both suits against
Nicaragua, holding that the rights of Costa Rica under the
boundary treaty of 1858 and the Cleveland award had
been violated, and that the establishment of the naval
base would menace the security of El Salvador and violate
her right of condominium in the Gulf of Fonseca. It
stated, therefore, that Nicaragua was under obligation to
take such measures as international law afforded to restore the
legal status existing before the Bryan-Chamorro Treaty.
In both cases, however, the Court refused to declare the
Treaty itself null and void, on the ground that it had no
jurisdiction over one of the contracting parties.[9]

[6] *Foreign Relations, 1915*, p. 1110.
[7] *Ibid.*, p. 1115.
[8] *Foreign Relations, 1916*, p. 890.
[9] The official text of the decisions was published in *Anales de la Corte de
Justicia Centroamericana*, Volumes V and VI. An English translation of the

Nicaragua, which had refused to admit the jurisdiction of the Court, and had protested strongly against its considering the complaints of Costa Rica and El Salvador, refused to recognize its decision in either case. The decision was also disregarded by the Government of the United States, which had taken the position in a circular instruction sent to its representatives in Central America on March 30, 1916, that the canal protocols with Nicaragua and Costa Rica had been concluded long before the 1907 treaties and that it was obviously not contemplated that the Court would attempt to assume jurisdiction in questions arising between the United States and Central American Governments. It said that the action of Costa Rica in resorting to the Court "cannot but be viewed by the United States as an unjustifiable effort to prevent Nicaragua from fulfilling her contractual obligations." [10] As stated above, it had already justified its action in signing the Canal Treaty in formal communications to Costa Rica and El Salvador.[11]

The cases relating to the Bryan-Chamorro Treaty were the last ones to come before the Court, for on March 9, 1917, the Nicaraguan Government gave notice of its intention to abrogate the treaty under which it had been established.[12] Although the expense of the Court was assigned as the principal reason for this action, it was obvious that the real motive was resentment at the decisions in favor of Costa Rica and El Salvador. The Court went out of existence on March 12, 1918.

POLITICAL EVENTS, 1917-21

The dissolution of the Central American Court removed one of the most important parts of the structure created

decision in the case of Costa Rica is published in *Foreign Relations, 1916*, p. 862-86 and one of the decision in the case of El Salvador in *Foreign Relations, 1917*, p. 1101-4.

[10] *Foreign Relations, 1916*, p. 831.
[11] *Foreign Relations, 1914*, p. 954, 964.
[12] *Foreign Relations, 1917*, p. 30.

by the 1907 Conference, and events which occurred soon afterward made it clear that the other provisions of the treaties were no longer so effective in assuring internal and international tranquillity in Central America as they had for a time appeared to be.

Curiously enough, the first instance after 1911 in which a constituted government was overthrown by revolution occurred in Costa Rica, on January 27, 1917, when Federico Tinoco, the Minister of War, overthrew President Alfredo González by a *golpe de cuartel*, or military conspiracy, in the capital. The United States publicly expressed its disapproval of Tinoco's action on February 9, and announced that it would "not give recognition or support to any Government which may be established unless it is clearly proven that it is elected by legal and constitutional means." On February 22, the Department of State published a further statement reading as follows: [13]

In order that citizens of the United States may have definite information as to the position of this Government in regard to any financial aid which they may give to, or any business transactions which they may have with those persons who overthrew the Constitutional Government of Costa Rica by an act of armed rebellion, the Government of the United States desires to advise them that it will not consider any claims which may in the future arise from such dealings, worthy of its diplomatic support.

Tinoco nevertheless maintained himself for two years, although he rapidly lost the popular support which he had enjoyed at the beginning of his administration and was compelled to resort to repressive measures to discourage opposition to his régime. The United States continued to refuse to recognize his administration, and endeavored to persuade him that he should withdraw in order to permit the establishment of a constitutional government in Costa Rica; but at the same time it refused to countenance

[13] For the text of these statements see *Foreign Relations, 1917*, p. 306 and 308.

revolutionary movements against him [14] and made representations to the Governments of Honduras and Nicaragua to discourage them from giving aid to Tinoco's opponents.[15]

In May 1919 a revolutionary force under Julio Acosta invaded Costa Rica from the Nicaraguan frontier and met with sufficient success to make Tinoco's position more and more difficult. On August 12 the dictator fled from the country, leaving the executive power in the hands of Juan Bautista Quirós, the first designate. Since the latter held his position under the Constitution adopted during the Tinoco régime, which the United States had considered invalid, he also was refused recognition. At the suggestion of the American Government, the presidency was then intrusted to one of the *designados* who had been elected before the Tinoco revolution.[16] Elections were held on December 7, 1919, and Señor Acosta was chosen President by a large majority. Probably because of the illness of President Wilson, he was not formally recognized by the United States until August 2, 1920.

In 1919 there was also a successful revolution in Honduras, and in the following year the long-established dictatorship of Estrada Cabrera was overthrown in Guatemala. During the same period new presidents came into office in El Salvador and Nicaragua. These changes produced an entirely new political alignment in Central America and introduced new elements of instability and international friction which seemed for a time to threaten a return of the conditions which had existed before 1907.

THE ATTEMPTED UNION, 1921

Fear of the repressive measures with which Estrada Cabrera had always treated any open opposition to his Government had led the group which finally overthrew the dictator to organize their movement for the ostensible

[14] *Ibid.*, p. 332.
[15] *Foreign Relations, 1918*, p. 270.
[16] Foreign Policy Association, Foreign Policy Reports, Vol. VII, p. 183.

purpose of establishing a Central American Union. The new rulers of Guatemala were therefore committed to an effort to realize this purpose, and there was much enthusiasm for the Union not only among their followers but also in El Salvador and Honduras, where sentiment for a Central American Federation had always been strong. On December 4, 1920, all of the five Republics sent delegates to a conference at San José, Costa Rica, where a Treaty of Union was drawn up and plans were made for a constitutional convention. A bitter controversy over the validity of the Canal Treaty with the United States led Nicaragua to withdraw from the conference, and Costa Rica, reverting to her traditional policy of aloofness in Central American affairs, failed to ratify the Treaty of Union; but the three northern countries proceeded to establish a Provisional Federal Council at Tegucigalpa, Honduras, in June 1921. The constituent assembly met in the same city a month later. In the meantime, Mr. Hughes had publicly expressed the interest of the United States in the effort to establish a Central American Republic and had indicated that the United States would view with friendly eyes a Union based on the free agreement of all the peoples concerned.[17]

Pending the establishment of a permanent Federal Government, which was to have taken place on February 1, 1922, the states composing the Union surrendered practically none of their functions to the Provisional Council at Tegucigalpa. Although the new Constitution theoretically went into effect October 1, 1921, the Council actually had no military forces, no revenues, and no real control over foreign relations. Under these circumstances there was no occasion for its recognition by the United States, although problems affecting the Union were discussed informally with representatives who were sent to Washington during the fall of 1921.

[17] Department of State Press Release of June 2, 1921.

The project was in this inchoate state when a *golpe de cuartel* brought a new government into power in Guatemala on December 6. Advocates of the Union urged the other two states to intervene to restore the former administration by force, a step which might have had the most serious consequences in view of the superior power and resources of Guatemala and the resentment which any incursion of foreign troops would have aroused. The United States, however, informed each of the Governments concerned on December 17 that it would view with the greatest concern any interference by one Central American state in the affairs of another and that it expected all of the Central American Governments to comply with their obligations under the 1907 treaties.[18] In January, after the Provisional Federal Council had refused to admit representatives of the new Guatemalan Government to the Federal Congress, Guatemala formally withdrew from the Union. Honduras and El Salvador soon afterward resumed their status as independent nations.

THE CENTRAL AMERICAN CONFERENCE OF 1923

During 1922 and 1923 the general situation in Central America was decidedly unsatisfactory. The weakness of some of the newly established governments encouraged the partisans of former régimes to carry on intrigues against them not only at home but also in neighboring states. The 1907 treaties seemed to have lost much of their influence and there were even doubts as to their continued validity. The relations between Honduras, Nicaragua and El Salvador, which had been especially strained, were somewhat improved by a meeting of their Presidents on board the U.S.S. *Tacoma* in August 1922, when an agreement was signed specifically recognizing the continued validity of the General Treaty of Peace and

[18] For the text of this statement see Foreign Policy Reports, above cited, Vol. VII, p. 189.

Amity of 1907, and containing other provisions calculated
to maintain peace.[19]   Guatemala and Costa Rica, however,
declined to adhere to this pact.

The Tacoma Agreement also proposed a new Central
American conference, to meet in the following December.
In October, the United States invited the five Central
American Governments to hold this meeting in Washington.   The Conference resulted in a number of treaties,
which for the most part restated and reinforced the principles laid down in 1907.[20]   The new General Treaty of
Peace and Amity obligated the contracting parties to refrain from interference in one another's internal affairs and
to settle all disputes by peaceful means.   For this latter
purpose, new machinery was established.   The Central
American Court, instead of being a permanent group of
politically appointed, salaried judges, was to be a panel
of jurists proposed by the contracting parties and by other
American Governments, from which three judges were to
be selected by the interested parties to try each case which
arose.   Further machinery for the settlement of disputes
was provided by the Convention for the Establishment of
International Commissions of Inquiry, which were to
elucidate the facts in controversies where questions of
fact relative to failure to comply with treaty provisions
were at issue.   This was the only convention drawn up
by the Conference to which the United States was a party,
although it had been represented by official delegates, at
the request of the Central American Governments,
throughout the proceedings.

Other treaties signed at the Conference were one containing rather ineffective provisions for the limitation of
armaments in Central America, one providing for the es-

[19] The text of the Tacoma Agreement, in English and Spanish, is printed
in the Report of the 1923 Conference on Central American Affairs, p. 6.

[20] For the report of the Conference and the texts of the treaties, see
Conference on Central American Affairs, Washington, Government Printing
Office, 1923.

tablishment of Central American commissions to study economic and social problems, and conventions dealing with extradition, electoral legislation, the protection of labor, agricultural experiments, free trade, the reciprocal exchange of students, and the practice of liberal professions. As in the case of some of the treaties signed in 1907, financial and other difficulties unfortunately prevented the realization of many of the economic and social reforms which these agreements envisaged.

NON–RECOGNITION OF REVOLUTIONARY GOVERNMENTS

One of the most important provisions of the new General Treaty was Article II, which provided

Desiring to make secure in the Republics of Central America the benefits which are derived from the maintenance of free institutions and to contribute at the same time toward strengthening their stability, and the prestige with which they should be surrounded, they declare that every act, disposition or measure which alters the constitutional organization in any of them is to be deemed a menace to the peace of said Republics, whether it proceed from any public power or from the private citizens.

Consequently, the Governments of the Contracting Parties will not recognize any other Government which may come into power in any of the five Republics through a *coup d'état* or a revolution against a recognized Government, so long as the freely elected representatives of the people thereof have not constitutionally reorganized the country. And even in such a case they obligate themselves not to acknowledge the recognition if any of the persons elected as President, Vice-President or Chief of State designate should fall under any of the following heads:

(1) If he should be the leader or one of the leaders of a *coup d'état* or revolution, or through blood relationship or marriage, be an ascendant or descendant or brother of such leader or leaders.

(2) If he should have been a Secretary of State or should have held some high military command during the accomplishment of the *coup d'état*, the revolution, or while the election was being carried on, or if he should have held this

office or command within the six months preceding the *coup d'état*, revolution, or the election.

Furthermore, in no case shall recognition be accorded to a government which arises from election to power of a citizen expressly and unquestionably disqualified by the Constitution of his country as eligible to election as President, Vice-President or Chief of State designate.

An agreement not to recognize revolutionary administrations pending the reorganization of the Government through a free election had been included in one of the 1907 treaties but had had little practical effect. The policy which the United States had hitherto followed toward revolutionary governments had varied with circumstances. In 1910 such governments had been promptly recognized in Nicaragua and Honduras. Under the Wilson Administration, attempts at revolution had in general been discouraged by moral support of the constituted authorities and sometimes by small naval demonstrations. The emphatic stand taken against Tinoco has already been mentioned. In 1919, however, when President Bertrand of Honduras had been forced to yield to a revolt, partly at least because of the United States Government's disapproval of his efforts to compel the election of his own brother-in-law, a new government was promptly recognized. In this case, there was a compliance with constitutional forms because the executive power was transferred to the President's legal successor, who held an election resulting in the victory of General López Gutiérrez, the principal leader of the revolution. Changes of government which occurred in Guatemala in 1920 and 1922 were similarly effected in accord with constitutional forms, though by means of force; and the fact that a military leader who seized power through a *golpe de cuartel* subsequently became President in the latter case was not regarded as a bar to recognition.

After the signature of the treaties of 1923, however, the

United States adopted as its own the policy which the five Central American Governments had formulated. Its application of this policy has been a subject of much controversy. Many critics, especially in Central America, have felt that the attempt to pass judgment on the character of a new administration was an undue interference in the internal affairs of the countries affected. They have also asserted that the rules laid down by the Treaty have discouraged justifiable revolts against governments which have abused their power, and that they might operate to weaken governments which really represented the wishes of the people, for refusal by the United States to recognize a Central American President necessarily serves as an invitation to further disorder. On the other hand, many of those who have closely observed day by day political developments in the less stable Central American countries consider it unquestionable that fear of non-recognition by the United States has often deterred political leaders from starting revolts which had as their only incentive a desire for office and personal gain.

The United States first announced its adherence to the new policy a few months after the Central American Conference, when political disturbances seemed imminent in Honduras.[21] Its warning to the rival factions in this case did not suffice to maintain peace, for after the failure of any of the three candidates to receive a majority in the presidential election of 1923, and the subsequent failure of the Congress to settle the question, President López Gutiérrez declared martial law and attempted to maintain himself in power after the end of his term. His Conservative opponents promptly started a revolt. After a civil war in which there was much loss of life and property, and during which a force of American marines was sent to Tegucigalpa to protect the American Legation, the

[21] Foreign Policy Association Reports, Vol. VII, p. 196.

President of the United States sent Mr. Sumner Welles to continue the efforts at mediation which the representatives of the American Government had been making since the beginning of the conflict. A peace agreement was signed on the U.S.S. *Denver* at Amapala on April 28, 1924, in accordance with which the Council of Ministers, which had assumed power after the death of General López Gutiérrez on March 10, accepted General Tosta, one of the revolutionary leaders, as Provisional President.

General Tiburcio Carías, who had been the Conservative candidate in 1923, seemed certain to be the candidate of the victorious party in the new elections which the Provisional Government was to hold. He had also been one of the chief leaders of the revolution, and the United States made it clear that it could not under the circumstances extend recognition to any government which he might establish.[22] General Carías consequently withdrew, and Dr. Paz Barahona, another member of the Conservative party, but a civilian, was elected President by a large majority.

In December 1930 President Chacón of Guatemala became seriously ill, and Señor Baudilla Palma, the second designate, assumed the executive power. He was compelled to resign by a military revolt under General Manuel Orellana, who himself assumed control. The Government of the United States is reported to have informed Orellana that he would not be recognized in view of Article II of the 1923 Treaty, thus causing him to withdraw in favor of Dr. Reyna Andrade, who was duly elected as first designate.[23]

Unless we include the case just referred to, there have been only two occasions since 1923 when the United States has actually refused to recognize a Central American Government because of its revolutionary origin. The first

[22] *Ibid.*, p. 196.
[23] *Ibid.*, p. 200.

was that of the Chamorro régime in Nicaragua in 1926, which will be discussed in the following chapter. The other was that of General Maximiliano Martínez in El Salvador.

General Martínez had been elected Vice President of El Salvador in February 1931. He was also Minister of War and in December 1931 he was placed in the presidency by a military *junta* which had seized control of affairs and forced President Araujo to resign. Since this was clearly a case to which Article II of the General Treaty applied, the new régime was not recognized by the United States. General Martínez has nevertheless maintained himself in power for more than two years. A serious outbreak, said to be inspired by local communist agitators, occurred in January 1932, but since that time the country has been fairly tranquil.

The discussion of the propriety of the provisions regarding the recognition of new governments has somewhat overshadowed other questions connected with the 1923 treaties, especially as the relatively satisfactory relations which have existed between the Central American Governments have not caused attention to be centered on the more important provisions designed to prevent international conflict. A dislike of what they consider American interference has led one section of Central American opinion to advocate the termination of the treaties, and it was in response to this feeling that the Government of Costa Rica officially denounced the General Treaty of Peace and Amity on December 23, 1932. The Martínez Government in El Salvador took similar action on December 26, 1932. On August 26, 1933, the Salvadorean Congress passed a resolution declaring the Treaty invalid on the ground that it had not been registered with the Secretariat of the League of Nations under Article 18 of the Covenant. The other Central American Governments, however, have shown no inclination to take similar action, and it seems probable that the Treaty will remain in force for the present as between Guatemala, Honduras and Nicaragua.

DOLLAR DIPLOMACY

In general, the diplomacy of the United States in Central America has been predominantly concerned with political questions,—the prevention of international conflict and the promotion of stable government in individual countries,—rather than with commerce or finance. Commercial questions have been unimportant, for the total trade of the five Central American countries is insignificant as compared, for example, with that of Cuba. During the period between 1910 and 1920, however, much attention was paid to problems of public finance, partly because of their bearing on governmental stability and partly because it was feared that international complications would result from the failure of many of the Central American Governments to meet their obligations to their foreign creditors. Financial reform was an especially important objective of American policy while Mr. Knox was Secretary of State.

Until within the last quarter century, nearly all Central American loans were contracted in London. In 1909, Guatemala, Honduras and Costa Rica were in default on a part or all of their foreign bonded indebtedness.[24] Each of these countries had contracted loans in London between 1867 and 1872, at prices varying from 70 to 80 per cent of the nominal value of the bonds, and at interest rates ranging from 6 to 10 per cent. The service of these bonds had been maintained for only a short time. In Guatemala and Costa Rica, the creditors had been compelled to accept successive agreements for reducing the principal and fund-

[24] The most complete information regarding the history of the Central American debts will be found in the Report of the Council of the Corporation of Foreign Bondholders, published annually in London. There is a briefer account of the situation before 1916 in Munro, *op. cit.*, Chapter XIII.

ing the interest, only to have the payments again suspended after a brief period, while Honduras had made no payments at all on its foreign debt for more than 30 years. The record of Nicaragua and El Salvador, which had obtained foreign loans at a later date and under somewhat different conditions, was better, although neither country had been free from default.

Honduras, whose total annual revenues did not exceed two or three million dollars, owed the stupendous sum of $124,000,000. Her Government had issued bonds to a nominal value of more than $25,000,000 between 1867 and 1870 for the construction of an interoceanic railroad across her territory, but the portion of the proceeds which had reached the national treasury had sufficed only to build approximately sixty miles of cheaply constructed line. Payments of interest had been suspended in 1872.

An arrangement for refunding this debt had been proposed in 1908 by the British bondholders, with the diplomatic support of the British Government, but had been opposed by the Government of the United States on the ground that it did not properly safeguard the interests of the Republic's American creditors. In April 1909 the Honduran Government sought the good offices of the United States to arrange a loan with American bankers, and a plan somewhat similar to that adopted a few years before in the Dominican Republic was worked out after prolonged negotiations.[25] The British bondholders agreed to accept approximately $4,500,000 in cancellation of their claim and the American bankers agreed to float a loan of $7,500,000 to provide funds for this purpose. An additional $2,500,000 was to be issued later for public improvements if conditions permitted.[26]

After the agreement with the bankers had been worked out, a treaty between Honduras and the United States

[25] The correspondence regarding these negotiations will be found in *Foreign Relations, 1912.*

[26] For an analysis of the plan, see *Foreign Relations, 1912,* p. 562, 577.

was signed at Washington on January 10, 1911, providing that the new loan should be secured by the collection of customs duties by a Collector General selected by the Government of Honduras from a list of three names presented by the Fiscal Agent of the loan and approved by the President of the United States. The Government of Honduras agreed to give full protection to the Collector General and the Government of the United States promised on its part to afford such protection as it might find requisite. The two Governments agreed to consult with one another in case difficulties should arise regarding the execution of the contract, and Honduras agreed not to make changes in the customs duties without consultation and agreement with the Government of the United States.[27] The loan treaty was at once submitted to the United States Senate and to the Honduran Congress. It encountered strong opposition in Honduras, and on January 31 the Congress rejected the treaty by a large majority, asserting that it was unconstitutional and a violation of Honduras' sovereignty.[28]

Soon afterward, a change of Government occurred. The treaty had been signed with President Dávila, the same chief executive who had been placed in office by Nicaraguan troops in 1907. After the fall of Zelaya, Dávila was deprived of his strongest supporter, and at the end of 1910 his opponents under the leadership of General Manuel Bonilla and an American soldier of fortune named Lee Christmas, and probably with assistance from Guatemala, invaded Honduras and won several substantial successes. Both the United States and Great Britain landed marines on the north coast, where the fighting was taking place, and the United States tendered its good offices at the end of January to bring about an agreement. A conference presided over by Mr. Thomas C. Dawson ar-

[27] The text of the treaty is printed in *Foreign Relations, 1912*, p. 560.
[28] *Ibid.*, p. 562.

ranged early in March for the installation of a bi-partisan Provisional Government under which a free election should be held, and this election, as was usual in such cases, resulted in the choice of General Bonilla as President.[29]

The new Chief Executive had apparently approved the conclusion of the loan contract with the United States, but he showed little interest in obtaining its ratification by Congress. Early in 1912 the American bankers withdrew, and the United States Senate, where the plan had encountered much opposition, recommitted the treaty to the Committee on Foreign Relations. Subsequent efforts to arrange for a loan by other American bankers came to nothing and the public debt of Honduras remained in default until 1926, when an arrangement was effected through the efforts of the British Legation at Tegucigalpa. The bondholders agreed to accept a total amount of $6,000,000 in full payment at the rate of $200,000 a year for thirty years. The consular invoice tax, collected at ports from which goods were shipped, was assigned as security for these payments, and the National City Bank of New York undertook to collect this tax on behalf of the bondholders.[30]

A treaty similar to that with Honduras was signed with Nicaragua in June 1911, but this, like the other, failed of ratification in the United States Senate. The plan of financial rehabilitation which was subsequently worked out in Nicaragua will be described in the next chapter.

Mr. Knox had apparently contemplated efforts to refund and adjust the foreign debts of all of the Central American countries, believing that foreign creditors might seize the customhouses as they had threatened to in the Dominican Republic if such action were not taken. He appears to have been convinced by the earlier results of the Dominican treaty that the establishment of financial

[29] *Foreign Relations, 1911*, p. 291–305.
[30] Raymond Leslie Buell, *The Central Americas*, Foreign Policy Association, Pamphlet Series No. 69, p. 14.

control was in itself a most important step toward political stability. In a statement regarding the Honduran loan treaty before the Senate Committee on Foreign Affairs, he pointed out that the expense to the United States of protecting life and property in Central America was estimated at over $1,000,000 annually, and he referred to the fact that there had been two military interventions in Honduras during the preceding six months. "Should the Convention be put into operation," he said, "no such necessity will be likely to arise." He emphasized his belief that the only object of Central American revolutions was to obtain control of the customs duties. He also indicated, however, that he did not contemplate making treaties like those with Honduras and Nicaragua with other Central American countries, for he felt that different conditions would make the "degree of intimacy" less in other cases.[81]

The strong opposition which was expressed in Central America, as well as the refusal of the United States Senate to approve the proposed treaties with Honduras and Nicaragua, caused the abandonment of any further effort to establish customs collectorships. Costa Rica and Guatemala, moreover, reached agreements with their foreign creditors in 1911 and 1913 which to a great extent eliminated the apparent danger of European intervention.

Costa Rica obtained a refunding loan from a syndicate of American, German, British and French bankers in 1911, after persuading her creditors to accept a substantial reduction of the debt, upon which no interest had been paid for ten years. The syndicate issuing the new bonds was to assume the collection of the customs duties only in case of default. It does not appear that the Government of the United States was involved in any way in the negotiations by which this settlement was effected.

[81] *Foreign Relations, 1912,* p. 583.

In Guatemala, the British Government had made urgent representations on behalf of the foreign creditors, who had received no payments since 1898 because the Government had diverted to other purposes the revenues set aside by the contract for the service of their bonds. A plan to refund the debt by a loan from American bankers was worked out with the active assistance of the Department of State, but was not accepted by the bondholders. The British Government refused to advise the bondholders to accept despite a strong plea from Secretary Knox, who described the proposed contract as a means of carrying out the United States Government's "broad policy with regard to Central America where its interests are necessarily of predominant importance." In 1913, an agreement for the resumption of payments on the existing bonds was forced upon the Guatemalan Government by the British Government, which sent a warship and threatened to suspend diplomatic relations within five days if the agreement were not signed.[32]

The American Government continued to show an interest in the efforts of the Central American countries to improve their financial administration and in several cases recommended experts to assist one or another of the Central American Republics in preparing or carrying out projects for currency reform, for new revenue legislation, or for other purposes. By its friendly advice and suggestions, it also exerted its influence on several occasions to discourage unfair or injudicious loans or other financial transactions with foreign interests.

In the case of the Salvador loan of 1922, it went somewhat farther. As a result of the war and the postwar depression, El Salvador was in urgent need of a large loan. The bankers who had been approached had declined to make a loan without security in the form of outside

[32] *Foreign Relations, 1912*, p. 500–511; *Foreign Relations, 1913*, p. 557–572.

financial control, but a plan had finally been worked out
for the establishment of a fiscal agency representing the
bankers, which would merely supervise the collection of
the pledged customs revenues so long as the service of the
loan was maintained. In case of default, the Republic
was to appoint a collector of customs nominated by the
bankers with the concurrence of the Secretary of State
of the United States, and all disputes arising under the
loan contract were to be referred for decision to the
Chief Justice of the United States Supreme Court or to
another member of the Federal judiciary. At the request
of the Salvadorean Government and the interested bankers,
the Secretary of State consented to assist in the manner
indicated in selecting a collector of customs in the event
of default, and to use his good offices in referring disputes
to the Chief Justice or another American judge if the
occasion should arise. The Department of State, however,
had no other relation to the loan.[83]

The Government of the United States does not appear
to have exercised any pressure, diplomatic or otherwise,
upon those Central American Governments which have
suspended the service of their foreign debts during the
depression. The provisions of the loan contracts for the
establishment of customs collectorships have not been
invoked either in El Salvador or in Costa Rica.

BOUNDARY DISPUTES

Aside from questions arising out of the internal politics
of individual states, the only important causes of international friction in Central America have been the
boundary disputes caused by the failure of the Spanish
authorities in colonial times to define clearly the limits of
the various provinces. The history of the controversy
between Costa Rica and Panama has already been de-

[83] State Department Press Release, October 18, 1923.

scribed.[34] The other boundary questions which have caused trouble in recent years have been those between Honduras and Guatemala and between Honduras and Nicaragua.

In 1917 the Cuyamel Fruit Company, under a concession from Honduras, started to build a railroad into the hitherto valueless region along the Motagua River, where two other American concerns, the United Fruit Company and the International Railways of Central America, held concessions from the Government of Guatemala.[35] The Government of the latter country ordered the construction stopped and sent troops into the territory. At the request of Honduras, the United States exercised its good offices to prevent an armed conflict, and in November both sides expressed a willingness to accept American mediation. A conference was held in Washington in 1918, at which the Guatemalan and Honduran representatives made a formal statement of their respective claims, and an economic survey of the region in dispute was made later in the same year by a representative of the American Geographical Society at the request of the Department of State. It proved impossible, however, to reach a solution which both parties would accept, and the mediation proceedings were finally suspended.

At the Washington Conference in 1923 Guatemala and Honduras announced that they had decided to submit the dispute to arbitration by the President of the United States.[36] The subsequent efforts of the two Governments to negotiate the necessary treaty for this purpose were,

[34] See Chapter II.
[35] The earlier correspondence regarding the mediation of the United States in this boundary dispute was published in *Foreign Relations* for 1917. A brief account up to 1930, covering both the Guatemala-Honduras and the Honduras-Nicaragua disputes, is given in a pamphlet issued by the Foreign Policy Association, *Unsettled Boundary Disputes in Latin America*, Information Service, Vol. V, No. 26, 1930.
[36] *Conference on Central American Affairs*, above cited, p. 56, 62.

however, unsuccessful. In 1927 new incidents occurred
on the frontier and the two Governments again asked the
United States to assist in reaching a settlement, but a
conference held at Cuyamel in the disputed territory,
under the chairmanship of the Hon. Roy T. Davis,
was unable even to establish a provisional boundary line
pending a definitive settlement of the dispute.

In 1930, after long and difficult negotiations in which
the United States was represented by Assistant Secretary
of State Francis White, the Guatemalan and Honduran
Governments were finally able to agree upon a treaty for
the settlement of the boundary by arbitration. Since there
was disagreement as to the jurisdiction of the International Central American Tribunal in the matter, it was
agreed that the arbitral court should first decide in effect
whether it should function as the Central American
Tribunal or as a special tribunal for the boundary question.
Upon deciding for the latter alternative, the Court proceeded to consider the boundary question itself. The
judges, who were Chief Justice Hughes, Dr. Bello Codesido
of Chile, and Dr. Castro Ureña of Costa Rica, rendered
a decision on January 23, 1933, in which they divided the
disputed territory between the parties.[37]

Attempts to settle the boundary between Honduras
and Nicaragua have been less successful. Under a treaty
signed in 1894, this question was submitted to arbitration
by the King of Spain, who handed down his decision in
1906. The issue since that time has been the validity of
this award, which Nicaragua refused to accept on the
ground that there had been various irregularities in the
procedure. When military incidents along the boundary
threatened to disturb the good relations between the two
countries in 1918, the proferred mediation of the United

[37] F. C. Fisher, "The Arbitration of the Guatemalan-Honduran Boundary
Dispute," *American Journal of International Law* (July, 1933), Vol. 27,
p. 403.

States was accepted by both sides.[38] No agreement was reached, however, at the conferences held during the next few months in Washington, and the question has remained open down to the present time.

POLITICAL PROGRESS IN CENTRAL AMERICA

The repeatedly expressed main objective of the United States' policy in Central America has been the elimination of the disorderly conditions which have prevented the economic development of the countries of the Isthmus and have frequently caused foreign intervention in their affairs. Since the Washington Conference in 1907, these disorderly conditions have unquestionably improved. Wars between the Central American states have apparently become a thing of the past. Efforts by one government to assist a revolution in another country, which were accepted as a normal practice twenty-six years ago, are no longer carried on openly or very effectively, if indeed they still occur. With the removal of this great cause of disturbance, several of the Central American Republics have been able to make distinct progress toward the development of political institutions based on constitutional methods. Costa Rica, except for the brief period of the Tinoco régime, has enjoyed real republican government for many years. In Nicaragua, after a series of elections supervised at the request of both factions by the United States, the leaders of the two great political parties are now endeavoring to work out a system of minority representation and bi-partisan electoral control which will prevent further civil strife. In Honduras, President Paz Barahona and his successor, President Mejía Colindres, won a distinguished place for themselves in Central American history in 1928 and 1932 by holding free and fair elections as the result of which the control of the Government was transferred in each case to the opposition candidate.

[38] *Foreign Relations, 1918*, p. 11–34.

Central America suffered, it is true, from the wave of revolt which swept over Latin America during the depression, but the disorder which occurred there was less serious and less prolonged than in many of the more advanced South American countries. A small uprising in Costa Rica and a more serious one in Honduras were suppressed by the constituted Governments and the disturbance caused by the military *coups d'état* in El Salvador and Guatemala was of short duration. It may take several years for the people of the Central American Republics to establish permanently stable political institutions, but the progress which has already been made toward this end has been sufficient materially to affect the basic factors governing the Central American policy of the United States.

CHAPTER VI

THE AMERICAN INTERVENTION
IN NICARAGUA

Political partisanship in Nicaragua has been especially intense because of the historic feud between León and Granada, the centers respectively of the Liberal and the Conservative parties. Other towns have aligned themselves with one or another of these two chief cities, and the entire population has taken an active interest in their struggles for control. Civil wars have been more frequent and more bitterly fought than in any of the other Central American countries.

THE REVOLUTION OF 1909–10

In 1909 the Liberal party under the dictatorship of José Santos Zelaya had maintained itself in power for sixteen years. There had been many revolts at home, and much friction with other Central American Governments. We have already seen something of the part which Zelaya's conflicts with his neighbors played in defeating the efforts of the United States to maintain peace in Central America between 1906 and 1909. As President Taft said in his annual message to Congress in 1909:

Since the Washington Conventions of 1907 were communicated to the Government of the United States as a consulting and advising party, this Government has been almost continuously called upon by one or another, and in turn by all five of the Central American republics, to exert itself for the maintenance of the conventions. Nearly every complaint has been against the Zelaya Government of Nicaragua, which has kept Central America in constant tension and turmoil.

Relations between the United States and the Zelaya Government were thus already strained when a revolution started on the east coast of Nicaragua in October 1909. They were broken off altogether in the following month when the Government's forces shot two American adventurers who had been taken prisoners while serving with the revolutionists. In a note addressed to the Nicaraguan Chargé d'Affaires at Washington, Secretary Knox condemned not only the shooting of the two Americans but Zelaya's whole conduct, at home and abroad, in the harshest language, and frankly expressed the opinion[1]

that the revolution represents the ideals and the will of a majority of the Nicaraguan people more faithfully than does the Government of President Zelaya.

Realizing that the open hostility of the United States made his further continuance in office impossible, Zelaya resigned in favor of Dr. José Madriz, another Liberal, and left the country on a Mexican warship.

The new Government, however, was not recognized by the United States, and the successes which it at first won against the revolutionists were nullified when an American naval commander at Bluefields refused to permit an attack on that town on the ground that fighting there would endanger the lives and properties of the foreigners who formed a substantial portion of the population. By August 1910 the revolution was in control of the entire Republic and General Juan J. Estrada, its leader, had been established as Provisional President at Managua.

The Dawson Agreement

The situation which confronted the new administration was by no means encouraging. General Estrada had been promised the Provisional Presidency chiefly because his former position as Governor and Commander of the troops at Bluefields under Zelaya had made his help indispensable

[1] *Foreign Relations, 1909*, p. 455.

to the success of the revolution. He and a few other leaders, like General José María Moncada, the new Minister of Government, were Liberals, but the great majority of the victorious army were Conservatives. The latter were little inclined to give loyal support to Estrada now that the revolution was over, and they were divided among themselves in factions headed by General Emiliano Chamorro, General Luís Mena and Don Adolfo Díaz. There was every prospect of a serious conflict when an attempt was made to select a permanent President; and the situation was the more dangerous because the Zelaya Liberals, despite their defeat, were still numerically strong and showed every inclination to resume the contest for power at any favorable opportunity. The condition of the national treasury was also a source of grave anxiety, because practically no funds were available and it was clear that a default on the foreign debt must soon occur.

Through the good offices of the representative of the United States, Mr. Thomas C. Dawson, Estrada, Díaz, Mena and Chamorro signed a series of agreements on October 27, 1910, under which a constituent assembly, to be convened as soon as possible, would elect Estrada as President and Díaz as Vice President for a two-year term, at the end of which Estrada would not be a candidate for reëlection. A mixed commission constituted in coöperation with the Government of the United States was to pass on all pecuniary claims against the Government, and a foreign loan was to be obtained, if possible, through the good offices of the United States.[2]

THE REVOLUTION OF 1912

The apparent harmony brought about by the Dawson Agreement was short-lived. The Constituent Assembly,

[2] The text of these agreements is printed in the pamphlet entitled *The United States and Nicaragua*, issued by the Department of State in 1932. This is a complete and carefully prepared history of American relations with Nicaragua, upon which a large part of the present chapter has been based.

composed mainly of Conservatives under the leadership of General Chamorro, quarreled with President Estrada and was promptly dissolved. General Chamorro left Nicaragua, and General Mena, the Minister of War, became for a time the chief leader of the Conservative faction in the Government. When a new Constituent Assembly met it was composed mainly of his followers, since his control of the army had enabled him to dominate the elections. On May 9, 1911, Mena compelled the President and General Moncada to withdraw from the Government, leaving it entirely in Conservative hands. Señor Díaz succeeded to the presidency, and worked in relative harmony with Mena until the latter aroused the opposition of the other Conservative leaders by having the Constituent Assembly elect himself as President for the next term. In July 1912 Chamorro, who had returned, was made Chief of the Army; and Mena left the capital to start a new revolution. He was at once joined by the Liberals in León and elsewhere. Since the greater part of the army remained loyal to him and he also retained control of nearly all of the supplies of war material, the Government was practically helpless. President Díaz was therefore compelled to request the armed intervention of the United States. American marines were landed to protect the Legation and to keep open communications with the capital, and the revolution was strongly condemned in a public pronouncement by the Department of State.[3] The American Government's attitude caused the greater part of the revolutionists to abandon the movement, and on September 25 General Mena surrendered to the American commander. The revolt ended when a force of Liberals, who had continued to hold a strong position overlooking Masaya, were dislodged by American marines.

This energetic action by the United States placed the Conservative party in undisputed control in Nicaragua

[3] *The United States and Nicaragua*, p. 21.

and inaugurated the first period of relative tranquillity which the Republic had known for many years. Señor Díaz continued as President during the term 1913–17, and was succeeded by General Chamorro. The Liberals did not even participate in the election of 1916, because the American Minister had warned them that the United States would not recognize their candidate, a close associate of ex-President Zelaya, if he should be elected.[4] The Liberals, who asserted that they were numerically the stronger party, protested violently against their continued exclusion from the Government, but they were discouraged from armed revolt by the belief that the Government at Washington would again intervene if necessary to maintain the Conservative authorities. A Legation Guard of about one hundred marines, which had remained in Managua after the suppression of the Mena revolt, was generally considered, and was presumably intended, to be an indication that the United States would oppose a renewal of civil war.

FINANCIAL AFFAIRS, 1911–14

While these events were occurring, the Nicaraguan Government had been endeavoring, with the active assistance of the Department of State, to find a way out of very grave financial difficulties. Although President Madriz had left a substantial sum in the treasury on his departure from Managua, this money was rapidly used up, largely in paying more or less justifiable claims of members of the victorious party against the national treasury. More funds were obtained for the same purpose by large new issues of inconvertible money, which helped to make worse the already disastrous situation of the currency and foreign exchange. The Government soon found difficulty in meeting necessary administrative expenses, and on July 1, 1911, it defaulted on the service of the bonds issued in 1909 in

[4] Nothing regarding this statement was published by the United States Government, but the fact that it was made was well known in Nicaragua.

London.[5] The British bondholders thus augmented the number of foreign creditors who were already pressing for an adjustment of their claims with the diplomatic support of their Governments.

The Dawson Agreement, as we have seen, had contemplated the rehabilitation of the finances and the adjustment of claims through measures to be taken in coöperation with the United States, and early in 1911, at the request of the Nicaraguan Government, the Department of State had sent Mr. Ernest H. Wands to make a study of the Republic's financial situation. On June 6, 1911, the Knox-Castrillo Convention was signed. By this treaty, Nicaragua agreed to refund her existing external and internal debt by means of a loan secured by the customs revenues, and to place the administration of the customs during the life of the loan in the hands of an official nominated by the Fiscal Agent of the loan and approved by the President of the United States.[6] The convention was promptly ratified by the Nicaraguan Constituent Assembly, but failed on May 12, 1912, to obtain a favorable report from the Committee on Foreign Relations of the United States Senate.

Pending the ratification of the convention by the United States, the Nicaraguan Government had entered into negotiations with Brown Brothers & Company and J. and W. Seligman & Company, who had agreed on June 21, 1911, to loan the Republic $15,000,000 if the convention were ratified by September 1.[7] When the United States Congress adjourned in the summer, thus

[5] *The United States and Nicaragua*, p. 18.
[6] The text is printed in *Foreign Relations, 1912*, p. 1074.
[7] See the preamble of the Treasury Bills Agreement of September 1, 1911. The text of this and all other important contracts and decrees relating to Nicaragua's financial affairs from 1911 to 1928 are printed in César Arana's excellent compilation entitled *Compilación de contratos celebrados con los Banqueros de New York, con el Ethelburga Syndicate de Lóndres y con El Banco Nacional de Nicaragua Inc.—Leyes relativos á los mismos contratos.* Managua, 1928-9. See Vol. I, p. 15, for the text of the Treasury Bills Agreement.

postponing for some months any possibility of final action on the convention, the banking group agreed to advance funds at once to meet a part of the Republic's most urgent requirements and especially to make possible an early reform of the currency. On September 1, 1911, they purchased short term 6 per cent treasury bills to the amount of $1,500,000, with the proceeds of which the Republic agreed to establish a National Bank, incorporated in the United States, with an initial capital of $100,000 subscribed by the Government, and to carry out in coöperation with the bankers a plan of currency reform. To secure the loan the collection of the customs was placed at once in the hands of a United States national nominated by the bankers and approved by the Department of State. On March 20, 1912, the Constituent Assembly approved a law establishing a monetary unit equal in value to the United States dollar. The old paper money was exchanged at a fixed rate for the notes of the new National Bank, and the parity of the new notes was to be assured through an exchange fund maintained by the Nicaraguan Government in New York.

The New York bankers had also been authorized as agents of Nicaragua to reach an adjustment with the British bondholders. Through their efforts, an agreement was signed on May 25, 1912, under which the interest on the 1909 bonds was reduced from six to five per cent on condition that the customs continue to be administered as provided in the Treasury Bills Agreement.

The Mixed Claims Commission had meanwhile been established under a decree approved by the Assembly on May 17, 1911. In view of the fact that American claims exceeded in amount those of all other nationalities, even including those of Nicaraguans,[8] it had been agreed that this body should consist of three members: one Nicaraguan selected by the Government, one American appointed by

[8] *The United States and Nicaragua*, p. 15.

the Government but upon nomination of the Government of the United States, and an umpire designated by the Department of State. The commission began work at once, and continued for over three years, despite the fact that no funds were available to pay its awards because of the failure to obtain a large foreign loan under the Knox-Castrillo Convention. It passed upon 7,908 claims, and made awards totalling $1,840,432 as against $13,808,161 demanded by the claimants. A sum of $538,749 was awarded on sixty-six American claims totalling $7,576,564.[9]

By the time when it became clear that the Knox-Castrillo Convention would not be ratified, a substantial part of the program envisaged by the treaty had thus been carried out in anticipation of obtaining a loan from which the advances already made by the bankers would be refunded. When the treaty failed of ratification in the United States Senate, both the Department of State and the bankers were already inextricably involved in the work of rehabilitating Nicaragua's finances. The heavy expense caused by the Mena revolt and the decline of Nicaragua's revenues made impossible the repayment of the small short term advances already made, and in fact compelled the bankers to advance further sums to enable the Government to maintain itself and to prevent the breakdown of the new currency system. The orginal treasury bills were refunded on October 8, 1913, and additional funds were obtained by the Government through the purchase by the bankers for $1,000,000 of a 51 per cent interest in the Pacific Railroad of Nicaragua, a Government-owned line extending from Corinto to Managua and Granada. At the same time, the bankers became owners of 51 per cent of the stock of the National Bank, by subscribing the greater part of the sum necessary to increase the capital of that institution to $300,000. After the outbreak of the European War, payment of interest both on the treasury bills and on the

---

[9] *Ibid.*, p. 15. See also the article by Judge Schoenrich, one of the members of the Commission, in the *American Journal of International Law*, Vol. IX, p. 858.

English bonds was suspended by agreements which were renewed from time to time during the next two years.

THE BRYAN–CHAMORRO TREATY

In making these agreements both the Nicaraguan Government and its foreign creditors had hoped for an early improvement in the Republic's financial position through the receipt of a direct payment from the Treasury of the United States. On February 8, 1913, a treaty had been signed with the American Minister under which the Government of the United States had agreed to pay $3,000,000 for the grant in perpetuity of the "exclusive proprietary rights necessary and convenient for the construction, operation and maintenance of an interoceanic canal" across Nicaragua. The United States was also granted a 99-year lease on Great and Little Corn Islands in the Caribbean Sea and the right for a similar period to establish a naval base on the Gulf of Fonseca. While this treaty was still under consideration by the United States Senate, the Nicaraguan Government suggested the inclusion of provisions similar to the "Platt Amendment" in the Cuban Treaty of 1903, giving to the United States the right to intervene in Nicaragua for the maintenance of the Republic's independence and the protection of life and property.[10] This amendment, however, proved unacceptable to the Foreign Relations Committee of the United States Senate, and a new treaty, omitting this feature, was signed on August 5, 1914.[11]

The agreements under which the New York bankers and the British bondholders consented to the suspension of payments on the Republic's debt had provided that all arrears should be paid in full upon the receipt of the money due from the United States under the treaty. The treaty, however, had provided that this money should be applied

[10] *Foreign Relations, 1914,* p. 953.

[11] For the text of the Treaty see Appendix, *infra,* p. 313. The protests of Costa Rica and El Salvador against this treaty have already been discussed in Chapter V.

upon the Republic's indebtedness or for other public purposes as determined by the two high contracting parties, and the Department of State, despite its earlier approval of the agreements with the bankers, was reluctant to see almost the entire amount paid to one class of creditors. Numerous other American and foreign claimants were clamoring for consideration, and the British Government had formally protested against any disposition of the treaty fund which did not include the payment of certain British revolutionary claims.[12] The bankers insisted upon payment in full, and thus delayed any distribution under the treaty for a considerable period.[13] Meanwhile, the Nicaraguan Government was in desperate need of funds with which to meet back salaries and current expenses, and its position was made especially difficult when the Collector General of Customs, at the expiration of the periods during which interest payments on the treasury bills and the British bonds had been suspended by agreement, began to retain all of the customs revenues.[14] In December 1916 the Department of State finally obtained the consent of the bankers to a postponement of a part of the amounts due them on condition that the Nicaraguan Government should adopt a general plan for the adjustment of its indebtedness. After prolonged negotiations, during which President Emiliano Chamorro successfully resisted efforts by the bankers and the Department of State to compel him to agree to the appointment of a Financial Adviser, a plan of financial control satisfactory to all concerned was finally worked out.[15]

The Financial Plan of 1917

A series of contracts known collectively as the Financial Plan of 1917 were signed on October 20 of that year.

[12] *Foreign Relations, 1915*, p. 1118.
[13] For the correspondence on this subject, see *Foreign Relations, 1916*, p. 898–917.
[14] *The United States and Nicaragua*, p. 28.
[15] For the text see Arana, *op. cit.*, Vol. II, p. 20–65.

The bankers agreed to a further extension of one-half of the principal of the outstanding treasury bills, and the British bondholders received the accrued interest on their bonds but agreed to a partial suspension of the service of the loan during the next three years.

The Collector General of Customs was to continue to administer the customs so long as any of the British bonds or the treasury bills outstanding under the plan or the new bonds which were to be issued in payment of claims should be outstanding. He was to pay preferentially the sums due for the service of the British bonds and for interest on the treasury bills, depositing the balance of the customs collections in the National Bank to the credit of the Nicaraguan Government. The internal revenues were to be collected as hitherto by Nicaraguan officials unless the amount collected should fall below an aggregate of $180,000 in any three consecutive months. If this should occur, however, they were to pass under the control of the American customs officials.

The Nicaraguan Government agreed to limit its budget to a sum of $90,000 monthly, although a further amount not exceeding $26,666.66 might be expended each month with the approval of a new body called the High Commission, of which one member was appointed by the President of Nicaragua, another by the Secretary of State of the United States, and a third, who would act only in the event of a disagreement, also by the Secretary of State. Any surplus remaining after these expenditures had been made was to be applied: 25 per cent to the deferred payments on the 1909 bonds; 25 per cent to the retirement of the treasury bills; and the remainder for public works.

The plan provided for the adjustment of the floating debt by a new Claims Commission, whose awards would be paid partly in cash and partly in new bonds. This commission, like the High Commission, was composed of a Nicaraguan member, a resident American member and

an American umpire. It passed upon all claims against
the Government including those adjudicated by the Mixed
Claims Commission of 1911, though the amounts awarded
by the latter were reduced only in cases where the claims
had passed into the hands of third parties. The awards
of the new commission, amounting to $5,304,386 out of a
total claimed of about $13,500,000, were paid largely
through an issue of Guaranteed Customs Bonds, for which
the High Commission above referred to acted as Fiscal
Agent.[16]

Financial Plan of 1920

In the years immediately following the adoption of the
Financial Plan of 1917, Nicaragua was unusually prosperous. It had been possible by June 30, 1920, to pay
off the principal of the treasury bills and the arrears due
on the British bonds, and to accumulate a surplus of
$1,000,000 in the treasury. This improved financial out-
look caused a revival of interest in the project for connect-
ing the interior of the Republic with the Atlantic coast
by a railway, an enterprise which had been the chief
purpose of the 1909 loan and one of the chief purposes
of the Knox-Castrillo Convention. A new series of contracts intended to pave the way for a future issue of bonds
for this railway were signed on October 5, 1920, but the
loan itself did not materialize because of a failure to agree
on the terms of issue. A new Financial Plan was adopted
at the same time without, however, changing materially
the system of financial control established in 1917.

Under the 1920 contract, the Nicaraguan Government
repurchased from the bankers the controlling interest in
the Pacific Railroad, which the latter had held since 1913,
for $1,750,000. Of the purchase price $300,000 was paid
in cash, and new treasury bills at 9 per cent, secured by
75 per cent of the surplus revenues, were issued to cover
the remainder.

[16] *The United States and Nicaragua*, p. 36–7.

FINANCES, 1924–29

When these new treasury bills were paid in full in 1924, the Pacific Railroad again became the unincumbered property of the Nicaraguan Government.   In September of the same year, the Government bought the stock in the National Bank for which the bankers had subscribed in 1913.[17]   The bankers thus had no further financial interest in Nicaragua, although the Customs Collectorship and the High Commission established under contracts with them continued in existence for the benefit of the British bondholders and the holders of the Guaranteed Customs Bonds.

When the bank again became the exclusive property of the Nicaraguan Government there was some alarm among business interests, and particularly among the holders of the Guaranteed Customs Bonds, which were payable in Nicaraguan currency, lest the Government should fail to maintain the stability of the currency system which had been established through the bankers' assistance.   President Martínez, however, not only announced his definite intention of maintaining the gold exchange standard but also requested the bankers to permit their representatives to remain on the boards of directors both of the bank and of the railroad, and to continue the existing management of both institutions, in order to assure their efficient conduct.[18]   This new relationship with the bankers continued until October 1929, when differences on matters of policy led the bankers to withdraw their representatives from the boards of directors and the managements of the two companies and to resign as bankers under the Financial Plan.[19]

The financial operations of the American bankers in Nicaragua, and the participation of the Department of State in the negotiation of the series of contracts above described, has been the subject of much unfriendly criti-

[17] *Ibid.*, p. 46.
[18] *Ibid.*, p. 46.
[19] *Ibid.*, p. 96.

cism. It has even been asserted that one of the chief objectives of American policy was to assist the bankers in making large profits from their relations with the Nicaraguan Government. Any study of the policy of the United States in Nicaragua would be incomplete without an effort to ascertain exactly what were the purpose and the results of the contracts with the bankers. The detailed study of these contracts will indicate that the profits derived by the bankers from their transactions with the Nicaraguan Government between 1911 and 1924 were as follows:

(1) Six per cent interest on the treasury bills issued between 1911 and 1917. The largest amount of such bills outstanding at any one time was apparently considerably less than $2,000,-000.

(2) Profits from the ownership of stock in the Pacific Railroad from 1913 to 1920 and from the resale of the stock to the Nicaraguan Government. Large amounts were paid in dividends during this period, but profits to the amount of about $700,000 were reinvested in the property. The bankers paid $1,000,000 for the stock in 1913 and sold it to the Government for $1,750,000 in 1920. The treasury bills given in part payment bore 9 per cent interest—a rate which was not out of line with prevailing money rates at the time.

(3) The profit from the ownership of a controlling interest in the National Bank and from the resale of the bank stock to the Government. During a part of the period when it was under the bankers' control, the Bank did ordinary commercial business as an affiliate of the Mercantile Bank of the Americas and was presumably of value as a part of that organization. When the bankers sold to the Government for $300,000 the stock for which they had paid $153,000 in 1913, representing 51 per cent of the institution's capital, the net assets of the Bank were reported to be $615,542.[20] The bankers required the Government to purchase at the same time the property and assets of a commercial subsidiary, then in liquidation, for which an additional $300,000 was paid. The assets of this company were valued at $300,478.13.[21]

[20] *Ibid.*, p. 46.
[21] Arana, *op. cit.*, Vol. III, p. 289.

POLITICAL AFFAIRS, 1917–25

The Conservative party remained in power during the Administrations of Emiliano Chamorro (1917–1920) and Diego Manuel Chamorro (January 1921–October 1923). Although the American Legation Guard of about 100 men assumed no responsibility for the maintenance of order, its continued presence in Managua was regarded as an evidence of the intention of the United States Government to support the constituted authorities, and there was no serious attempt at revolution. Such minor disturbances as occurred were easily put down by the Nicaraguan Government's own forces. The country benefited from the establishment of stable government, but there was naturally much discontent and unrest among the Liberals. In Nicaragua, as in most of the other Central American countries, intimidation and fraud too often made elections a mere form, and revolution had always been the only effective method of changing governments. It was difficult to justify the indefinite continuance of a policy which prevented revolution without affording the Government's opponents, who were believed by many observers to constitute a majority of the people, an opportunity to come into office by peaceful means.

Before the election of 1920, therefore, the Department of State had suggested that the Nicaraguan Government invite an expert to make suggestions for the reform of the electoral system. President Chamorro had refused to accept this suggestion, but had given assurances that he would conduct a free and fair election under the existing laws. The American Minister issued a public statement on July 1, 1920, emphasizing the complete impartiality of the United States in the approaching contest and the desire of the American Government that the election be free and fair. He was later compelled to express to President Chamorro the grave apprehension caused by reports of abuses and political arrests during the registration of voters. President Chamorro apparently took some steps to correct these abuses, but the election was nevertheless held under conditions which aroused violent protests from the Liberal party, and resulted in the victory of the Conservative candidate, one of President Chamorro's relatives.[22]

The United States raised no question as to the validity of the election or the recognition of the new President. Major Jesse I. Miller, who had been sent to Nicaragua by the Department of State as an observer, had reported that he had observed no violence or intimidation during the electoral period, although there had been fraud both in the registration of voters and the counting of ballots. Major Miller believed, however, that no fair election would have been possible under the existing laws and that the two parties were so nearly equal in strength as to make it impossible to say that either enjoyed a majority.[23]

Before the inauguration of the new President, the Department of State informed the Nicaraguan Government that it felt that the electoral system must be reformed at once, and obtained a promise to employ an expert suggested by the Government of the United States who should draft a new electoral law. Dr. Harold W. Dodds, the Secretary of the National Municipal League, was selected for this purpose, and the law which he prepared after visiting Nicaragua in 1922 was approved by the Nicaraguan Congress on March 16, 1923. The United States Government successfully interposed to prevent changes by which some members of the Congress wished to eliminate important features of the act.[24]

With a good prospect for the holding of a fair election at the end of President Diego Chamorro's term in 1924, it became possible to consider the early withdrawal of the

[22] *The United States and Nicaragua*, p. 39–43.
[23] *Ibid.*, p. 42.
[24] *A Brief History of the Relations between the United States and Nicaragua, 1909 to 1928*, p. 22, Government Printing Office, Washington, 1928.

Legation Guard. The Department of State felt "that this withdrawal could be effected with safety only after a strong Government backed by the majority of the people had been established." [25] It seemed doubtful, however, whether any Government could maintain itself unless it were supported by an adequate military force, especially as dissatisfaction among the Liberals after the election of 1920 had found expression in a number of small disorders during 1921 and 1922. The policy of the American Government was therefore directed toward "(1) passage of a new electoral law, and the assistance of an American electoral mission in putting into effect this law both during registration and election; and (2) the reorganization of the army by converting it into an efficient constabulary under American instruction." [26]

On November 14, 1923, the American Minister to Nicaragua informed the Nicaraguan Government that the United States desired to withdraw the Legation Guard as soon as practicable and that, in view of the steps already taken by the Nicaraguan Government to assure freedom and fairness in the approaching elections, the Government of the United States felt that the marines could be withdrawn from Managua upon the installation of the new administration. They would remain in Nicaragua during the intervening period only if the Nicaraguan Government considered that their presence would assist the constituted authorities in assuring complete freedom. The United States offered to assist the Nicaraguan Government in the installation of the new electoral system through the medium of qualified technical experts, and it also offered "to assist the Nicaraguan Government in the organization and training of an efficient constabulary which would assure the maintenance of order after the marines are withdrawn." The note concluded with an expression

[25] *The United States and Nicaragua*, p. 47.
[26] *Ibid.*, p. 47.

of the hope that the general treaty of peace and amity signed at Washington on February 7, 1923, would have been ratified by the Central American Governments before the new administration came into office, so that persons who might attempt to overthrow the constituted authorities in Nicaragua would know in advance that they could not expect recognition either from the other Central American Governments or from the United States.[27]

The Nicaraguan Government's reply to this note expressed general accord with the program proposed by the United States and expressly accepted the conditions under which the United States was willing to permit the Legation Guard to remain in Nicaragua during the electoral period.[28]

On October 12, 1923, when instructions to present the note of November 14 were already on the way to Managua, President Diego Manuel Chamorro died and was replaced by the Vice President, Señor Bartolomé Martínez. This event completely altered the political situation in Nicaragua because Martínez represented a wing of the Conservative party which opposed the control hitherto exercised by the Granada "oligarchy." With the support of several Liberal leaders, Martínez at first indicated that he would himself be a candidate in the approaching elections, but he abandoned this idea after the Government of the United States, in reply to his request for its views, had pointed out that it could not very well recognize a President expressly disqualified, as Martínez would be, by the Nicaraguan constitution.[29] He then threw his support to a Liberal-Conservative coalition known as the Transaction, which nominated Carlos Solórzano, a Con-

[27] *Ibid.*, p. 47–49.
[28] Department of State press release, February 7, 1924.
[29] *The United States and Nicaragua*, p. 49–50. Article 104 of the Nicaraguan Constitution reads in translation: "No citizen who holds the office of President either as the duly elected incumbent or accidentally, shall be eligible to the office of President or Vice President for the next term."

servative of Managua, as President and Dr. Juan B. Sacasa, a Liberal from León, as Vice President. The Granada Conservatives supported General Emiliano Chamorro, while a Liberal faction which had not joined the coalition nominated Luís Corea.

Meanwhile, the new electoral law had been put into operation for the first time during the registration of voters in March 1924. As suggested in the American Legation's note of November 14, Dr. Dodds had been requested by the Nicaraguan Government to assist in the administration of the law, and the registration had taken place under unusually satisfactory conditions. When the time came to make preparations for the election itself, however, President Martínez refused to accept further assistance from American experts. He ostensibly reconsidered this decision less than a week before the election, and suggested that observers from the Legation Guard be present during the voting, but the United States declined to act upon this suggestion because it considered it impossible at so late a date to take any steps adequate to insure fairness. In the meantime, Martínez had issued decrees making certain changes in the electoral law against which his opponents loudly protested. As compared with 115,000 total registration, 84,000 votes were cast. Of these, Solórzano received 48,000, Chamorro 28,000 and Corea 7,000. Many of the customary abuses seem to have occurred, and the completion of the electoral process was made possible only by Martínez' arbitrary action in removing the Conservative majority of the National Electoral Board, which had refused to certify the result. After canvassing the other possible courses of action, however, the United States decided, though apparently with some reluctance, to recognize the Solórzano Government. Prior to his inauguration, Solórzano gave the American Legation definite assurances that the 1928 elections would be carried out "in full freedom and fairness" under the

Dodds Law; that the proposed constabulary would be organized immediately with the assistance of the United States; that adequate measures would be adopted with the coöperation of the United States for the solution of the Republic's economic problems; and that as many political elements as possible would be given participation in his administration.[30]

WITHDRAWAL OF THE LEGATION GUARD

In accord with its announced policy, the United States had made arrangements to withdraw the Legation Guard immediately after the inauguration of the new administration on January 1, 1925. On January 7, however, President Solórzano asked that the Guard might remain until the Nicaraguan Government could organize the new constabulary, and the United States acceded to this request on condition that the organization of this force should be undertaken immediately and carried out energetically. The Solórzano Government was nevertheless very slow in taking action, and in March the Department of State indicated that unless something were done at once the Guard would be withdrawn. An act providing for the constabulary was passed by the Nicaraguan Congress in May, and President Solórzano asked the United States to recommend persons qualified to organize it. Since there was no authority at that time for members of the United States armed forces to undertake such work, Major C. B. Carter, a former Philippine constabulary officer, was designated to head the new organization. Major Carter arrived in July, and the Legation Guard was withdrawn from Managua on August 1.[31]

The new constabulary was still in an embryonic state when events occurred which led to one of the worst civil wars in Nicaragua's history. The political situation of the Solórzano Government had from the first been ex-

[30] *The United States and Nicaragua*, p. 52.
[31] *Ibid.*, p. 54.

ceedingly difficult. The President and his immediate personal followers were Conservatives, but the Liberals in accord with a preëlection agreement had been given two cabinet posts and several appointments as provincial governors, while membership in the courts had been divided as evenly as possible between the two parties. There was much distrust and friction within the administration, and this made it more difficult for the President to cope with the intrigues of the opposition led by General Chamorro.

THE CHAMORRO COUP D'ÉTAT

On August 28, 1925, Conservative military officers under the leadership of the President's own brother-in-law invaded a social function at Managua and imprisoned several prominent Liberals, including the Minister of Finance. Although the captives were released the next day, the two Liberal cabinet officers resigned. The President's evident weakness in dealing with his Conservative subordinates encouraged new efforts to create political disturbances, and on October 25 supporters of General Chamorro seized the Loma, the principal fortress overlooking the city of Managua. Chamorro compelled the President to sign an agreement repudiating his pact with the Liberals and eliminating the members of that party from the Government, while Chamorro himself became commander in chief of the Army. He also obtained $10,000 from the public treasury to pay the expenses of his *coup d'état*.

The Department of State, which had warned Chamorro before President Solórzano's inauguration that it would give its moral support to the constituted authorities in the event of revolutionary disturbances, informed him after the *coup d'état* that no government assuming power by force could hope for American recognition. It continued its normal diplomatic relations with President Solórzano, however, and refused to accede to the Liberals' request that it seek the coöperation of the other Central American Governments in restoring the former state of affairs.

Chamorro proceeded nevertheless to make himself President of the Republic. His first move was to eliminate the Vice President, who had been in hiding at León since the seizure of the Loma. Dr. Sacasa fled from Nicaragua in November, after 1,200 men had been quartered in his native city with the statement that they would remain there until his resignation was obtained. In January the Congress, from which the supporters of the coalition had been expelled on the ground that they were illegally seated after the 1924 election, declared the vice presidency vacant and elected Chamorro as first *designado*. It then granted Solórzano an indefinite leave of absence. Chamorro thus assumed the Presidency. On April 13 he had the Congress remove four Liberal judges of the Supreme Court, thus bringing all branches of the Government under the control of his own party.

The United States and the other Central American Governments refused to recognize the new régime on the ground that it had come into power by a *coup d'état* and clearly fell within the provisions of the Central American Treaty of 1923. Dr. Sacasa, who claimed that he should rightfully have occupied the Presidency after the withdrawal of Solórzano, had meanwhile visited Washington to seek the intercession of the American Government. He was informed that while the latter would never recognize the Chamorro régime, it was under no obligation under the 1923 treaty to intervene to restore the constitutional order in Nicaragua and that it would not look with sympathy on a resort to arms to bring about a constitutional régime.

The Revolution of 1926–27

The Liberals nevertheless started a revolution on the east coast in May, but this was easily suppressed by Chamorro's troops.   They began a more formidable movement on both coasts in August 1926.   This was suppressed in the western provinces but continued on the east coast where the revolutionists obtained control of several towns.   In August, the United States again emphatically warned Chamorro that it would not recognize him and insisted upon his entering into negotiations with the Liberals.   A peace conference which took place at Corinto through the good offices of the United States failed because the two parties could not agree upon a person to take over the presidency.   Hostilities were resumed on October 30, after a thirty days' truce.

On the same day, in accordance with a promise which he had made to the American Chargé d'Affaires before the peace conference, Chamorro turned over the presidency to the second *designado,* Señor Uriza.   The Conservative leaders then took steps to establish a régime which could hope to obtain recognition from the United States. Eighteen Senators and Deputies who had been removed by Chamorro were invited to return and resume their seats, though several supporters of the coalition who had been seated by Congress in 1925 were replaced by Conservatives who had been declared elected by the National Board of Elections before that body was removed by Martínez.   On November 11, 1926, the reconstituted Congress with 51 present out of a legal membership of 67 elected Adolfo Díaz as *designado* by 44 votes against 2 for ex-President Solórzano.   Five Liberals refrained from voting on the ground that an infraction of the rules of procedure had prevented a full attendance of the members of their party.   Señor Díaz thus became President of the Republic.

The constitutionality of Díaz' election has been the subject of much controversy.   His supporters asserted that the procedure which was followed was the only one possible in view of the provision of Article 106 of the constitution to the effect that:

In case of the absolute or temporary default of the President of the Republic, the executive power shall devolve upon the Vice President, and in default of the latter upon one of the Designates in the order of their election. In the latter case, should Congress be in session, it shall be its duty to authorize the intrustment of the office to the representative whom it may designate, who must fulfill the requirements for President of the Republic.

Solórzano had resigned and Vice President Sacasa was absent from Nicaragua, and thus could not assume office. The Liberals, on the other hand, asserted that Sacasa had been the constitutional President of Nicaragua since the resignation of Solórzano and that he had not lost his rights by the fact that he had been compelled to leave Nicaragua by threats of violence. The Government of the United States accepted the former point of view and recognized President Díaz on November 17. A public statement issued by the Secretary of State on that day explaining the legal basis of this decision stated that Diaz had indicated that he would make overtures of peace and amnesty to his opponents and would offer the Liberals a participation in the new Government. Mr. Kellogg expressed the hope that these proposals would be accepted in the interests of peace.[32] The peace offers which Señor Díaz subsequently made, however, were rejected by the Liberals, who again insisted upon the appointment of an impartial Provisional President as the basis of any settlement.

On December 1, Dr. Sacasa landed at Puerto Cabezas and set up what claimed to be the constitutional Government of Nicaragua. Later in the same month, the Liberals won the decisive victory of Pearl Lagoon, which gave them control of the greater part of the east coast. In January General Moncada, the head of the Liberal army, marched into the interior and small bands of Liberals rose in arms in the west coast districts to support him. A large part of the city of Chinandega was destroyed by fire fol-

[32] *Ibid.*, p. 64.

lowing a battle there and the whole conflict assumed a more and more sanguinary and destructive character.

By this time it was evident that the revolutionists were receiving substantial aid from official or private sources in Mexico. That country had been the only power which had recognized Dr. Sacasa as President of Nicaragua, and there was conclusive evidence that arms and ammunition, some of which had apparently belonged to the Mexican Government, had been sent to the Liberals in ships fitted out in Mexican ports with the knowledge and in some cases with the encouragement of Mexican officials. The failure of the peace conference at Corinto in October had been due partly to the fact that the Liberal delegates asserted that the acceptance of any compromise candidate for the presidency would be a breach of faith with their Mexican allies.[33]

The fighting on the east coast had seriously endangered the lives and interests of the American and British citizens who formed a large part of the population and controlled most of the industry and trade of that region. Both sides had attempted to impose taxes on foreign commerce, and the work of the customs service had become very difficult. Several warships had consequently been sent to various Nicaraguan ports, and American forces had established a neutral zone for the protection of foreigners at Bluefields during the outbreak in May and again when hostilities recommenced in August.

On November 15, 1926, President Díaz formally requested the assistance of the United States in protecting American lives and property. He also asked for help in reaching a solution of the crisis which would "avoid further hostilities and invasions on the part of the Government of Mexico." The Department of State replied that it could only give him such moral support as it accorded

[33] See President Coolidge's special message to Congress, January 10, 1927, Sixty-ninth Congress, Second Session, House Document No. 633.

to any friendly Government threatened by a revolutionary movement. In February it declined to consider a proposal from President Díaz for a treaty under which the United States would maintain the territorial integrity and the internal stability of Nicaragua. The Government of the United States continued, however, to take measures for the protection of American interests. Neutral zones were established at several of the principal towns on the east coast, and in January, after the British and Italian representatives at Managua had urged that measures be taken to protect their nationals, the Legation Guard was reëstablished in that city. This action soon led to the establishment of a neutral zone along the whole line of the railway, with American marines in the principal towns, to keep open communication with the coast. In March, when the American consular agent at Matagalpa was attacked by unknown parties, marines were sent to that city. By March 15, 1927, the American forces in Nicaragua amounted to 2,000 men.

As time went on, the Díaz Administration received an increasing measure of assistance from the United States. The embargo on the export of arms to Nicaragua, which had been imposed by President Coolidge on September 15, 1926, was relaxed in December to permit shipments by private firms to the Nicaraguan Government, since it was considered unfair to prevent the recognized authorities from obtaining war supplies when the revolutionists were receiving them in large quantities from Mexican and other sources.[34] On February 25, 1927, the United States Government itself sold a quantity of rifles, machine guns and ammunition to the Díaz Government from surplus army stocks, following a precedent established by a similar sale to the Mexican Government in 1923. In March, it raised no objection to a small loan to Nicaragua by American bankers, although it "did not suggest or recommend this

[34] *Ibid.*, p. 6.

loan and assumed no responsibility in connection with the transaction." [35] The revolutionists, moreover, complained that many of the military measures taken by the United States for the protection of foreigners had the effect of hampering their military operations.

Acrimonious discussion in Congress and in the American press made it clear that a large section of American public opinion disapproved of the policy which the Government of the United States had adopted. Furthermore, reports of events in Nicaragua, often distorted by persons who wished for commercial or political reasons to create hostility to the United States, were causing an increasingly unfriendly feeling throughout Latin America, with unfortunate effects upon American interests there.[36] President Coolidge, however, emphatically defended the propriety and necessity of the steps which had been taken in a special message which he sent to Congress on January 10, 1927. After describing the Nicaraguan situation at length, and referring especially to the aid received by the revolutionists from Mexican sources, the President said:

Manifestly the relation of this Government to the Nicaraguan situation, and its policy in the existing emergency, are determined by the facts which I have described. The proprietary rights of the United States in the Nicaraguan canal route, with the necessary implications growing out of it affecting the Panama Canal, together with the obligations flowing from the investments of all classes of our citizens in Nicaragua, place us in a position of peculiar responsibility. I am sure it is not the desire of the United States to intervene in the internal affairs of Nicaragua or of any other Central American republic. Nevertheless it must be said that we have a very definite and special interest in the maintenance of order and good government in Nicaragua at the present time, and that the stability, prosperity, and independence of all Central American countries can never be a matter of indifference to us. The United States can not,

[35] *The United States and Nicaragua*, p. 70.

[36] For a brief discussion of Latin American opinion regarding the Nicaraguan affair, see Isaac Joslin Cox, *Nicaragua and the United States, 1909–1927* (World Peace Foundation), p. 786 ff.

therefore, fail to view with deep concern any serious threat to stability and constitutional government in Nicaragua tending toward anarchy and jeopardizing American interests, especially if such state of affairs is contributed to or brought about by outside influences or by any foreign power. It has always been and remains the policy of the United States in such circumstances to take the steps that may be necessary for the preservation and protection of the lives, the property, and the interests of its citizens and of this Government itself. In this respect I propose to follow the path of my predecessors.

Consequently, I have deemed it my duty to use the powers committed to me to insure the adequate protection of all American interests in Nicaragua, whether they be endangered by internal strife or by outside interference in the affairs of that Republic.

THE STIMSON MISSION

In April 1927 President Coolidge sent the Hon. Henry L. Stimson to Nicaragua as his personal representative with broad powers to act on behalf of the United States.[37] Both sides by this time apparently realized the impossibility of hoping for the restoration of peace without American assistance. While General Moncada had reached the interior of the Republic, he had achieved no decisive victory over the Government forces there and the military situation appeared to be approaching a stalemate. Guerrilla bands more or less loosely connected with the regular forces on either side were committing depredations and molesting noncombatants throughout the country, and the increasing cruelty and demoralization which always characterize a long drawn out Central American civil war were making all of the saner elements in the country more and more anxious for a return of peace.[38] Both sides had already indicated a willingness for a settlement based on the supervision of the approaching presidential elections by the United States, but the Liberals had con-

[37] Mr. Stimson has described the events of his mission in his book entitled *American Policy in Nicaragua*, New York, 1927.
[38] Stimson, *op. cit.*, p. 53.

tinued to insist that Díaz withdraw in favor of a neutral Provisional President. After a study of the situation, however, Mr. Stimson reached the conclusion that Díaz' continuance in office until a new constitutional government could be chosen offered the only practicable solution, because it was impossible to find any Nicaraguan who could be said to be entirely neutral and impartial and because any attempt to have the Congress elect a substitute for President Díaz under the provisions of the Nicaraguan Constitution "would almost certainly in the present situation become the occasion of further bitter factional strife." [39]

Mr. Stimson, therefore, worked out a solution on this basis. On April 22, President Díaz proposed the following peace terms to the revolutionists: [40]

1. Immediate general peace and delivery of arms simultaneously by both parties into American custody;
2. General amnesty and return of exiles and return of confiscated property;
3. Participation in the Díaz cabinet by representative Liberals;
4. The organization of a Nicaraguan constabulary on a nonpartisan basis, to be commanded by American officers;
5. Supervision of 1928 and subsequent elections by Americans who would have ample police power to make effective such supervision;
6. A temporary continuance of a sufficient force of American marines to secure the enforcement of peace terms.

Mr. Stimson then held an interview with General Moncada at Tipitapa, at which he informed the Liberal leaders [41]

that the United States Government intended to accept the request of the Nicaraguan Government to supervise the elections of 1928; that the retention of President Díaz during the remainder of his term was regarded as essential to that plan and would be insisted upon; that a general disarmament was also

[39] *The United States and Nicaragua*, p. 74.
[40] *Ibid.*, p. 73.
[41] *Ibid.*, p. 74.

necessary for the proper conduct of such an election; and that American forces would be authorized to accept the custody of the arms of the Government and those others willing to lay them down, and to disarm the rest.

Similar statements were made to the accredited representatives of Dr. Sacasa, who had been brought from Puerto Cabezas to the west coast on an American destroyer. General Moncada agreed to persuade his troops to lay down their arms. He warmly approved the proposed supervision of the 1928 election, and, although he objected to the President's continuing in office, he said that he would not oppose the American troops if the United States insisted on this point.

At a second conference at Tipitapa on May 11, General Moncada informed Mr. Stimson that his army had consented to the proposed general disarmament in reliance upon the promise of a fair election under American control in 1928. Mr. Stimson thereupon gave the Liberal leader a letter stating that the President of the United States had consented to supervise the election, to assign American officers to train and command a nonpartisan constabulary to prevent fraud or intimidation, and to leave in Nicaragua until after the election a sufficient force of marines to support the constabulary and to assure proper conditions for the voting. Mr. Stimson's letter also stated that a general amnesty had already been granted, and that he had received assurances from President Díaz that the various branches of the Government would be reorganized in such a way as to restore to the Liberals the offices which members of their party had held before the Chamorro *coup d'état*.

Although Dr. Sacasa refused to accept the terms thus agreed upon, since he maintained that he himself was constitutionally the President of Nicaragua, his opposition did not prevent the execution of the agreement because his forces in the field were willing to proceed under it.

Dr. Sacasa left Puerto Cabezas on May 20. He indicated before his departure that his followers would coöperate in the 1928 election as well as in measures for the restoration of normal conditions.

The peace agreement was carried out without serious difficulty. The troops on both sides were disarmed by the American marines, $10 being paid for each serviceable rifle or machine gun surrendered. The training of the *Guardia Nacional* by American marine officers began on May 12, although the formal agreement between the two Governments covering the details of organization was not signed until December 22. Pending the organization of the new force, the American marines took over the maintenance of order.

The promised political changes were duly carried out by President Díaz. The Liberals declined to accept positions in the cabinet, but the Congress, the Supreme Court and the lower courts were reconstituted as nearly as possible with the members who had been serving before the Chamorro *coup d'état* and special elections were held in certain Liberal districts where disturbed conditions had prevented the choice of new members of Congress in 1926. Liberal governors acceptable to General Moncada were appointed in six departments where the Liberals were especially numerous. A Claims Commission, with a representative of each party and an American chairman, called for the presentation of all claims against the Government arising out of the civil war.

In working out with the Nicaraguan leaders a plan for the conduct of the 1928 election, Mr. Stimson had felt that the United States should not assume the responsibility of supervision unless its representatives were given sufficient authority definitely to assure a free and fair exercise of the suffrage. His personal study of the recent efforts to hold a plebiscite in Tacna-Arica had convinced him of the impossibility of establishing proper conditions for an election without a sufficient control of the police power to maintain order and to prevent intimidation. He had therefore regarded a complete disarmament of the military forces on both sides and the creation of a new nonpartisan constabulary under American officers as indispensable.[42] Since the constabulary obviously would not be able for some time to maintain order without assistance and since its American officers must necessarily be supported and protected in the meantime, the plan adopted involved the retention in Nicaragua of a considerable force of American marines. After the Tipitapa agreement, therefore, the American marines assumed temporarily the greater part of the responsibility for maintaining order. Forces of the new constabulary were available in a short time to assist in this work and to take over the actual policing of the towns, but with the appearance of a new and unexpected military problem in the North the task of maintaining order became much more difficult and the marines became involved in operations of a far more serious character than could reasonably have been anticipated.

SANDINO

The disarmament of the guerrilla bands operating in the interior had been carried out with only a few minor conflicts, during which two marines and eleven Nicaraguans had been killed. The only considerable force which remained under arms was that commanded by Augusto César Sandino, one of the generals in the Liberal army, who had pretended to accept the proposal for a general disarmament in a letter written to Moncada on May 9, but had then withdrawn with his troops into a mountainous, sparsely settled district in the north of the Republic. Two months later, on July 16, with a force of about 400 men, he made a night attack on a detachment of 39

[42] Stimson, *op. cit.*, p. 58–63.

marines and 47 guardia at Ocotal, and the little garrison was saved from annihilation only by the timely arrival of a squadron of American airplanes the next morning. His forces suffered severe losses in this affair, but he continued guerrilla operations in the north, ambushing small marine or guardia patrols and occasionally attacking a weakly garrisoned town. Although additional marines were sent to Nicaragua and an energetic campaign was carried on against him, Sandino and his forces were able to evade capture because of the inaccessible character of the country and because of the ease with which his followers could hide their arms and apparently become simple peasants when pursuit became too hot. Repeated efforts by the American and Nicaraguan authorities and by members of his own family to persuade him to discuss terms on which he would lay down his arms were as unsucessful as were the military operations.

Sandino's activities affected very little the normal political and economic life of Nicaragua except in the remote and unimportant northern districts, where his depredations caused much loss of life and destruction of property. Even there it was possible to afford sufficient military protection in the towns and villages to prevent any serious interference with the 1928 election, although on one occasion the cold-blooded murder of several Liberal political workers, presumably under his orders, shocked the members of both parties. So far as could be determined by a foreign observer, Sandino received little sympathy and practically no effective assistance from the population of the interior, which was much more interested in the contest for control between the two great political parties, to one or another of which nearly every Nicaraguan is an enthusiastic adherent. Outside of Nicaragua, however, Sandino's avowed championship of Nicaragua's independence against foreign aggression won him much sympathy.

The Election of 1928

On May 15, 1927, President Díaz had formally requested American supervision of the 1928 election. He proposed that the electoral machinery should be under the complete control of a commission composed of a representative of each party with an American chairman, and that this commission should have the right to command the services of the new constabulary to insure the proper conduct of the registration and the voting. He also requested that a sufficient force of American marines should remain in the country pending the organization of the constabulary. The President of the United States formally acceded to this request for assistance on June 10 [43] and on July 2 he announced that he would nominate General Frank R. McCoy as chairman of the Electoral Commission.

A new electoral law was enacted by the Nicaraguan Senate on January 10, 1928, but when it reached the Chamber of Deputies, where the followers of General Chamorro were still in the majority, changes which would seriously have diminished the effectiveness of the electoral supervision were made, ostensibly for constitutional reasons. The Department of State insisted that the Stimson Agreement must be carried out not merely technically but also in spirit, and after prolonged negotiations another law in satisfactory form was passed by the Senate in March. It was again defeated in the Chamber of Deputies, but President Díaz, who had consistently carried out his own promises under the Stimson Agreement, issued an Executive Decree granting the necessary authority to the American electoral officials on March 21.

Several troublesome questions arose in connection with the nomination of candidates. General Chamorro, despite the provisions of Article 104 of the Nicaraguan Consti-

[43] *The United States and Nicaragua*, p. 80.

tution[44] was apparently one of the leading contenders for the Conservative nomination. When he called on the Secretary of State in Washington, on October 22, 1927, however, he was handed a written statement reading as follows:[45]

On January 1, 1929, the Government of the United States will be confronted by the necessity of deciding whether it can consistently recognize the incoming administration in Nicaragua as the constitutional government of that country. While the United States is not supporting or opposing any political candidate it is most desirous that there should be no question at that time as to the eligibility under the Constitution of the person who may have prevailed at the presidential elections, since it wishes to extend the fullest and most sympathetic cooperation to the new government.

In these circumstances and in view of the reports that General Chamorro contemplates becoming a candidate for the presidency of Nicaragua in the 1928 elections, the Government of the United States has no choice but to point out that it regards General Chamorro as ineligible under the provisions of the Nicaraguan constitution to the office of President of Nicaragua during any part of the term commencing January 1, 1929.

He subsequently announced that he would not be a candidate, but he was still the acknowledged leader of a very strong faction in opposition to the administration Conservatives headed by President Díaz. The rivalry between these factions made it appear for a time that one of the chief purposes of the American supervision,—to give the two great political parties an opportunity to measure their strength on equal terms,—would be defeated by the failure of the Conservatives to unite upon a candidate. The National Board of Elections refused to recognize either faction as representing the party to the exclusion of the other, and on July 26 the Conservatives finally united on the candidacy of Adolfo Benard, a prominent citizen of Granada.

[44] See *supra*, p. 244.
[45] *The United States and Nicaragua*, p. 83.

On August 20 the Conservative member of the National Board of Elections challenged the eligibility of General Moncada, the Liberal candidate, on various grounds, but his contention was overruled by the majority of the board. While the United States Government made no public statement of its own views as to the propriety of General Moncada's candidacy in view of the provisions of the Central American Treaty of 1923, it may be supposed that it considered the treaty inapplicable in this case because the revolution headed by Moncada had not resulted in the overthrow of the constitutional government and because of the circumstances under which the election was being held.

The registration of voters took place in September and the election itself on November 4. General Moncada received 76,676 votes to 56,987 for Señor Benard, and he was consequently inaugurated as President of Nicaragua on January 1, 1929.

In October, before the election, General Moncada and Señor Benard had exchanged letters agreeing that the successful candidate, whichever he might be, would request the United States also to supervise the presidential election to be held in 1932.

Now that we are witnessing the justice with which those in charge of the American supervision are proceeding [General Moncada wrote], when with generous and praiseworthy earnestness they are extending to us their hand in the development of republican institutions, by means of a true and honest freedom in elections, we who desire an era of peace and industry for Nicaragua might agree to accept this same supervision for one or several further periods of constitutional government. . . .[46]

CAMPAIGN AGAINST SANDINO, 1929–32

It was considered impossible to withdraw the American marines from Nicaragua immediately after the election

[46] *Ibid.*, p. 89.

because the training of the National Guard had not reached a point where that organization could deal with the continuing insurgent activities in the north. Financial difficulties had prevented the enlistment of an adequate number of men, and eighteen months had been too short a time in which to train a Nicaraguan officer personnel. Shortly after President Moncada's inauguration, however, he was informed by the American military authorities that American assistance in maintaining order could not be counted on for an indefinite period and that steps should therefore be taken as soon as possible to strengthen the Guardia. President Moncada was in full agreement with this policy.[47] The Marine Brigade was therefore reduced from the maximum of 5,673 navy and marine personnel on shore just before the 1928 election, to 2,215 men on September 1, 1929, and 1,384 on September 1, 1930.[48]

Sandino left Nicaragua in June 1929, and took up his residence temporarily at Mérida, Mexico. By the latter part of that year conditions in the north had greatly improved, and only small, poorly armed bands remained in the field. The return of the insurgent chief in the spring of 1930 caused renewed activities among his followers and there were many conflicts in the north during the next two years.

By the end of 1930, however, the Guardia had assumed almost the entire responsibility for these operations and was discharging its task in a highly creditable manner. On February 13, 1931, the United States Government announced its intention of withdrawing all marines from combatant duty within the next few months, leaving in Nicaragua only the American officers in the Guardia with an instruction battalion for their support and an aviation section to carry supplies to the northern provinces where

[47] *Annual Report of the Secretary of the Navy, 1929*, p. 6.
[48] *Ibid.*, p. 5; *Annual Report, 1930*, p. 100.

communication by road was impossible. This step was intended to pave the way for the withdrawal of all marine forces immediately after the election of 1932.[49] The program was carried out, and by April 1, 1932, there were in Nicaragua only 753 marine and naval personnel besides the 205 American officers in the Guardia.[50]

On March 31, 1931, the city of Managua was destroyed by an earthquake and fire in which nearly 1,000 people were killed and practically the whole population was rendered homeless. While all available guardia and marine forces were engaged in relief work and the normal activities of the Government were completely paralyzed, Sandino's forces made a surprise attack on the east coast, sacking the town of Cabo Gracias and murdering a large number of civilians, including nine Americans and a few other foreigners. Eight employees of the Standard Fruit and Steamship Company were killed in cold blood after being captured.[51] When this occurred, the Department of State sent the following instructions to its representatives in Nicaragua: [52]

In view of outbreak of banditry in portions of Nicaragua hitherto free from such violence, you will advise American citizens that this Government can not undertake general protection of Americans throughout that country with American forces. To do so would lead to difficulties and commitments which this Government does not propose to undertake. Therefore, the Department recommends to all Americans who do not feel secure under the protection afforded them by the Nicaraguan Government through the Nicaraguan National Guard to withdraw from the country, or at least to the coast towns whence they can be protected or evacuated in case of necessity. Those who remain do so at their own risk and must not expect American forces to be sent inland to their aid.

[49] The United States and Nicaragua, p. 107.
[50] Ibid., p. 108.
[51] Press release, April 16, 1931, Department of State, Press Releases, April 18, 1931, p. 278-9.
[52] The United States and Nicaragua, p. 105.

When this action was criticized in Congress and in the American press, Secretary Stimson pointed out that the existing situation in Nicaragua was very different from that in 1926, when the United States had been able to protect foreigners by the establishment of neutral zones. There was at that time [53]

no organized attempt to murder private citizens of any country. The problem was only to protect them from the inevitable catastrophe of war. . . . Now we have a situation where small groups of confessed outlaws—treated as outlaws by the Nicaraguan Government—are making their way through the jungle to the east coast, with the avowed intention of murdering and pillaging the civilian inhabitants of the country. The terrain where this is taking place is one of the thickest jungles in the world . . . a region where it would be almost impossible for regular troops to operate effectively even if it were attempted.

Pointing out that the Nicaraguan Government was making every effort to deal with the situation with its own forces, Mr. Stimson continued:

Purely from the standpoint of protection, the most effective way to protect the American and foreign civilians who have been suddenly exposed to this danger in the forests of eastern Nicaragua is to give them warning of the danger and an opportunity to escape to the protection of the coast towns; and then for this specially trained constabulary to operate in the jungle against the bandits. If the number of constabulary now on the east coast is not sufficient for that purpose, there are certainly enough elsewhere to reinforce them against these comparatively small bands of outlaws. American naval vessels are standing by at all the threatened east-coast ports with orders to protect life and property at these ports. These ships will remain until the danger is over.

While the Nicaraguan Government was endeavoring to increase the efficiency of the Guardia, and to destroy banditry through military operations, it was at the same time endeavoring to do away with the economic conditions

[53] *Ibid.*, p. 105.

which made banditry possible. So far as funds permitted, President Moncada had carried on a program of road and railroad construction both to give employment to persons who might otherwise become bandits and to open up the country for military and commercial purposes. The depression, however, made this policy very difficult. Despite all efforts to improve the situation, Sandino was still active in the north at the end of President Moncada's Administration, and was in fact carrying his depredations into regions nearer to the more important towns and agricultural districts of the Republic.

SUPERVISION OF ELECTIONS, 1930 AND 1932

In accord with the agreement entered into with his Conservative opponent before the election of 1928, President Moncada soon after his inauguration formally requested the Government of the United States to designate an American citizen to serve as Chairman of the National Board of Elections. This invitation was accepted in May 1930, when Captain Alfred Wilkinson Johnson of the United States Navy was nominated to supervise the Congressional election held in November of that year. On January 4, 1932, Admiral Clark Howell Woodward was similarly nominated to serve as Chairman of the National Board of Elections during the approaching presidential election.[54]

Shortly after Admiral Woodward's appointment, President Moncada sent members of both Nicaraguan political parties to Washington as his personal representatives to discuss with the Secretary of State a plan to choose a constitutional convention, rather than new members of Congress, at the approaching election. The President expressed the opinion that the electoral laws, the Canal Treaty of 1914 and the agreement for the establishment of

[54] *Ibid.*, p. 115–17.

the National Guard were in conflict with the Constitution as it stood, and that amendments should also be adopted to assure the representation of both political parties in certain branches of the Government. General Moncada appears to have obtained some support for this project among the leaders of the Conservative party, but he encountered strong opposition from many of his fellow Liberals, who suspected, despite the President's reiterated denials, that his real purpose was to continue his own control over the Government.

After consulting with the Nicaraguan commissioners, the Secretary of State convinced them that there could be no real question as to the constitutionality of the Canal Treaty, and pointed out that any changes deemed necessary to give specific recognition to the Guardia could easily be secured, as could provisions for minority representation, through the normal procedure for amending the existing Constitution without attempting to adopt a new one. He said that the whole question was of course one for decision by the Nicaraguans themselves, but that in view of its doubt as to the advisability and the legality of the proposed action the United States would not be willing to supervise the 1932 elections if the Nicaraguan Government should decide to have a constitutional assembly chosen. The plan to make immediate changes in the Constitution was therefore abandoned.[55]

The Liberal party had been divided, not only upon the question of the proposed constitutional convention, but also by rivalry for the control of the party machinery. The supporters and the opponents of the President had established two separate organizations, each of which demanded recognition from the National Board of Elections as the legitimate representative of the Liberal party. Admiral Woodward finally ordered that a "plebiscite" be held to determine which candidate should be placed on

[55] *Ibid.*, p. 120–124.

the ballot in the Liberal column, but before the vote was taken the two factions agreed upon the nomination of Dr. Sacasa, who had been the head of the revolutionary government on the east coast in 1927. The Conservatives, after some hesitation as to the advisability of participating in the election at all, in view of the lack of funds for the campaign, nominated Adolfo Díaz for President and General Emiliano Chamorro for Vice President.

The methods adopted in supervising the election of 1932 differed somewhat from those employed in 1928 and 1930, when Americans had been present at every polling place throughout the Republic and large forces of marines had been available to maintain order and to protect the electoral personnel. By 1932 the American forces had been reduced, as we have seen, to a small instruction battalion and an aviation section at Managua, and the responsibility for maintaining order had been transferred entirely to the Guardia. Both to avoid sending Americans into districts where their nationality would expose them to attack by the Sandinistas, and to give Nicaraguan citizens experience in electoral matters, Nicaraguans were appointed as chairmen in 247 of the 429 local electoral boards. This arrangement, which was especially appropriate in view of the fact that subsequent elections would presumably not be supervised by the United States, made it possible to conduct the election with the reduced personnel available as the result of the action of the United States Congress in prohibiting the use of funds for sending additional marines to Nicaragua for electoral purposes.[56] Freedom and fairness in the voting appear to have been guaranteed as effectively as in the two preceding elections, for the central committee of the Conservative party, after the canvas of the votes by Congress had established the defeat of their candidates by a substantial majority, pub-

[56] A provision to this effect was contained in the Naval Appropriation Act for 1933.

lished a manifesto in the Nicaraguan newspapers of December 17, in which they recognized that the result of the election represented the decision of the majority of the voters and pledged their coöperation to the new Administration.

THE INTERPARTY AGREEMENTS

This manifesto, with a Liberal manifesto published on the same day promising fair treatment to all Nicaraguan citizens under the new administration, showed how completely the attitude of the two political parties had changed since the civil war of 1926–7. For some months before the election, the principal leaders of both factions had in fact been coöperating in plans to assure the maintenance of stable government and the settlement of political questions by free and fair elections after the assistance of the United States for these purposes should no longer be available. Their efforts culminated in a series of four interparty agreements, which were signed in October and November 1932. The first of these, though not made public, is understood to have provided for united action in dealing with Sandino. The others provided for participation by the minority party in the work of the Government,—to be brought about so far as possible by immediate executive and congressional action, and to be established on a permanent basis by amendment of the Constitution. Under the new system, both parties would be assured representation in the Congress, the courts, and the municipal governments, and the President of the Republic would have permanent bipartisan commissions to advise and to a certain extent to control him in the conduct of foreign relations and financial affairs. The electoral machinery was to be strengthened and an effort was to be made to assure the appointment of a citizen acceptable to both parties as Chairman of the National Board of Elections.[57]

[57] The text of the second, third and fourth agreements was published in *La Prensa* of Managua, November 17, 1932.

A part of this program was soon afterward carried out. The Conservatives were given representation in the Courts of Appeal when new judges were elected by the Congress in December 1932, and a commission was appointed by Congress a few months later to draw up the constitutional amendments necessary to establish minority representation in other branches of the Government.

A separate agreement, for the maintenance of the non-partisan character of the Guardia, was signed by the Presidential and Vice Presidential candidates of each party on November 5, 1932. The numerous officers who were subsequently appointed from civil life to replace the Americans hitherto serving in the organization were selected in approximately equal numbers from the two great political parties.[58]

On January 2, 1933, the day after the inauguration of Dr. Sacasa as President of the Republic, the last of the American marines were withdrawn from Nicaragua.

THE AGREEMENT WITH SANDINO

With the withdrawal of the American marines, the objective for which Sandino had avowedly been fighting had been realized. There was small prospect of his continuing to obtain foreign support, and the two great political parties had shown that they were determined to assist the Government in putting an end to his operations. He was persuaded, therefore, to enter into peace negotiations, and on February 2, 1933, his representatives signed an agreement with the accredited representatives of the Conservative and Liberal parties providing that his followers should be granted an amnesty and should be permitted to establish an agricultural colony on unoccupied public lands in the valley of the Coco River. He undertook to disarm all of his forces except one hundred men

[58] Department of State, *Press Releases*, December 17, 1932, p. 439.

who were to be incorporated in the Guardia for the purpose of maintaining order in the new colony; and it was agreed that public works should be inaugurated, especially in the northern provinces, in which as many of his followers as possible should be employed. This peace pact was formally accepted by the Nicaraguan Government, and was carried out without serious difficulty.

RECENT FINANCIAL CONDITIONS

Nicaragua's recent political progress, as exemplified in the coöperation of the two parties in measures designed to prevent a recurrence of internal strife and in the establishment of peace and order throughout the Republic, has been the more noteworthy because it has been accomplished in spite of formidable financial and economic difficulties. Nicaragua not only felt the full effects of the world depression, which so disastrously affected political conditions in many other Latin American countries, but also had to repair the losses caused by the civil war of 1926–7, by Sandino's depredations, and by the earthquake which destroyed her capital in 1931. Confronted with abnormal expenses for these purposes and for the military operations in the north, the Government has nevertheless maintained the payment of interest on its public debt, although it has been compelled to obtain the consent of its creditors to a suspension of the amortization for the calendar years 1932 and 1933.[59]

The public debt consists at present of the British bonds of 1909, of which £487,780 were outstanding on February 28, 1933, and of the Guaranteed Customs Bonds, issued to Nicaraguan and foreign claimants in part payment of the awards of the Claims Commission established in 1918, of which $1,117,750 were outstanding on the

[59] Republic of Nicaragua, *Report of the Collector General of Customs and High Commissions for 1932*, p. 38–42.

same date.[60] Under the existing contracts, the Customs Collectorship and the High Commission established by the Financial Plan of 1917 will remain in existence until both of these issues are repaid. Since 1928, the Collector General of Customs has also been resident American member of the High Commission. The principal duty of the latter organization, except when funds have been placed under its control by the Nicaraguan Government for special reasons, is to act as Fiscal Agent for the Guaranteed Customs Bonds.

The currency system, which was one of the chief results of the financial program adopted in 1911, has remained substantially intact, although it has of course been subjected to a severe strain by recent financial conditions. Except for a brief period during the European war, the *cordoba* was maintained at par until the depression. Late in 1931, it was necessary to institute a system of exchange control, and in the following year an issue of currency secured by government bonds to the amount of $1,500,000 was made to meet urgent public necessities. Despite these measures, it does not appear that there has been any great depreciation of the *cordoba,* even in clandestine transactions.

Claims arising from the civil war of 1926–7 and the subsequent military operations have been submitted to the consideration of a commission established in 1929, consisting of a member from each political party and a chairman nominated by the Secretary of State of the United States. Although special revenues have been set aside for the purpose, funds have been available to pay only a part of the awards thus far made, preference being given to those smallest in amount.[61] The work of the commission was greatly delayed by the destruction of all Government records in the earthquake.

[60] *Ibid.,* p. 11.
[61] *The United States and Nicaragua,* p. 94–5.

The National Bank and the National Railroad are still operated by companies incorporated in the United States, although the entire stock of both companies is owned by the Nicaraguan Government. The bank is managed by an Austrian citizen and the railroad by an American, and the Government has sought to avoid the disadvantages of a purely political control by asking several American citizens to serve on the boards of directors of both companies. In 1930 it appointed the International Acceptance Bank of New York as its depository and fiscal agent in the United States, but this bank did not assume any of the functions of the "bankers" under the Financial Plans of 1917 and 1920.[62]

[62] *Ibid.*, p. 96.

APPENDIX

TREATIES BETWEEN THE UNITED STATES AND THE CARIBBEAN STATES

I. PANAMA

Convention for the Construction of a Ship Canal to Connect the Waters of the Atlantic and Pacific Oceans [1]

Signed at Washington, November 18, 1903; ratification advised by the Senate, February 23, 1904; ratified by the President, February 25, 1904; ratified by Panama, December 2, 1903; ratifications exchanged at Washington, February 26, 1904; proclaimed, February 26, 1904.

The United States of America and the Republic of Panama being desirous to insure the construction of a ship canal across the Isthmus of Panama to connect the Atlantic and Pacific oceans, and the Congress of the United States of America having passed an act approved June 28, 1902, in furtherance of that object, by which the President of the United States is authorized to acquire within a reasonable time the control of the necessary territory of the Republic of Colombia, and the sovereignty of such territory being actually vested in the Republic of Panama, the high contracting parties have resolved for that purpose to conclude a convention and have accordingly appointed as their plenipotentiaries,—

The President of the United States of America, John Hay, Secretary of State, and

The Government of the Republic of Panama, Philippe Bunau-Varilla, Envoy Extraordinary and Minister Plenipotentiary of the Republic of Panama, thereunto specially empowered by said government, who after communicating with each other their respective full powers, found to be in good and due form, have agreed upon and concluded the following articles:

ARTICLE I. The United States guarantees and will maintain the independence of the Republic of Panama.

[1] Reprinted from *Treaty Series* No. 431; Malloy, William M., *Treaties, Conventions, etc.*, II, p. 1349.

ARTICLE II. The Republic of Panama grants to the United States in perpetuity the use, occupation and control of a zone of land and land under water for the construction, maintenance, operation, sanitation and protection of said Canal of the width of ten miles extending to the distance of five miles on each side of the center line of the route of the Canal to be constructed; the said zone beginning in the Caribbean Sea three marine miles from mean low water mark and extending to and across the Isthmus of Panama into the Pacific ocean to a distance of three marine miles from mean low water mark with the proviso that the cities of Panama and Colon and the harbors adjacent to said cities, which are included within the boundaries of the zone above described, shall not be included within this grant. The Republic of Panama further grants to the United States in perpetuity the use, occupation and control of any other lands and waters outside of the zone above described which may be necessary and convenient for the construction, maintenance, operation, sanitation and protection of the said Canal or of any auxiliary canals or other works necessary and convenient for the construction, maintenance, operation, sanitation and protection of the said enterprise.

The Republic of Panama further grants in like manner to the United States in perpetuity all islands within the limits of the zone above described and in addition thereto the group of small islands in the Bay of Panama, named Perico, Naos, Culebra and Flamenco.

ARTICLE III. The Republic of Panama grants to the United States all the rights, power and authority within the zone mentioned and described in Article II of this agreement and within the limits of all auxiliary lands and waters mentioned and described in said Article II which the United States would possess and exercise if it were the sovereign of the territory within which said lands and waters are located to the entire exclusion of the exercise by the Republic of Panama of any such sovereign rights, power or authority.

ARTICLE IV. As rights subsidiary to the above grants the Republic of Panama grants in perpetuity to the United States the right to use the rivers, streams, lakes and other bodies of water within its limits for navigation, the supply of water or waterpower or other purposes, so far as the use of said rivers, streams, lakes and bodies of water and the waters thereof may be necessary and convenient for the construction, maintenance, operation, sanitation and protection of the said Canal.

ARTICLE V. The Republic of Panama grants to the United States in perpetuity a monopoly for the construction, maintenance and operation of any system of communication by means of canal or railroad across its territory between the Caribbean Sea and the Pacific ocean.

ARTICLE VI. The grants herein contained shall in no manner invalidate the titles or rights of private land holders or owners of private property in the said zone or in or to any of the lands or waters granted to the United States by the provisions of any Article of this treaty, nor shall they interfere with the rights of way over the public roads passing through the said zone or over any of the said lands or waters unless said rights of way or private rights shall conflict with rights herein granted to the United States in which case the rights of the United States shall be superior. All damages caused to the owners of private lands or private property of any kind by reason of the grants contained in this treaty or by reason of the operations of the United States, its agents or employees, or by reason of the construction, maintenance, operation, sanitation and protection of the said Canal or of the works of sanitation and protection herein provided for, shall be appraised and settled by a joint Commission appointed by the Governments of the United States and the Republic of Panama, whose decisions as to such damages shall be final and whose awards as to such damages shall be paid solely by the United States. No part of the work on said Canal or the Panama railroad or on any auxiliary works relating thereto and authorized by the terms of this treaty shall be prevented, delayed or impeded by or pending such proceedings to ascertain such damages. The appraisal of said private lands and private property and the assessment of damages to them shall be based upon their value before the date of this convention.

ARTICLE VII. The Republic of Panama grants to the United States within the limits of the cities of Panama and Colon and their adjacent harbors and within the territory adjacent thereto the right to acquire by purchase or by the exercise of the right of eminent domain, any lands, buildings, water rights or other properties necessary and convenient for the construction, maintenance, operation and protection of the Canal and of any works of sanitation, such as the collection and disposition of sewage and the distribution of water in the said cities of Panama and Colon, which, in the discretion of the United States may be necessary and convenient for the construction, maintenance, operation, sanitation and protection of the said Canal and railroad. All such works of sanitation, collection and disposition of sewage and distribution of water in the cities of Panama and Colon shall be made at the expense of the United States, and the Government of the United States, its agents or nominees shall be authorized to impose and collect water rates and sewerage rates which shall be sufficient to provide for the payment of interest and the amortization of the principal of the cost of said works within a period of fifty years and upon the expiration of said term of fifty years the system of sewers and water works shall revert to and become the properties of the cities of Panama and Colon respectively, and the use of the water shall be free to the inhabitants of Panama and Colon, except to the extent that water rates may be necessary for the operation and maintenance of said system of sewers and water.

The Republic of Panama agrees that the cities of Panama and Colon shall comply in perpetuity with the sanitary ordinances whether of a preventive or curative character prescribed by the United States and in case the Government of Panama is unable or fails in its duty to enforce this compliance by the cities of Panama and Colon with the sanitary ordinances of the United States the Republic of Panama grants to the United States the right and authority to enforce the same.

The same right and authority are granted to the United States for the maintenance of public order in the cities of Panama and Colon and the territories and harbors adjacent thereto in case the Republic of Panama should not be, in the judgment of the United States, able to maintain such order.

ARTICLE VIII. The Republic of Panama grants to the United States all rights which it now has or hereafter may acquire to the property of the New Panama Canal Company and the Panama Railroad Company as a result of the transfer of sovereignty from the Republic of Colombia to the Republic of Panama over the Isthmus of Panama and authorizes the New Panama Canal Company to sell and transfer to the United States its rights, privileges, properties and concessions as well as the Panama Railroad and all the shares or part of the shares of that company; but the public lands situated outside of the zone described in Article II of this treaty now included in the concessions to both said enterprises and not required in the construction or operation of the Canal shall revert to the Republic of Panama except any property now owned by or in the possession of said companies within Panama or Colon or the ports or terminals thereof.

ARTICLE IX. The United States agrees that the ports at either entrance of the Canal and the waters thereof, and the Republic of Panama agrees that the towns of Panama and Colon shall be free for all time so that there shall not be imposed or collected custom house tolls, tonnage, anchorage, lighthouse, wharf, pilot, or quarantine dues or any other charges or taxes of any kind upon any vessel using or passing through the Canal or belonging to or employed by the United States, directly or indirectly, in connection with the construction, maintenance, operation, sanitation and protection of the main Canal, or auxiliary works, or upon the cargo, officers, crew, or passengers of any such vessels, except such tolls and charges as may be imposed by the United States for the use of the Canal and other works, and except tolls and charges imposed by the Republic of Panama upon merchandise destined to be introduced for the consumption of the rest of the Republic of Panama, and upon vessels touching at the ports of Colon and Panama and which do not cross the Canal.

The Government of the Republic of Panama shall have the right to establish in such ports and in the towns of Panama and Colon such houses and guards as it may deem necessary to collect duties on importations destined to other portions of Panama and to prevent contraband trade. The United States shall have the right to make use of the towns and harbors of Panama and Colon as places of anchorage, and for making repairs, for loading, unloading, depositing, or transshipping cargoes either in transit or destined for the service of the Canal and for other works pertaining to the Canal.

ARTICLE X. The Republic of Panama agrees that there shall not be imposed any taxes, national, municipal, departmental, or of any other class, upon the Canal, the railways and auxiliary works, tugs and other vessels employed in the service of the Canal, store houses, work shops, offices, quarters for laborers, factories of all kinds, warehouses, wharves, machinery and other works, property, and effects appertaining to the Canal or railroad and auxiliary works, or their officers or employees, situated within the cities of Panama and Colon, and that there shall not be imposed contributions or charges of a personal character of any kind upon officers, employees, laborers, and other individuals in the service of the Canal and railroad and auxiliary works.

ARTICLE XI. The United States agrees that the official dispatches of the Government of the Republic of Panama shall be transmitted over any telegraph and telephone lines established for canal purposes and used for public and private business at rates not higher than those required from officials in the service of the United States.

ARTICLE XII. The Government of the Republic of Panama shall permit the immigration and free access to the lands and workshops of the Canal and its auxiliary works of all employees and workmen of whatever nationality under contract to work upon or seeking employment upon or in any wise connected with the said Canal and its auxiliary works, with their respective families, and all such persons shall be free and exempt from the military service of the Republic of Panama.

ARTICLE XIII. The United States may import at any time into the said zone and auxiliary lands, free of custom duties, imposts, taxes, or other charges, and without any restrictions, any and all vessels, dredges, engines, cars, machinery, tools, explosives, materials, supplies, and other articles necessary and convenient in the construction, maintenance, operation, sanitation and protection of the Canal and auxiliary works, and all provisions, medicines, clothing, supplies and other things necessary and convenient for the officers, employees, workmen and laborers in the service and employ of the United States and for their families. If any such articles are disposed of for use outside of the zone and auxiliary lands granted to the United States and within the territory of the Republic, they shall be subject to the same import or other duties as like articles imported under the laws of the Republic of Panama.

ARTICLE XIV. As the price or compensation for the rights, powers and privileges granted in this convention by the Republic of Panama to the United States, the Government of the United States agrees to pay to the Republic of Panama the sum of ten million dollars ($10,000,000) in gold coin of the United States on the exchange of the ratification of this convention and also an annual payment during the life of this convention of two hundred and fifty thousand dollars ($250,000) in like gold coin, beginning nine years after the date aforesaid.

The provisions of this Article shall be in addition to all other benefits assured to the Republic of Panama under this convention.

But no delay or difference of opinion under this Article or any other provisions of this treaty shall affect or interrupt the full operation and effect of this convention in all other respects.

ARTICLE XV. The joint commission referred to in Article VI shall be established as follows:

The President of the United States shall nominate two persons and the President of the Republic of Panama shall nominate two persons and they shall proceed to a decision; but in case of disagreement of the Commission (by reason of their being equally divided in conclusion) an umpire shall be appointed by the two Governments who shall render the decision. In the event of the death, absence, or incapacity of a Commissioner or Umpire, or of his omitting, declining or ceasing to act, his place shall be filled by the appointment of another person in the manner above indicated. All decisions by a majority of the Commission or by the Umpire shall be final.

Article XVI. The two Governments shall make adequate provision by future agreement for the pursuit, capture, imprisonment, detention and delivery within said zone and auxiliary lands to the authorities of the Republic of Panama of persons charged with the commitment of crimes, felonies or misdemeanors without said zone and for the pursuit, capture, imprisonment, detention and delivery without said zone to the authorities of the United States of persons charged with the commitment of crimes, felonies and misdemeanors within said zone and auxiliary lands.

Article XVII. The Republic of Panama grants to the United States the use of all the ports of the Republic open to commerce as places of refuge for any vessels employed in the Canal enterprise, and for all vessels passing or bound to pass through the Canal which may be in distress and be driven to seek refuge in said ports. Such vessels shall be exempt from anchorage and tonnage dues on the part of the Republic of Panama.

Article XVIII. The Canal, when constructed, and the entrances thereto shall be neutral in perpetuity, and shall be opened upon the terms provided for by Section I of Article three of, and in conformity with all the stipulations of, the treaty entered into by the Governments of the United States and Great Britain on November 18, 1901.

Article XIX. The Government of the Republic of Panama shall have the right to transport over the Canal its vessels and its troops and munitions of war in such vessels at all times without paying charges of any kind. The exemption is to be extended to the auxiliary railway for the transportation of persons in the service of the Republic of Panama, or of the police force charged with the preservation of public order outside of said zone, as well as to their baggage, munitions of war and supplies.

Article XX. If by virtue of any existing treaty in relation to the territory of the Isthmus of Panama, whereof the obligations shall descend or be assumed by the Republic of Panama, there may be any privilege or concession in favor of the Government or the citizens and subjects of a third power relative to an interoceanic means of communication which in any of its terms may be incompatible with the terms of the present convention, the Republic of Panama agrees to cancel or modify such treaty in due form, for which purpose it shall give to the said third power the requisite notification within the term of four months from the date of the present convention, and in case the existing treaty contains no clause permitting its modifications or annulment, the Republic of Panama agrees to procure its modification or annulment in such form that there shall not exist any conflict with the stipulations of the present convention.

ARTICLE XXI. The rights and privileges granted by the Republic of Panama to the United States in the preceding Articles are understood to be free of all anterior debts, liens, trusts, or liabilities, or concessions or privileges to other Governments, corporations, syndicates or individuals, and consequently, if there should arise any claims on account of the present concessions and privileges or otherwise, the claimants shall resort to the Government of the Republic of Panama and not to the United States for any indemnity or compromise which may be required.

ARTICLE XXII. The Republic of Panama renounces and grants to the United States the participation to which it might be entitled in the future earnings of the Canal under Article XV of the concessionary contract with Lucien N. B. Wyse now owned by the New Panama Canal Company and any and all other rights or claims of a pecuniary nature arising under or relating to said concession, or arising under or relating to the concessions to the Panama Railroad Company or any extension or modification thereof; and it likewise renounces, confirms and grants to the United States, now and hereafter, all the rights and property reserved in the said concessions which otherwise would belong to Panama at or before the expiration of the terms of ninety-nine years of the concessions granted to or held by the above mentioned party and companies, and all right, title and interest which it now has or may hereafter have, in and to the lands, canal, works, property and rights held by the said companies under said concessions or otherwise, and acquired or to be acquired by the United States from or through the New Panama Canal Company, including any property and rights which might or may in the future either by lapse of time, forfeiture or otherwise, revert to the Republic of Panama under any contracts or concessions, with said Wyse, the Universal Panama Canal Company, the Panama Railroad Company and the New Panama Canal Company.

The aforesaid rights and property shall be and are free and released from any present or reversionary interest in or claims of Panama and the title of the United States thereto upon consummation of the contemplated purchase by the United States from the New Panama Canal Company, shall be absolute, so far as concerns the Republic of Panama, excepting always the rights of the Republic specifically secured under this treaty.

ARTICLE XXIII. If it should become necessary at any time to employ armed forces for the safety or protection of the Canal, or of the ships that make use of the same, or the railways and auxiliary works, the United States shall have the right, at all times and in its discretion, to use its police and its land and naval forces or to establish fortifications for these purposes.

ARTICLE XXIV. No change either in the Government or in the laws and treaties of the Republic of Panama shall, without the consent of the United States, affect any right of the United States under the present convention, or under any treaty stipulation between the two countries that now exists or may hereafter exist touching the subject matter of this convention.

If the Republic of Panama shall hereafter enter as a constituent into any other Government or into any union or confederation of states, so as to merge her sovereignty or independence in such Government, union or confederation, the rights of the United States under this convention shall not be in any respect lessened or impaired.

ARTICLE XXV. For the better performance of the engagements of this convention and to the end of the efficient protection of the Canal and the preservation of its neutrality, the Government of the Republic of Panama will sell or lease to the United States lands adequate and necessary for naval or coaling stations on the Pacific coast and on the western Caribbean coast of the Republic at certain points to be agreed upon with the President of the United States.

ARTICLE XXVI. This convention when signed by the Plenipotentiaries of the Contracting Parties shall be ratified by the respective Governments and the ratifications shall be exchanged at Washington at the earliest date possible.

In faith whereof the respective Plenipotentiaries have signed the present convention in duplicate and have hereunto affixed their respective seals.

Done at the City of Washington the 18th day of November in the year of our Lord nineteen hundred and three.

JOHN HAY [SEAL]
P. BUNAU VARILLA [SEAL]

II. DOMINICAN REPUBLIC

1. Convention respecting Assistance of the United States in the Collection and Application of the Customs Revenues of the Dominican Republic [2]

Signed at Santo Domingo, February 8, 1907; ratification advised by the Senate, with amendments, February 25, 1907; ratified by the President, June 22, 1907; ratified by the Dominican Republic, June 18, 1907; ratifications exchanged at Washington, July 8, 1907; proclaimed, July 25, 1907.

Whereas during disturbed political conditions in the Dominican Republic debts and claims have been created, some by regular and some by revolutionary governments, many of doubtful validity in whole or in part, and amounting in all to over $30,-000,000 nominal or face value;

And Whereas the same conditions have prevented the peaceable and continuous collection and application of National revenues for payment of interest or principal of such debts or for liquidation and settlement of such claims; and the said debts and claims continually increase by accretion of interest and are a grievous burden upon the people of the Dominican Republic and a barrier to their improvement and prosperity;

And Whereas the Dominican Government has now effected a conditional adjustment and settlement of said debts and claims under which all its foreign creditors have agreed to accept about $12,407,000 for debts and claims amounting to about $21,184,-000 of nominal or face value, and the holders of internal debts or claims of about $2,028,258 nominal or face value have agreed to accept about $645,827 therefor, and the remaining holders of internal debts or claims on the same basis as the assets already given will receive about $2,400,000 therefor, which sum the Dominican Government has fixed and determined as the amount which it will pay to such remaining internal debt holders; making the total payments under such adjustment and settlement, including interest as adjusted and claims not yet liquidated, amount to not more than about $17,000,000;

And Whereas a part of such plan of settlement is the issue and sale of bonds of the Dominican Republic to the amount of $20,-000,000 bearing five per cent interest payable in fifty years and redeemable after ten years at 102½ and requiring payment of at least one per cent per annum for amortization, the proceeds of

[2] Reprinted from *Treaty Series* No. 465; Malloy, William M., *Treaties, Conventions, etc.*, I, p. 418.

said bonds, together with such funds as are now deposited for the benefit of creditors from customs revenues of the Dominican Republic heretofore received, after payment of the expenses of such adjustment, to be applied first to the payment of said debts and claims as adjusted and second out of the balance remaining to the retirement and extinction of certain concessions and harbor monopolies which are a burden and hindrance to the commerce of the country and third the entire balance still remaining to the construction of certain railroads and bridges and other public improvements necessary to the industrial development of the country;

And Whereas the whole of said plan is conditioned and dependent upon the assistance of the United States in the collection of customs revenues of the Dominican Republic and the application thereof so far as necessary to the interest upon and the amortization and redemption of said bonds, and the Dominican Republic has requested the United States to give and the United States is willing to give such assistance:

The Dominican Government, represented by its Minister of State for Foreign Relations, Emiliano Tejera, and its Minister of State for Finance and Commerce, Federico Velásquez H., and the United States Government, represented by Thomas C. Dawson, Minister Resident and Consul General of the United States to the Dominican Republic, have agreed:

I. That the President of the United States shall appoint, a General Receiver of Dominican Customs, who, with such Assistant Receivers and other employees of the Receivership as shall be appointed by the President of the United States in his discretion, shall collect all the customs duties accruing at the several customs houses of the Dominican Republic until the payment or retirement of any and all bonds issued by the Dominican Government in accordance with the plan and under the limitations as to terms and amounts hereinbefore recited; and said General Receiver shall apply the sums so collected, as follows:

First, to paying the expenses of the receivership; second, to the payment of interest upon said bonds; third, to the payment of the annual sums provided for amortization of said bonds including interest upon all bonds held in sinking fund; fourth, to the purchase and cancellation or the retirement and cancellation pursuant to the terms thereof of any of said bonds as may be directed by the Dominican Government; fifth, the remainder to be paid to the Dominican Government.

The method of distributing the current collections of revenue in order to accomplish the application thereof as hereinbefore provided shall be as follows:

The expenses of the receivership shall be paid by the Receiver as they arise. The allowances to the General Receiver and his assistants for the expenses of collecting the revenues shall not exceed five per cent unless by agreement between the two Governments.

On the first day of each calendar month the sum of $100,000 shall be paid over by the Receiver to the Fiscal Agent of the loan, and the remaining collection of the last preceding month shall be paid over to the Dominican Government, or applied to the sinking fund for the purchase or redemption of bonds, as the Dominican Government shall direct.

Provided, that in case the customs revenues collected by the General Receiver shall in any year exceed the sum of $3,000,000, one half of the surplus above such sum of $3,000,000 shall be applied to the sinking fund for the redemption of bonds.

II. The Dominican Government will provide by law for the payment of all customs duties to the General Receiver and his assistants, and will give to them all needful aid and assistance and full protection to the extent of its powers. The Government of the United States will give to the General Receiver and his assistants such protection as it may find to be requisite for the performance of their duties.

III. Until the Dominican Republic has paid the whole amount of the bonds of the debt its public debt shall not be increased except by previous agreement between the Dominican Government and the United States. A like agreement shall be necessary to modify the import duties, it being an indispensable condition for the modification of such duties that the Dominican Executive demonstrate and that the President of the United States recognize that, on the basis of exportations and importations to the like amount and the like character during the two years preceding that in which it is desired to make such modification, the total net customs receipts would at such altered rates of duties have been for each of such two years in excess of the sum of $2,000,000 United States gold.

IV. The accounts of the General Receiver shall be rendered monthly to the Contaduria General of the Dominican Republic and to the State Department of the United States and shall be subject to examination and verification by the appropriate officers of the Dominican and the United States Governments.

V. This agreement shall take effect after its approval by the

Senate of the United States and the Congress of the Dominican Republic.

Done in four originals, two being in the English language, and two in the Spanish, and the representatives of the high contracting parties signing them in the City of Santo Domingo this 8th day of February, in the Year of our Lord 1907.

THOMAS C. DAWSON
EMILIANO TEJERA
FEDERICO VELÁZQUEZ H.

2. Convention of Ratification as Contained in the Agreement of Evacuation of June 30, 1922 [3]

Signed at Santo Domingo, June 12, 1924; ratification advised by the Senate, January 21, 1925; ratified by the President, June 1, 1925; ratified by the Dominican Republic, June 30, 1925; ratifications exchanged at Santo Domingo, December 4, 1925; proclaimed, December 8, 1925.

Whereas, in the month of May, 1916, the territory of the Dominican Republic was occupied by the forces of the United States of America, during which occupation there was established, in substitution of the Dominican Government, a Military Government which issued governmental regulations under the name of Executive Orders and Resolutions and Administrative Regulations, and also celebrated several contracts by virtue of said Executive Orders or by virtue of some existing laws of the Republic;

Whereas, the Dominican Republic has always maintained its right to self-government, the disoccupation of its territory and the integrity of its sovereignty and independence; and the Government of the United States has declared that, on occupying the territory of the Dominican Republic, it never had, nor has at present, the purpose of attacking the sovereignty and independence of the Dominican Nation; and these rights and declarations gave rise to a Plan or *Modus Operandi* of Evacuation signed on June 30, 1922, by Monseñor A. Nouel, General Horacio Vasquez, Don Federico Velásquez y H., Don Elías Brache, hijo, and Don Francisco J. Peynado, and the Department of State, represented by the Honorable William W. Russell, Envoy Extraordinary and Minister Plenipotentiary of the United States in the Dominican Republic, and the Honorable Sumner Welles, Commissioner of the President of the United States, which met

[3] Reprinted from *Treaty Series* No. 729.

with the approval of the Dominican people, and which approval was confirmed at the elections that took place on March 15, of the present year;

Whereas, although the Dominican Republic has never delegated authority to any foreign power to legislate for it, still, it understands that the internal interests of the Republic require the validation or ratification of several of the Executive Orders and Resolutions, published in the Official Gazette, as well as the Administrative Regulations and Contracts of the Military Government celebrated by virtue of said Orders or of any Law of the Republic; and, on its part, the United States considers that it is also to its interest that said acts be validated or ratified; for these reasons one of the stipulations in the above-mentioned Plan of Evacuation provides for the celebration of a Treaty or Convention of Ratification or Validation of said Orders, Resolutions, Regulations and Contracts;

Therefore, the United States of America and the Dominican Republic, desirous of celebrating the above-mentioned Treaty or Convention, have named for this purpose their Plenipotentiaries as follows:

The President of the United States, William W. Russell, Envoy Extraordinary and Minister Plenipotentiary of the United States in Santo Domingo, and,

The Provisional President of the Dominican Republic, Don Horacio Vasquez, Don Frederico Velásquez y H., and Don Francisco J. Peynado, who, after having exchanged their full powers, and after having found them in due and proper form, have agreed upon the following:

I. The Dominican Government hereby recognizes the validity of all the Executive Orders and Resolutions, promulgated by the Military Government and published in the Official Gazette, which may have levied taxes, authorized expenditures, or established rights on behalf of third persons, and the administrative regulations issued, and contracts which may have been entered into, in accordance with those Orders or with any law of the Republic. Those Executive Orders and Resolutions, Administrative Regulations and Contracts are those listed below:

[Here follows the list.]

The Dominican Government likewise agrees that those Executive Orders, those resolutions, those administrative regulations, and those contracts shall remain in full force and effect unless and until they are abrogated by those bodies which, in accordance with the Dominican Constitution, can legislate. But, this ratification, in so far as concerns those of the above mentioned Executive Orders, resolutions, administrative regulations, and contracts, which have been modified or abrogated by other Executive Orders, resolutions, or administrative regulations of the Military Government, only refers to the legal effects which they created while they were in force.

The Dominican Government further agrees that neither the subsequent abrogation of those Executive Orders, resolutions, administrative regulations, or contracts, or any other law, Executive Order, or other official act of the Dominican Government, shall affect the validity or security of rights acquired in accordance with those orders, those resolutions, those administrative regulations and those contracts of the Military Government; the controversies which may arise related with those rights acquired will be determined solely by the Dominican Courts, subject, however, in accordance with the generally accepted rules and principles of international law, to the right of diplomatic intervention if those Courts should be responsible for cases of notorious injustice or denial of justice. The determination of such cases in which the interests of the United States and the Dominican Republic only are concerned shall, should the two Governments disagree, be by arbitration. In the carrying out of this agreement, in each individual case, the High Contracting Parties, once the necessity of arbitration is determined, shall conclude a special agreement defining clearly the scope of the dispute, the scope of the powers of the arbitrators, and the periods to be fixed for the formation of the arbitral tribunal and the several stages of the procedure. It is understood that on the part of the United States, such special agreements will be made by the President of the United States, by and with the advice and consent of the Senate thereto, and on the part of the Dominican Republic shall be subject to the procedure required by the Constitution and laws thereof.

II. The Dominican Government, in accordance with the provisions of Article I, specifically recognizes the bond issue of 1918 and the twenty-year five and one-half per cent Customs Administration Sinking Fund Gold Bond Issue authorized in 1922, as legal, binding, and irrevocable obligations of the Republic, and pledges its full faith and credit to the maintenance of the service of those bond issues. With reference to the stipulation contained in Article 10 of the Executive Order No. 735, in accordance with which the loan of five and one-half per cent authorized in 1922 was issued, which provides:—

'That the present customs tariff will not be changed during the life of this loan without previous agreement between the Dominican Government and the Government of the United States;'

the two Governments concerned agree in interpreting this stipulation in the sense that, in accordance with article 3 of the Convention of 1907, a previous agreement between the Dominican Government and the United States shall be necessary to modify the import duties of the Dominican Republic, it being an indispensable condition for the modification of such duties that the Dominican Executive demonstrate and that the President of the United States recognize that, on the basis of exportations and importations to the like amount and the like character during the two years preceding that in which it is desired to make such modification, the total net customs receipts would at such altered rates of duties have been, for each of such two years, in excess of the sum of $2,000,000 United States gold.

III. The Dominican Government and the Government of the United States agree that the Convention signed on February 8, 1907, between the United States and the Dominican Republic, shall remain in force so long as any bonds of the issues of 1918 and 1922 shall remain unpaid, and that the duties of the General Receiver of Dominican Customs appointed in accordance with that Convention shall be extended to include the application of the revenues pledged for the service of those bond issues in accordance with the terms of the Executive Orders and of the contracts under which the bonds were issued.

IV. This arrangement shall take effect after its approval by the Senate of the United States and the Congress of the Dominican Republic.

Done in four originals, two in the English language, and two in the Spanish, and the representatives of the High Contracting Powers signing them in the City of Santo Domingo, this twelfth day of June, nineteen hundred and twenty-four.

[SEAL] WILLIAM W. RUSSELL
[SEAL] HORACIO VASQUEZ
[SEAL] FED^{co} VELÁSQUEZ Y H.
[SEAL] FRAN^c J. PEYNADO

3. Convention to Replace the Convention of February 8, 1907, between the two Governments Providing for the Assistance of the United States in the Collection and Application of the Customs Revenues of the Dominican Republic [4]

Signed at Washington, December 27, 1924; ratification advised by the Senate, January 21, 1925; ratified by the President, January 26, 1925; ratified by the Dominican Republic, August 17, 1925; ratifications exchanged at Washington, October 24, 1925; proclaimed, October 26, 1925.

Whereas a convention between the United States of America and the Dominican Republic providing for the assistance of the United States in the collection and application of the customs revenues of the Dominican Republic, was concluded and signed by their respective Plenipotentiaries at the City of Santo Domingo, on the eighth day of February, one thousand nine hundred and seven, and

Whereas that convention was entered into to enable the Dominican Government to carry out a plan of settlement for the adjustment of debts and claims against the Government; and

Whereas, in accordance with that plan of settlement, the Dominican Republic issued in 1908, bonds to the amount of $20,000,000, bearing 5 per cent interest, payable in 50 years and redeemable after 10 years at 102½, and requiring payment of at least 1 per cent per annum for amortization; and

Whereas additional obligations have been incurred by the Dominican Government in the form of the issuance, in 1918, of bonds to the amount of $5,000,000, bearing 5 per cent interest, payable in 20 years, and redeemable at par on each interest date as the amount of amortization fund available on such interest dates will permit, and requiring payment of at least 5 per cent per annum for amortization; and in the form of the issuance of bonds, in 1922, to the amount of $10,000,000, bearing 5½ per cent interest, payable in 20 years, and redeemable after 8 years at 101 and requiring payment after such period of at least $563,916.67 per annum for amortization; and

Whereas certain of the terms of the contracts under which these bonds have been issued have proven by experience unduly onerous to the Dominican Republic and have compelled it to devote a larger portion of the customs revenues to provide the interest and sinking fund charges pledged to the service of such bonds than is deemed advisable or necessary; and

[4] Reprinted from *Treaty Series* No. 726.

Whereas it is the desire of the Dominican Government and appears to be to the best interest of the Dominican Republic to issue bonds to a total amount of $25,000,000, in order to provide for the refunding on terms more advantageous to the Republic of its obligations represented by the bonds of the three issues above mentioned still outstanding and for a balance remaining after such operation is concluded to be devoted to permanent public improvements and to other projects designed to further the economic and industrial development of the country; and

Whereas the whole of this plan is conditioned and dependent upon the assistance of the United States in the collection of customs revenues of the Dominican Republic and the application thereof so far as necessary to the interest upon and the amortization and redemption of said bonds, and the Dominican Republic has requested the United States to give and the United States is willing to give such assistance:

The United States of America, represented by Charles Evans Hughes, Secretary of State of the United States of America; and the Dominican Republic, represented by Señor José del Carmen Ariza, Envoy Extraordinary and Minister Plenipotentiary of the Dominican Republic in Washington, have agreed:

ARTICLE I. That the President of the United States shall appoint, a General Receiver of Dominican Customs, who, with such Assistant Receivers and other employees of the Receivership as shall be appointed by the President of the United States in his discretion, shall collect all the customs duties accruing at the several customs houses of the Dominican Republic until the payment or retirement of any and all bonds issued by the Dominican Government in accordance with the plan and under the limitations as to terms and amounts hereinbefore recited; and said General Receiver shall apply the sums so collected, as follows:

First, to paying the expenses of the receivership; second, to the payment of interest upon all bonds outstanding; third, to the payment of the annual sums provided for amortization of said bonds including interest upon all bonds held in sinking fund; fourth, to the purchase and cancellation or the retirement and cancellation pursuant to the terms thereof of any of said bonds as may be directed by the Dominican Government; fifth, the remainder to be paid to the Dominican Government.

The method of distributing the current collections of revenue in order to accomplish the application thereof as hereinbefore provided shall be as follows:

The expenses of the receivership shall be paid by the Receiver as they arise. The allowances to the General Receiver and his assistants for the expenses of collecting the revenues shall not exceed five per cent unless by agreement between the two Governments.

On the first day of each calendar month shall be paid over by the Receiver to the Fiscal Agent of the loan a sum equal to one twelfth of the annual interest of all the bonds issued and of the annual sums provided for amortization of said bonds and the remaining collection of the last preceding month shall be paid over to the Dominican Government, or applied to the sinking fund for the purchase or redemption of bonds or for other purposes as the Dominican Government shall direct.

Provided, that in case the customs revenues collected by the General Receiver shall in any year exceed the sum of $4,000,000, 10 per cent of the surplus above such sum of $4,000,000 shall be applied to the sinking fund for the redemption of bonds.

ARTICLE II. The Dominican Government will provide by law for the payment of all customs duties to the General Receiver and his assistants, and will give to them all needful aid and assistance and full protection to the extent of its powers. The Government of the United States will give to the General Receiver and his assistants such protection as it may find to be requisite for the performance of their duties.

ARTICLE III. Until the Dominican Republic has paid the whole amount of the bonds of the debt, its public debt shall not be increased except by previous agreement between the Dominican Government and the United States.

ARTICLE IV. The Dominican Government agrees that the import duties will at no time be modified to such an extent that, on the basis of exportations and importations to the like amount and the like character during the two years preceding that in which it is desired to make such modification, the total net customs receipts would not at such altered rates have amounted for each of such two years to at least $1\frac{1}{2}$ times the amount necessary to provide for the interest and sinking fund charges upon its public debt.

ARTICLE V. The accounts of the General Receiver shall be rendered monthly to the Ministry of Finance and Commerce of the Dominican Republic and to the State Department of the United States and shall be subject to examination and verification by the appropriate officers of the Dominican and the United States Governments.

Article VI. The determination of any controversy which may arise between the Contracting Parties in the carrying out of the provisions of this Convention shall, should the two Governments be unable to come to an agreement through diplomatic channels, be by arbitration. In the carrying out of this agreement in each individual case, the Contracting Parties, once the necessity of arbitration is determined, shall conclude a special agreement defining clearly the scope of the dispute, the scope of the powers of the arbitrators, and the periods to be fixed for the formation of the arbitral tribunal and the several stages of the procedure. The special agreement providing for arbitration shall, in all cases, be signed within a period of three months from the date upon which either one of the Contracting Parties shall notify the other Contracting Party of its desire to resort to arbitration. It is understood that on the part of the United States, such special agreements will be made by the President of the United States by and with the advice and consent of the Senate thereto, and on the part of the Dominican Republic, shall be subject to the procedure required by the Constitution and laws thereof.

Article VII. This agreement shall take effect after its approval by the Contracting Parties in accordance with their respective Constitutional methods. Upon the exchange of ratifications of this convention, which shall take place at Washington as soon as possible, the Convention between the United States of America and the Dominican Republic providing for the assistance of the United States in the collection and application of the customs revenues, concluded and signed at the City of Santo Domingo on the 8th day of February, 1907, shall be deemed to be abrogated.

Done in duplicate in the English and Spanish languages at the City of Washington this 27th day of December, nineteen hundred and twenty-four.

Charles Evans Hughes [seal]
J. C. Ariza [seal]

III. HAITI

1. Treaty respecting Finances, Economic Development and Tranquillity of Haiti [5]

Signed at Port-au-Prince, September 16, 1915; ratification advised by the Senate, February 28, 1916; ratified by the President, March 20, 1916; ratified by Haiti, September 17, 1915; ratifications exchanged at Washington, May 3, 1916; proclaimed, May 3, 1916.

Preamble

The United States and the Republic of Haiti desiring to confirm and strengthen the amity existing between them by the most cordial coöperation in measures for their common advantage;

And the Republic of Haiti desiring to remedy the present condition of its revenues and finances, to maintain the tranquillity of the Republic, to carry out plans for the economic development and prosperity of the Republic and its people;

And the United States being in full sympathy with all of these aims and objects and desiring to contribute in all proper ways to their accomplishment;

The United States and the Republic of Haiti have resolved to conclude a Convention with these objects in view, and have appointed for that purpose, Plenipotentiaries,

The President of the United States, Robert Beale Davis, Junior, Chargé d'Affaires of the United States;

And the President of the Republic of Haiti, Louis Borno, Secretary of State for Foreign Affairs and Public Instruction, who, having exhibited to each other their respective powers, which are seen to be full in good and true form, have agreed as follows:—

Article I. The Government of the United States will, by its good offices, aid the Haitian Government in the proper and efficient development of its agricultural, mineral and commercial resources and in the establishment of the finances of Haiti on a firm and solid basis.

Article II. The President of Haiti shall appoint, upon nomination by the President of the United States, a General Receiver and such aids and employees as may be necessary, who shall collect, receive and apply all customs duties on imports and ex-

[5] Reprinted from *Treaty Series* No. 623; *Treaties, Conventions, etc.*, III, p. 2673.

ports accruing at the several custom houses and ports of entry of the Republic of Haiti.

The President of Haiti shall appoint, upon nomination by the President of the United States, a Financial Adviser, who shall be an officer attached to the Ministry of Finance, to give effect to whose proposals and labors the Minister will lend efficient aid. The Financial Adviser shall devise an adequate system of public accounting, aid in increasing the revenues and adjusting them to the expenses, inquire into the validity of the debts of the Republic, enlighten both Governments with reference to all eventual debts, recommend improved methods of collecting and applying the revenues, and make such other recommendations to the Minister of Finance as may be deemed necessary for the welfare and prosperity of Haiti.

ARTICLE III. The Government of the Republic of Haiti will provide by law or appropriate decrees for the payment of all customs duties to the General Receiver, and will extend to the Receivership, and to the Financial Adviser, all needful aid and full protection in the execution of the powers conferred and duties imposed herein; and the United States on its part will extend like aid and protection.

ARTICLE IV. Upon the appointment of the Financial Adviser, the Government of the Republic of Haiti, in coöperation with the Financial Adviser, shall collate, classify, arrange and make full statement of all the debts of the Republic, the amounts, character, maturity and condition thereof, and the interest accruing and the sinking fund requisite to their final discharge.

ARTICLE V. All sums collected and received by the General Receiver shall be applied, first, to the payment of the salaries and allowances of the General Receiver, his assistants and employees and expenses of the Receivership, including the salary and expenses of the Financial Adviser, which salaries will be determined by previous agreement; second, to the interest and sinking fund of the public debt of the Republic of Haiti; and, third, to the maintenance of the constabulary referred to in Article X, and then the remainder to the Haitian Government for purposes of current expenses.

In making these applications the General Receiver will proceed to pay salaries and allowances monthly and expenses as they arise, and on the first of each calendar month, will set aside in a separate fund the quantum of the collection and receipts of the previous month.

ARTICLE VI. The expenses of the Receivership, including salaries and allowances of the General Receiver, his assistants and employees, and the salary and expenses of the Financial Adviser, shall not exceed five per centum of the collections and receipts from customs duties, unless by agreement by the two Governments.

ARTICLE VII. The General Receiver shall make monthly reports of all collections, receipts and disbursements to the appropriate officer of the Republic of Haiti and to the Department of State of the United States, which reports shall be open to inspection and verification at all times by the appropriate authorities of each of the said Governments.

ARTICLE VIII. The Republic of Haiti shall not increase its public debt except by previous agreement with the President of the United States, and shall not contract any debt or assume any financial obligation unless the ordinary revenues of the Republic available for that purpose, after defraying the expenses of the Government, shall be adequate to pay the interest and provide a sinking fund for the final discharge of such debt.

ARTICLE IX. The Republic of Haiti will not without a previous agreement with the President of the United States, modify the customs duties in a manner to reduce the revenues therefrom; and in order that the revenues of the Republic may be adequate to meet the public debt and the expenses of the Government, to preserve tranquillity and to promote material prosperity, the Republic of Haiti will coöperate with the Financial Adviser in his recommendations for improvement in the methods of collecting and disbursing the revenues and for new sources of needed income.

ARTICLE X. The Haitian Government obligates itself, for the preservation of domestic peace, the security of individual rights and full observance of the provisions of this treaty, to create without delay an efficient constabulary, urban and rural, composed of native Haitians. This constabulary shall be organized and officered by Americans, appointed by the President of Haiti, upon nomination by the President of the United States. The Haitian Government shall clothe these officers with the proper and necessary authority and uphold them in the performance of their functions. These officers will be replaced by Haitians as they, by examination, conducted under direction of a board to be selected by the senior American officer of this constabulary and in the presence of a representative of the Haitian Government, are found to be qualified to assume such duties. The constabulary herein provided for, shall, under the direction of the Haitian Government, have supervision and control of arms and ammunition, military supplies, and traffic therein, throughout the country. The high contracting parties agree that the stipulations in this Article are necessary to prevent factional strife and disturbances.

ARTICLE XI. The Government of Haiti agrees not to surrender any of the territory of the Republic of Haiti by sale, lease, or otherwise, or jurisdiction over such territory, to any foreign government or power, nor to enter into any treaty or contract with any foreign power or powers that will impair or tend to impair the independence of Haiti.

ARTICLE XII. The Haitian Government agrees to execute with the United States a protocol for the settlement, by arbitration or otherwise, of all pending pecuniary claims of foreign corporations, companies, citizens or subjects against Haiti.

ARTICLE XIII. The Republic of Haiti, being desirous to further the development of its natural resources, agrees to undertake and execute such measures as in the opinion of the high contracting parties may be necessary for the sanitation and public improvement of the Republic, under the supervision and direction of an engineer or engineers, to be appointed by the President of Haiti upon nomination by the President of the United States, and authorized for that purpose by the Government of Haiti.

ARTICLE XIV. The high contracting parties shall have authority to take such steps as may be necessary to insure the complete attainment of any of the objects comprehended in this treaty; and, should the necessity occur, the United States will lend an efficient aid for the preservation of Haitian Independence and the maintenance of a government adequate for the protection of life, property and individual liberty.

ARTICLE XV. The present treaty shall be approved and ratified by the high contracting parties in conformity with their respective laws, and the ratifications thereof shall be exchanged in the City of Washington as soon as may be possible.

ARTICLE XVI. The present treaty shall remain in full force and virtue for the term of ten years, to be counted from the day of exchange of ratifications, and further for another term of ten years if, for specific reasons presented by either of the high contracting parties, the purpose of this treaty has not been fully accomplished.

In faith whereof, the respective Plenipotentiaries have signed the present Convention in duplicate, in the English and French languages, and have thereunto affixed their seals.

Done at Port-au-Prince, Haiti, the 16th day of September in the year of our Lord one thousand nine hundred and fifteen.

ROBERT BEALE DAVIS, JR. [SEAL]
Chargé d'Affaires of the United States

LOUIS BORNO [SEAL]
Secrétaire d'Etat des Relations Extérieures et de l'Instruction Publique

2. Additional Act Extending the Duration of the Treaty of September 16, 1915 [6]

Signed at Port au Prince, March 28, 1917.

The Republic of Haiti having recognized as urgent the necessity of a loan for a term of more than ten years destined for the amelioration of its financial and economic situation, considering from now this necessity as a specific reason susceptible of giving to the Convention of September 16, 1915, a duration of twenty years and desiring in consequence to exercise the right which it holds from Article XVI of this Convention;

And the United States of America, conforming itself to Article first of the said Convention and assuring its good offices for the full accomplishment of its aims and objects,

Have decided to conclude an additional act to this Convention, with a view to facilitating a prompt realization of the loan and to offer to the capitalists the serious guarantee which they claim of an uninterrupted stability indispensable to the development of the wealth of the Republic of Haiti;

And have been appointed as Plenipotentiaries,

By the President of the United States of America,

Mr. Arthur Bailly-Blanchard, Envoy Extraordinary and Minister Plenipotentiary of the United States of America,

By the President of the Republic of Haiti,

Mr. Louis Borno, Secretary of State of Foreign Affairs and Public Worship,

Who having exhibited to each other their respective full powers found to be in good and true form, have agreed as follows:

ARTICLE 1. The two High Contracting Parties declare to

[6] Reprinted from *Treaty Series* No. 623A; *Treaties, Conventions, etc.,* III, p. 2677.

admit the urgent necessity for a loan for a period of more than ten years for the benefit of the Republic of Haiti as one of the specific reasons indicated in Article XVI of the Convention of September 16, 1915, and agree to fix at twenty years the life of the said Convention.

ARTICLE 2. The present act shall be approved by the High Contracting Parties in conformity with their respective established procedures and the approvals thereof shall be exchanged in the city of Port-au-Prince as soon as may be possible.

Signed and sealed in duplicate in the English and French languages, at Port-au-Prince, Haiti, the 28th day of March, 1917.

[SEAL]   A. BAILLY-BLANCHARD
[SEAL]   LOUIS BORNO

3. Protocol respecting Establishment of Claims Commission [7]

Signed at Port au Prince, October 3, 1919.

ARTICLE I. In pursuance of the objects of the Treaty concluded September 16, 1915, between the United States of America and the Republic of Haiti to establish the finances of Haiti on a firm and solid basis, the Government of the United States and the Government of Haiti through duly authorized representatives agree upon this Protocol for the purpose of carrying out the objects of the aforesaid Treaty and of giving effect to Article 12 thereof. It is clearly understood that this Protocol does not in fact or by implication extend the provisions of the Treaty of September 16, 1915, hereinbefore mentioned.

ARTICLE II. Since the settlement by arbitration or otherwise of all pending pecuniary claims of foreign corporations, companies, citizens or subjects against Haiti, makes it necessary to assemble, analyze and adjust such claims, the Government of Haiti agrees to constitute forthwith a Claims Commission of three members, one member to be nominated by the Secretary of State for Finance of Haiti; one member to be nominated by the Secretary of State of the United States, and the third member who shall not be a citizen either of Haiti or of the United States to be nominated by the Financial Adviser, the three members so nominated to be appointed by the Government of Haiti.

[7] Reprinted from *Treaty Series* No. 643; *Treaties, Conventions, etc.*, III, p. 2678.

In case a vacancy occurs in the office of any member by reason of his disability or for any other cause, a new member shall be nominated and appointed in the same manner as was the former incumbent.

ARTICLE III. The Claims Commission shall have jurisdiction to examine and pass upon all pecuniary claims against Haiti. It is understood, however, that the Commission shall not have jurisdiction to consider or pass upon:

(1) The indebtedness represented by the three bond issues of 1875, 1896 and 1910, now outstanding;

(2) That to the Banque Nationale de la République d'Haïti, as of December 31, 1916, as acknowledged by the Haytian Government on the 12th of April, 1919;

(3) The sum due as interest as this sum will have been verified and admitted by the Financial Adviser, upon the bonds of the Compagnie Nationale des Chemins de Fer d'Haïti, duly authorized and bearing the guarantee of the Haytian Government, to the amount of $3,544,-548.74; and

(4) So much of the sum due to the Compagnie des Chemins de Fer de la Plaine du Cul-de-Sac on account of the interest guarantee upon its bonds as has as not hitherto been in dispute between the railroad and the Haytian Government, the Government having recognized its obligation to pay to the Compagnie des Chemins de Fer de la Plaine du Cul-de-Sac a sum equal to $41,280 per annum, less the net profits of the railroad.

It is further understood that the claims heretofore presented to the Claims Commission appointed by the decree of November four nineteen sixteen need not be presented de novo to the new Claims Commission who will review the findings of the Commission appointed by the decree of November four nineteen sixteen in respect of these claims, may require the production of further evidence where they deem this necessary and shall make such final awards as seem to them just and equitable.

ARTICLE IV. The Claims Commission shall proceed, as soon as constituted, to hold meetings at Port-au-Prince, or elsewhere in the Republic of Haiti, to formulate rules of procedure for the filing and adjudication of claims.

The Claims Commission may fix the date after which claims may not be filed, but such date shall not be less than six months after the date of the first public announcement by the Commission of its readiness to receive claims. The Commission shall be bound to examine and decide upon every claim within two years from the day of its first meeting. A majority vote of the Commissioners shall constitute a binding decision upon any claim.

ARTICLE V. The Claims Commission shall determine the proportion of each award which is to be paid in cash and the proportion to be paid in bonds of Haiti; and it shall state these amounts respectively in its certificate of award which is to be issued to each creditor in whose favor an award is made, and which is to be surrendered by him to the Secretary of State for Finance upon payment of the award.

ARTICLE VI. In order to make possible the settlement of the awards rendered by the Claims Commission and the refunding of those obligations specifically mentioned in Numbers 1, 2, 3 and 4 in Article III above, and otherwise to establish the finances of Haiti on a firm and solid basis, the Republic of Haiti agrees to issue, upon the terms and at a time to be fixed in accord with the Financial Adviser, but not later than two years after the date of the signature of this Protocol a national loan of 40,000,-000 dollars gold ($40,000,000), payable in thirty years by annual drawings at par, or by purchase below par in the open market. It is agreed that the Government of Haiti shall have the right to pay off the entire loan at any time upon reasonable previous notice after fifteen years from the date of issue.

ARTICLE VII. It is further agreed that this loan, to the issuance of which the President of the United States consents, will be used to pay or otherwise provide for the obligations specifically mentioned and numbered 1, 2, 3 and 4 in Article III hereof, and also the awards rendered by the Claims Commission provided for herein. Provision shall be made for the exchange of the bonds of this loan for the bonds of the issues of 1875, 1896 and 1910, such exchange to take place with due regard for the interest rates of the respective bonds and to be carried on between the Secretary of State for Finance of the Republic of Haiti, in accord with the Financial Adviser, and such agency as may represent the holders of said bonds. After two years from the date of the official announcement of the beginning of the conversion the bonds of this loan not used for the purpose of conversion shall be returned to the Secretary of State for Finance of Haiti at Port-au-Prince for the use of the Government. The holders of any said old bonds which shall not have been presented for exchange within this period of two years shall apply for redemption of the same directly to the Secretary of State for Finance of Haiti. Any surplus remaining after the foreign and domestic indebtedness has been paid or otherwise provided for shall be applied by the Republic of Haiti, in accord with the Financial Adviser, to the construction of necessary public works or to the service of the loan hereinabove authorized.

ARTICLE VIII. It is agreed that the payment of interest and the amortization of this loan will constitute a first charge upon all the internal revenues of Haiti, and a second charge upon the customs revenues of Haiti next in order, until the expiration of the Treaty of September 16, 1915, after payment of salaries, allowances and expenses of the General Receiver and the Financial Adviser and their assistants; and it is further agreed that the control by an officer or officers duly appointed by the President of Haiti, upon nomination by the President of the United States, of the collection and allocation of the hypothecated revenues, will be provided for during the life of the loan after the expiration of the aforesaid Treaty so as to make certain that adequate provision be made for the amortization and interest of the loan.

ARTICLE IX. Each member of the Claims Commission will receive $8,000 gold per annum as salary, and $2,000 gold per annum as expenses; and the Commission is authorized, after approval of the Secretary of State for Finance in accord with the Financial Adviser, to retain the services of such assistants and experts and otherwise to incur such actual and necessary expenses as may be required for the proper discharge of its duties; and it is agreed that upon proper certification by the Secretary of State for Finance, such salaries, allowances and expenses thus authorized will be paid from the General Treasury of the Republic.

ARTICLE X. The Government of Haiti agrees to empower the Commission by appropriate legislation or otherwise to compel the attendance at its sessions in Haiti of witnesses whose testimony is desired in connection with any claim pending before the Commission, and to require the production of papers which the Commission may deem necessary for it to consider. The Government of Haiti further agrees to enact such legislation as may be necessary to give effect to the provisions of this Protocol.

ARTICLE XI. This Protocol will take effect immediately upon signature by the Minister of the United States to Haiti representing the Government of the United States, and by the Secretary of State for Foreign Affairs of Haiti representing the Government of Haiti.

In witness whereof this agreement has been signed and sealed by Mr. Arthur Bailly-Blanchard, Envoy Extraordinary and Minister Plenipotentiary of the United States of America on behalf of the United States, and by Mr. Constantin Benoit, Secretary of State for Foreign Affairs of Haiti on behalf of the République of Haiti.

Done in duplicate in the English and French languages at the City of Port-au-Prince on the third day of October, one thousand nine hundred and nineteen

[SEAL]   A. BAILLY-BLANCHARD
[SEAL]   C. BENOIT
av

4. Haitianization Agreement of August 5, 1931 [8]

The undersigned plenipotentiaries, duly authorized by their respective governments, have agreed upon the following Accord:

ARTICLE I. The services of the Engineers provided for by Article XIII of the Treaty of September 16, 1915, for the sanitation and public improvement of the Republic, and by the Accord of July 17, 1923, regarding the Service Technique d'Agriculture, as well as their foreign aids and employees, shall definitely cease on September 30, 1931, except as provided below in Articles III and IV.

ARTICLE II. Accordingly, on October 1, 1931, the Government of Haiti will assume rightfully and definitely the administration and control of the Direction General des Travaux Publics, of the Service d'Hygiene, and of the Service Technique d'Agriculture, and the President of the Republic will deliver, in conformity with the Constitution and the laws, commissions to the Haitian engineers, physicians, and employees deemed necessary for the functioning of the above mentioned Services.

ARTICLE III. In that which concerns the Service National d'Hygiène, it is understood that in conformity with the laws in force it will have, under the direction of the Secretary of State for the Interior, throughout the Republic, the administration, inspection, and supervision of all of the public services of hygiene, sanitation and quarantine, of the hospitals, rural dispensaries, poor relief, insane asylums and sanitary garages, of the Medical School, the Health Center, the laboratories, etc.

Nevertheless, in the cities of Port-au-Prince and Cape Haitian,

[8] Reprinted from Department of State, *Press Releases*, August 15, 1931, p. 145; Executive Agreement Series, No. 22.

and their immediate environs (that is within a radius of two miles of the cities proper but including also Petionville) where, pending other arrangements and until the conclusion of a protocol for their evacuation, American troops are stationed, an American Scientific Mission shall be especially charged in accord with the laws and regulations now in force with the control of sanitation and chlorination of water.

The Service National d'Hygiène will be entitled, if it so requests, to receive the advice and recommendations of the above mentioned Scientific Mission within the restricted field of sanitation.

The Government agrees to leave to the Mission the sanitary garages at Port-au-Prince and Cape Haitian and the motor equipment strictly necessary for its activities but the Service National d'Hygiène may always requisition the material thus loaned by agreement with the Mission if the need therefor should arise.

The Government of Haiti agrees that in case of epidemic or grave danger menacing the public health within the above mentioned cities of Cape Haitian and Port-au-Prince the Mission will coöperate with the National Public Health Service to combat the danger and for this purpose shall be authorized to make all necessary recommendations, and to make use of all the facilities and all of the organizations of the above mentioned Service; and the Haitian Government, under such circumstances, will take the necessary measures and provide the necessary credits.

ARTICLE IV. The Mission provided for in the preceding article will comprise 3 American medical officers nominated by the Government of the United States and appointed by the President of Haiti. Their status will be assimilated so far as the salary that they receive from the public treasury is concerned to that of Public Health Officers first class provided for by the Law of August 8, 1926. The Mission may also include, in addition, as a maximum 6 hospital corpsmen of the United States Navy who will be paid in conformity with a budget approved by the Minister of Interior upon the basis of the Law of December 5, 1924.

The Mission will have the right to suitable offices at Cape Haitian and Port-au-Prince.

The funds necessary for the payment of the Haitian personnel and for the functioning of the sanitary services in the cities of Cape Haitian and Port-au-Prince will be provided for in a budget which shall be approved in advance by the Minister of Interior.

ARTICLE V. The Accord of August 24, 1918, regarding the communication of projects of Haitian laws to the Legation of the United States of America at Port-au-Prince, is and remains abrogated from this date.

If, nevertheless, the Government of the United States should deem a given law to be seriously inconsistent with any rights arising from provisions of agreements still in force, it will present its views to the Haitian Government through diplomatic channels for all proper purposes.

ARTICLE VI. The Accord of December 3, 1918, relating to the visa of the Financial Adviser on orders of payment issued by the Secretary of State for Finance, on the Receiver-General of Customs, or on the National Bank of the Republic of Haiti, is and remains abrogated. The Minister of Finance shall reach an agreement with the Financial Adviser on the procedure governing the service of payments.

The abrogation of the visa implies an obligation on the part of the Government of Haiti until the liquidation of the services of the Financial Adviser-General Receiver to make its expenditures within the limits of laws and credits voted or decreed with the accord of the Financial Adviser. The Haitian Government will reach agreements with the Financial Adviser regarding the measures affecting sources of revenue pending the liquidation of the services of the Financial Adviser-General Receiver.

ARTICLE VII. The land title registry office (Bureau d'Enregistrement) shall be entirely detached from the Office of the Financial Adviser-General Receiver and will pass under the complete control of the Secretary of Finance upon the signature of this Accord.

ARTICLE VIII. In view of the difficulties which have arisen with regard to the Law of May 26, 1931, it is understood that the travelling or representation allowances of the Legislative Body as provided for in the above mentioned Law, will be paid without delay, starting from April 6, 1931, and up to September 30, 1931, from the general funds of the Treasury. After September 30, 1931, these allowances will be paid in accordance with a balanced budget.

ARTICLE IX. Since the Government of the United States believes that the discharge of the civilian officials and employees in the Services mentioned above in Articles I and II of the present Accord, will be unduly precipitate, and has requested an indemnity for them, the Secretary of State for Finance in accord with the Financial Adviser is authorized to indemnify them upon an equitable basis from the general funds of the Treasury.

Specialists in the Service Technique who, upon the express request of the Government of Haiti, shall desire to remain in their former positions and sign the necessary contracts for this purpose with the Secretary of State for Agriculture shall not have the right to any indemnity by virtue of the liquidation of the Treaty Services.

ARTICLE X. The two Governments agree to continue their discussions regarding the other problems arising from the Treaty.

ARTICLE XI. While awaiting the settlement of the question of the Garde, the two Governments agree to maintain the "status quo" established by existing laws and agreements and to respect said laws and agreements.

Signed at Port-au-Prince in duplicate in the English and French languages, this fifth day of August, 1931.

[SIGNED] DANA G. MUNRO
A. N. LEGER

5. Agreement between the United States of America and the Republic of Haiti [9]

Signed at Port au Prince, August 7, 1933.

SECTION I

HAITIANIZATION OF THE GARDE D'HAITI AND WITHDRAWAL OF MILITARY FORCES FROM HAITI

The undersigned plenipotentiaries, duly authorized by their respective Governments, have agreed upon the following Accord:

ARTICLE I. The American officers now serving with the Garde d'Haiti will be replaced in such a manner that by October 1, 1934, the Garde shall be completely commanded by Haitian officers.

ARTICLE II. On October 1, 1934, the Garde, under complete command of Haitian officers, will be turned over to a Colonel in active service whom the President of the Republic shall designate as Commandant.

[9] Reprinted from Department of State, *Press Releases*, August 19, 1933, p. 103.

ARTICLE III. The promotions to be effected until the complete Haitianization of the Garde will be made after examinations held in the presence of the representative of the Government of Haiti in conformity with Article X of the Treaty of September 16, 1915.

ARTICLE IV. To complete the instruction, training and discipline of the Garde the President of Haiti, may, if he consider it desirable, request the President of the United States to designate a Military Mission of not more than seven members among the American officers who have served in Haiti. The powers to be granted to this Mission will be determined by a decree of the President of Haiti. The services of this Mission shall terminate at the request of either party to the agreement upon sixty days' notice given by either party.

ARTICLE V. The withdrawal of the Marine Brigade of the United States and the American Scientific Mission established by the Accord of August 5, 1931, shall commence on October 1, 1934, and shall be completed within thirty days.

ARTICLE VI. The Government of Haiti, in order to preserve public order, assumes the obligation of maintaining strict discipline in the Garde and of applying for this purpose the present regulations of the Garde d'Haiti.

It will enact a statute which will fix the conditions of appointment, promotion and retirement in the Garde. It will also take all legislative measures recognized as necessary to guarantee public peace and security.

SECTION II

FINANCIAL ARRANGEMENT

ADJUSTMENT OF THE FINANCIAL GUARANTEES STIPULATED IN THE PROTOCOL OF 1919 AND THE LOAN CONTRACT OF 1922

ARTICLE VII. Beginning January 1, 1934, the services of the Financial Adviser-General Receiver and of the Deputy General Receiver shall be carried on, in fulfillment of the obligations and guarantees undertaken in order to obtain the loan issued in accord with the Protocol of October 3, 1919, by a Fiscal Representative and a Deputy Fiscal Representative, appointed by the President of the Republic upon nomination of the Preisdent of the United States, who shall exercise the powers hereinafter set forth.

ARTICLE VIII. As the Customs Revenues constitute the principal pledge to the holders of the bonds of the 1922 loan, the Fiscal Representative will have under his direction, until the complete amortization or the prior refunding of the loan under reference, the Customs Service and the application of the laws relative thereto. In addition he shall inspect the activities of the Internal Revenue Service and make appropriate recommendations for its proper operation; he shall be in charge of the existing Service of Payments, reserve being made of the provisions of Article XII hereafter; he shall maintain adequate records of receipts and disbursements which records shall be open to inspection and verification by the appropriate authorities; and he shall submit monthly reports of his activities to the Secretary of State for Finance and the Secretary of State of the United States.

In order properly to carry out his duties, the Fiscal Representative shall have such employees and assistants as may appear necessary. The number of Americans so employed shall not exceed eighteen. The President of Haiti, upon the presentation which will be made to him by the Secretary of State for Finance, will commission as of January 1, 1934, the employees occupying positions of authority and trust under the Fiscal Representative and recommended by the latter. Thereafter, any position which may become vacant among the commissioned employees shall be filled by examination, the form and procedure of which shall be determined by an accord between the Secretary of State for Finance and the Fiscal Representative. The successful competitor in such examination shall be recommended for the vacancy and will be commissioned by the President of Haiti. Such commissioned employees may be suspended without pay by the Fiscal Representative, on charges filed with the Secretary of State for Finance and such employee or assistant shall not be reinstated unless the charges shall have been disproved to the satisfaction of the Secretary of State for Finance, and of the Fiscal Representative. Pending the hearing of the charges made, the Fiscal Representative, after a report to the Secretary of State for Finance, may fill the vacancy provisionally, if necessary, until the charges have been disproved or a new commission issued.

ARTICLE IX. The salaries of the Fiscal Representative and of the Deputy Fiscal Representative shall be made the subject of an accord between the two Governments. These salaries, together with the expenses of the activities of the Fiscal Representative, but excluding the expenses of the Internal Revenue Inspection Service, may not exceed five per centum of customs receipts except by agreement between the two Governments.

ARTICLE X. The Internal Revenue Service, the personnel of which shall be exclusively Haitian, shall be placed in charge of a Haitian Director under the Secretary of State for Finance.

Nevertheless, if the Fiscal Representative should notify the Secretary of State for Finance and the Director General of Internal Revenue in writing that there is reason to suppose any officer or employee of the Internal Revenue Service is inefficient, or that his action is not correct, such officer or employee shall be suspended, and not reinstated unless the charges shall have been disproved to the satisfaction of the Secretary of State for Finance.

The expenses of the Internal Revenue Service shall be paid from the funds set aside for this purpose by the National Bank of the Republic of Haiti in accordance with schedules of payments agreed upon between the Secretary of State for Finance and the Fiscal Representative. These expenses shall not exceed ten per centum of internal revenue receipts, and the expenses of the Internal Revenue Inspection Service shall not exceed five per centum of internal revenue receipts. Any sums not required by the Internal Revenue Inspection Service within this allowance shall be made available to the Internal Revenue Service.

ARTICLE XI. On and after January 1, 1934, all monies received by or for the Haitian Government shall be deposited in the National Bank of the Republic of Haiti to the credit of the Haitian Government with the exception of the five per centum of customs revenues foreseen in Article IX above and the amounts needed for payments connected with execution of the loan contracts, which amounts shall be credited to the Fiscal Representative. The National Bank of the Republic of Haiti also shall set aside preferentially each month to the credit of the Fiscal Representative the amounts provided in Article X above for the expenses of the Internal Revenue Service and of the Internal Revenue Inspection Service.

In order to assure the maintenance of public order, the monthly allocation for the Garde d'Haiti will be set aside preferentially by the National Bank of the Republic of Haiti for the exclusive use of the Garde from the funds thereafter remaining.

ARTICLE XII. All payments of Government funds shall continue to be made by checks prepared by the Service of Payments. The existing arrangement, as agreed upon between the two Governments on August 5, 1931, shall continue to govern this service except that all checks henceforth will be signed by the Secretary of State for Finance, or his delegate, reserve being made in the case of those checks drawn against the funds deposited at the National Bank of the Republic of Haiti to the credit of the Fiscal Representative, which checks shall be signed only by the latter, or his delegate.

ARTICLE XIII. Each year, by January 31st at the latest the Fiscal Representative shall present a detailed estimate of receipts for the following fiscal year. Except by special agreement, the budget of the Republic shall not exceed the amount of probable ways and means which the Secretary of State for Finance and the Fiscal Representative shall have agreed upon.

ARTICLE XIV. The Haitian Government may authorize any appropriations whatsoever if unobligated funds are available, or derivable at an early date from the ordinary revenues, to cover such appropriations after setting up such reserves as may appear to the Secretary of State for Finance and the Fiscal Representative to be necessary.

ARTICLE XV. In case of a probable budgetary deficit, expenditures must be brought to the level of ways and means, either by reducing expenditures or by the creation of new receipts. In every case, it will not be possible without the accord of the Fiscal Representative to cover a deficit by calling upon the reserve funds of the Government.

ARTICLE XVI. There shall be included annually in the budget of the Republic the amounts necessary for the regular service of the funded debt and other contractual obligations, as well as two lump sums representing five per centum of customs and five per centum of internal revenues, respectively, for the payment of the expenses of the Fiscal Representative, and those of the Internal Revenue Inspection Service, and finally a lump sum representing ten per centum of internal revenue receipts for the payment of the expenses of the Internal Revenue Service. The balance may be apportioned by the Haitian Government between the budgets of the various departments as it may see fit. If the revenues received in any month shall be insufficient to meet the full debt service and expenses of collection, the Government will make available the amount required to make up the difference.

ARTICLE XVII. Without the accord of the Fiscal Representative no new financial obligation will be assumed unless the ordinary revenues of the Republic, after defraying the expenses of the Government, shall be adequate to assure the final discharge of such obligations.

ARTICLE XVIII. The Government will not dispose of its investments except with the accord of the Fiscal Representative.

ARTICLE XIX. The present finance law shall be the organic act of the Republic so far as concerns the administration of the government finances.

ARTICLE XX. The Government of Haiti agrees not to reduce the tariff nor to modify the taxes and internal revenues in such a manner as to reduce the total amount thereof without the accord of the Fiscal Representative.

ARTICLE XXI. The customhouses of the Republic will have an exclusively Haitian personnel and the title of Director shall be reëstablished in lieu of that of Collector. However, inspectors of the Customs Service may be assigned, either temporarily or permanently, to oversee the operation and the strict application of the customs laws.

ARTICLE XXII. In case of payment under protest of customs duties or internal revenue taxes, and where restitution of such payment is requested, a written claim shall be presented to the competent service within a time limit of thirty working days beginning with the date on which the duties or taxes were paid. If the decision is not accepted, the matter shall be presented to a commission composed of a representative of the Secretary of State for Finance and a representative of the Fiscal Representative.

If there should still be failure to reach an agreement, the claim for restitution shall be decided by legal proceedings, but the State may not be liable for any compensatory or punitive damages.

ARTICLE XXIII. In view of the fact that under normal conditions the operation of the sinking fund will result in retirement of the outstanding series of the loan authorized by the law of June 26, 1922, approximately by the year 1944, and inasmuch as any further issue of the loan would necessarily extend the operation of this agreement, to a period beyond that year, which extension is contrary to their desire, it is hereby agreed by both Governments that the loan shall be considered closed and that no additional series shall be issued thereunder.

ARTICLE XXIV. In case there should appear to be occasion for judicial proceedings against the Fiscal Representative or his

American assistants, the two Governments, in order to avoid possible misunderstanding, agree to examine each case impartially and to agree upon the legal action which might be appropriate.

ARTICLE XXV. The Haitian Government, upon the signature of the present agreement, will issue irrevocable instructions to the National Bank of the Republic of Haiti in order that there may be full and complete execution of the clauses herein respecting the deposit and disbursement of the funds of the Government.

ARTICLE XXVI. The Haitian Government reserves the right to retire the bonds issued in accord with the Protocol of October 3, 1919, in advance of their due date; and the Government of the United States will not invoke the provisions of Article VI of the Protocol as an obstacle to such retirement before the expiration of the period of fifteen years fixed therein, provided that the Haitian Government is able to make an arrangement for this purpose satisfactory to the holders of the outstanding bonds.

In this case the provisions of this accord shall automatically become null and void and of no effect upon the completion of the funding operation. The Haitian Government in order to hasten the retirement of the loan of 1922 may continue as rapidly as its resources will permit, to buy on the open market bonds of the several series of the said loan.

ARTICLE XXVII. Any controversy which may arise between the two Governments on the subject of the clauses of the present accord shall be submitted to arbitration in case it cannot be settled through diplomatic channels, in accordance with the Arbitration Treaty of January 7, 1909 between the two countries.

Signed at Port-au-Prince in duplicate in the English and French languages, this seventh day of August, 1933.

[SEAL] NORMAN ARMOUR
[SEAL] A. BLANCHET.

IV. NICARAGUA

Convention respecting Nicaraguan Canal Route [10]

Signed at Washington, August 5, 1914; ratification advised by the Senate, with amendments, February 18, 1916; ratified by the President, June 19, 1916; ratified by Nicaragua, April 13, 1916; ratifications exchanged at Washington, June 22, 1916; proclaimed, June 24, 1916.

The Government of the United States of America and the Government of Nicaragua being animated by the desire to strengthen their ancient and cordial friendship by the most sincere coöperation for all purposes of their mutual advantage and interest and to provide for the possible future construction of an interoceanic ship canal by way of the San Juan River and the great Lake of Nicaragua, or by any route over Nicaraguan territory, whenever the construction of such canal shall be deemed by the Government of the United States conducive to the interests of both countries, and the Government of Nicaragua wishing to facilitate in every way possible the successful maintenance and operation of the Panama Canal, the two Governments have resolved to conclude a Convention to these ends, and have accordingly appointed as their plenipotentiaries:

The President of the United States, the Honorable William Jennings Bryan, Secretary of State; and

The President of Nicaragua, Señor General Don Emiliano Chamorro, Envoy Extraordinary and Minister Plenipotentiary of Nicaragua to the United States;

Who, having exhibited to each other their respective full powers, found to be in good and due form, have agreed upon and concluded the following articles:

ARTICLE I. The Government of Nicaragua grants in perpetuity to the Government of the United States, forever free from all taxation or other public charge, the exclusive proprietary rights necessary and convenient for the construction, operation and maintenance of an interoceanic canal by way of the San Juan River and the great Lake of Nicaragua or by way of any route over Nicaraguan territory, the details of the terms upon which such canal shall be constructed, operated and maintained to be agreed to by the two governments whenever the Government of the United States shall notify the Government

[10] Reprinted from *Treaty Series* No. 624; *Treaties, Conventions, etc.,* III, p. 2740.

of Nicaragua of its desire or intention to construct such canal.

ARTICLE II. To enable the Government of the United States to protect the Panama Canal and the proprietary rights granted to the Government of the United States by the foregoing article, and also to enable the Government of the United States to take any measure necessary to the ends contemplated herein, the Government of Nicaragua hereby leases for a term of ninety-nine years to the Government of the United States the islands in the Caribbean Sea known as Great Corn Island and Little Corn Island; and the Government of Nicaragua further grants to the Government of the United States for a like period of ninety-nine years the right to establish, operate and maintain a naval base at such place on the territory of Nicaragua bordering upon the Gulf of Fonseca as the Government of the United States may select. The Government of the United States shall have the option of renewing for a further term of ninety-nine years the above leases and grants upon the expiration of their respective terms, it being expressly agreed that the territory hereby leased and the naval base which may be maintained under the grant aforesaid shall be subject exclusively to the laws and sovereign authority of the United States during the terms of such lease and grant and of any renewal or renewals thereof.

ARTICLE III. In consideration of the foregoing stipulations and for the purposes contemplated by this Convention and for the purpose of reducing the present indebtedness of Nicaragua, the Government of the United States shall, upon the date of the exchange of ratification of this Convention, pay for the benefit of the Republic of Nicaragua the sum of three million dollars United States gold coin, of the present weight and fineness, to be deposited to the order of the Government of Nicaragua in such bank or banks or with such banking corporation as the Government of the United States may determine, to be applied by Nicaragua upon its indebtedness or other public purposes for the advancement of the welfare of Nicaragua in a manner to be determined by the two High Contracting Parties, all such disbursements to be made by orders drawn by the Minister of Finance of the Republic of Nicaragua and approved by the Secretary of State of the United States or by such person as he may designate.

ARTICLE IV. This Convention shall be ratified by the High Contracting Parties in accordance with their respective laws, and the ratifications thereof shall be exchanged at Washington as soon as possible.

In witness whereof the respective plenipotentiaries have signed the present treaty and have affixed thereunto their seals.

Done at Washington, in duplicate, in the English and Spanish languages, on the 5th day of August, in the year nineteen hundred and fourteen.

WILLIAM JENNINGS BRYAN   [SEAL]
EMILIANO CHAMORRO   [SEAL]